best
hikes
with

dogs
OREGON

Ellen Morris Bishop

THE MOUNTAINEERS BOOKS

THE MOUNTAINEERS BOOKS
*is the nonprofit publishing arm of The Mountaineers Club, an organization
founded in 1906 and dedicated to the exploration, preservation, and
enjoyment of outdoor and wilderness areas.*

1001 SW Klickitat Way, Suite 201, Seattle, WA 98134

© 2004 by Ellen Morris Bishop

First edition: first printing 2004, second printing 2005, third printing 2005, fourth
printing 2006

Published simultaneously in Great Britain by Cordee, 3a DeMontfort Street, Leicester,
England, LE1 7HD

Manufactured in the United States of America

Acquiring Editor: Christine Ummel Hosler
Project Editor: Christine Ummel Hosler
Copy Editor: Brenda Pittsley
Cover and Book Design: The Mountaineers Books
Layout: Mayumi Thompson
Cartographer: Moore Creative Designs

All photographs by the author unless otherwise noted.

Cover photograph: *Dundee.* Photo by Ellen Morris Bishop.

Maps shown in this book were produced using National Geographic's *TOPO!*
software. For more information, go to *www.nationalgeographic.com/topo.*

Library of Congress Cataloging-in-Publication Data
Bishop, Ellen Morris.
  Best hikes with dogs : Oregon / Ellen Morris Bishop.— 1st ed.
    p. cm.
Includes bibliographical references (p.   ).
  ISBN 0-89886-944-7 (pbk.)
  1. Hiking with dogs—Oregon—Guidebooks. 2. Trails—Oregon—Guidebooks.
3. Oregon—Guidebooks. I. Title.
  SF427.455.B57 2004
  917.95—dc22

                         2003023322

 Printed on recycled paper

CONTENTS

Cascade Mountains

Klamath Mountains

Blue Mountains, Wallowa Mountains, and Eastern Oregon

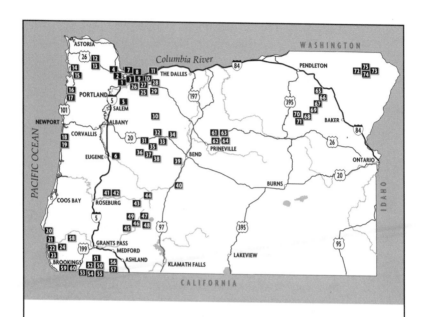

LEGEND

═══════════	Interstate Highway
───────────	Paved Road
═══════════	Gravel Road
= = = = = = = =	Dirt Road
■ ■ ■ ■ ■ ■ ■ ■ ▶	Featured Trail
··················	Connecting Trail
— · — · — · —	Wilderness Boundary
▬ · ▬ · ▬ · ▬	State Boundary
⌒⌒⌒⌒	River/Creek
⬭	Lake
·─·─·─·─·─·	Power Transmission Line

84	Interstate
20	U.S. Highway
410	Oregon Route
9712	Forest Road
643	Trail Number
] [	Bridge
🚩	Trailhead
⛺	Campground
▲	Peak
⛨	Ranger Station
■	Building
⛷	Ski Area

HIKE SUMMARY TABLE

Trail	Easy on paws	Easy hike 4 miles or less	Possible overnight trip	Alongside stream most of hike	Lake(s) to swim in	Unleashed okay	Solitude	Alpine scenery	Forested trail for the entire hike	Good for senior dogs	Best for well-conditioned dogs
Willamette Valley and Portland Area											
1 Tryon Creek State Park	•	•		•					•	•	
2 Forest Park Wildwood Trail (whole trail)	•									•	•
3 Powell Butte		•									
4 Sauvie Island: Warrior Rock Trail	•				•					•	
5 Silver Falls State Park: Smith Creek Trail	•			•					•		•
6 Howard Buford County Recreation Area: Mount Pisgah		•									
Columbia River Gorge											
7 Larch Mountain (almost) to Multnomah Falls	•								•		•
8 Angels Rest											
9 Latourell Falls: Upper Trail									•		
10 Oneonta Gorge: Triple Falls				•					•		
11 Wahclella Falls		•		•					•	•	
Coast and Coast Range											
12 Banks–Vernonia State Trail: Vernonia to Braun									•	•	
13 Banks–Vernonia State Trail: Tophill to Buxton	•								•	•	
14 Harts Cove at Cascade Head	•					•	•		•		
15 Cascade Head Trail	•					•	•		•	•	
16 Cape Lookout: South Trail		•				•			•		
17 Cape Lookout: North Trail	•					•			•		
18 Cape Perpetua: Cummins Ridge to Gwynn Creek			•			•	•		•		•
19 Cape Perpetua: Giant Spruce Trail	•	•							•	•	

Trail	Easy on paws	Easy hike 4 miles or less	Possible overnight trip	Alongside stream most of hike	Lake(s) to swim in	Unleashed okay	Solitude	Alpine scenery	Forested trail for the entire hike	Good for senior dogs	Best for well-conditioned dogs
20 Humbug Mountain State Park: Summit Trail									•		•
21 Humbug Mountain State Park: Old Coast Highway									•		
22 Floras Lake State Park: Blacklock Point	•				•						
23 Samuel H. Boardman State Scenic Corridor							•		•		•
24 Francis Shrader Old Growth Trail	•	•							•	•	
Cascade Mountains											
25 Wildwood Recreation Area and Salmon-Huckleberry Wilderness											•
26 Burnt Lake	•		•	•	•	•			•		•
27 Ramona Falls			•			•			•		
28 Mirror Lake and Tom, Dick, and Harry Mountain			•		•						
29 Badger Creek Trail			•	•		•	•		•		•
30 Olallie Lake Scenic Area: Red Lake Trail			•		•	•		•	•		•
31 Three Sisters Wilderness: Matthieu Lakes and Collier Cone			•		•	•			•		•
32 Metolius River Trail	•		•						•	•	
33 South Breitenbush River National Recreational Trail	•					•			•	•	
34 Jefferson Park via South Breitenbush Trail			•		•	•		•	•		•
35 Mount Washington Wilderness: Patjens Lakes	•		•		•	•			•	•	
36 Deschutes River			•						•	•	
37 Three Sisters Wilderness: Green Lakes to Soda Creek	•		•	•	•	•		•	•		•

Trail	Easy on paws	Easy hike 4 miles or less	Possible overnight trip	Alongside stream most of hike	Lake(s) to swim in	Unleashed okay	Solitude	Alpine scenery	Forested trail for the entire hike	Good for senior dogs	Best for well-conditioned dogs
38 Three Sisters Wilderness: Sisters Mirror Lake	•	•				•			•	•	
39 Todd Lake		•			•	•		•	•		•
40 Newberry National Volcanic Monument: Peter Skene Ogden Trail	•		•				•		•		
41 North Umpqua Trail: Tioga Segment, Miles 1–16						•	•		•		•
42 North Umpqua Trail: Hot Springs Segment, Miles 47–54	•		•			•			•		
43 North Umpqua Trail: Dread and Terror Segment, Miles 54–63	•		•			•	•		•		
44 North Umpqua Trail: Maidu Lake Segment, Miles 69–79	•		•	•	•	•	•	•	•		•
45 Upper Rogue River Trail: Takelma Gorge Segment, Miles 6–10	•		•			•			•	•	
46 Upper Rogue River Trail: Knob Falls Segment, Miles 10–14		•	•	•		•	•				•
47 Upper Rogue River Trail: Natural Bridge to Big Bend Segment, Miles 14–21			•			•			•	•	
48 Union Creek Trail	•		•						•	•	
49 Muir Creek Trail to Hummingbird Meadows			•					•	•	•	
Klamath Mountains											
50 Summit Lake						•	•		•		
51 Squaw Lakes Trail	•	•	•		•				•	•	
52 Applegate Lake: French Gulch–Payette Trail	•		•		•	•				•	
53 Echo Lake			•			•	•	•	•		•
54 Cook and Green Trail			•			•	•		•		•
55 Middle Fork Applegate River				•		•			•	•	

Trail	Easy on paws	Easy hike 4 miles or less	Possible overnight trip	Alongside stream most of hike	Lake(s) to swim in	Unleashed okay	Solitude	Alpine scenery	Forested trail for the entire hike	Good for senior dogs	Best for well-conditioned dogs
56 Big Pine Loop	•	•							•	•	
57 Taylor Creek Trail						•	•		•		
58 Rogue River Trail: Illahee to Paradise Bar			•	•		•			•		•
59 Vulcan Lake		•			•	•		•			
60 Chetco Lake						•	•		•		•
Blue Mountains, Wallowa Mountains, and Eastern Oregon											
61 Twin Pillars Trail	•		•				•		•	•	
62 Lookout Mountain Trail						•	•	•	•		•
63 Independent Mine to Lookout Mountain Summit						•	•	•			
64 Round Mountain Trail						•	•	•			
65 Elkhorn Crest Trail to Anthony Lake						•	•	•			•
66 Hoffer Lakes	•	•		•	•			•	•	•	
67 Crawfish Lake			•								
68 Baldy Creek Trail	•		•	•	•	•	•	•	•	•	
69 North Fork John Day Wilderness: Elkhorn Crest Loop			•	•		•	•	•			•
70 North Fork John Day Wilderness: North Fork Campground to Granite Creek			•	•		•	•		•		•
71 North Fork John Day Wilderness: Granite Creek to Big Creek			•	•		•	•		•		•
72 Eagle Cap Wilderness: Bear Creek	•		•	•		•	•	•	•	•	
73 Eagle Cap Wilderness: Hurricane Creek	•		•	•		•		•	•	•	
74 Eagle Cap Wilderness: Maxwell Lake			•		•	•		•	•		•
75 Eagle Cap Wilderness: West Fork Lostine River to Sky Lake			•	•	•	•	•	•			•

PART 1

Hiking Tips for Dogs and People

*The one absolutely unselfish friend
that man can have in this selfish world,
the one that never deserts him,
the one that never proves ungrateful or
treacherous, is the dog.*

— Samuel Taylor Coleridge (Table Talk, 1830)

S ay the word "dog," and it's likely you will smile. For the past 15,000 years, dogs have been our nonjudgmental friends, playmates, steadfast backcountry partners, and purveyors of solace. No wonder we want to take them hiking.

A well-trained, well-behaved dog can enhance your backcountry experience, opening up a new world of smells and textures and offering protection simply by being along for the trip—a dog in the hiking party makes you less likely to be threatened by predators of all species.

Not all dogs are Lassie, however, and even with a dog as your companion, you should use caution when hiking and carry first-aid supplies. Yet the stories of dogs bringing help to injured owners *are* legion. Dogs are also great icebreakers on the trail. Other hikers are more likely to pause to greet the two of you, though they usually address the dog first.

Like humans, dogs need training, conditioning, and the right gear if they are to enjoy their hike. Regular daily exercise is essential for you both. Up-to-date vaccinations, a current identification tag, along with good obedience skills and socialization training, are important prerequisites for any pet on the trails.

Many dog owners want to take Rover along on hikes. However, taking a dog means assuming extra responsibilities, including cleanup,

Rope makes a great toy for an impromptu game.

acceptable canine social behavior, and proper care of the dog's health on the trail. Whenever you are in the backcountry with your dog, you are an ambassador for all dogs who accompany hikers.

Hikers are generally tolerant of dogs, but a small, vocal minority would like to ban them from the trail. Their objections rest on three concerns: 1) potential harassment or harm to wildlife and ecologically sensitive environments; 2) dogs and dog waste creating unsanitary conditions; and 3) dogs biting or presenting other hazards to people, especially children. Some who object to dogs on the trail also incorrectly believe that dogs communicate disease to wildlife, spread giardiasis and other waterborne diseases, and, by their presence, discourage wildlife from using an area.

Hikers who take dogs along must ensure that dogs are controlled and will not chase or harass wildlife—including squirrels and other small animals. Cleanup is essential. Dog poop left along the trail is unsanitary and unsightly. Dogs who take to the trail must be friendly to humans and other dogs. The following tips are designed to help you develop a well-trained, happy trail dog; achieve this, and the two of you will better enjoy any trail you choose.

Gear for Fido and You

When hiking with your dog, there are a few supplies you should always take along. And with a proper pack, Rover can help carry them.

The Ten Essentials for People

For decades hikers have been coached to pack the Ten Essentials, key items to help them survive a wilderness emergency. The list has recently been modified into ten functional systems that hikers need to consider when heading into the outdoors.

1) **Navigation (map and compass).** Carry a topographic map of the area you will hike, and learn how to read it. Also carry a compass and learn how to use it, including the local magnetic declination. An altimeter can be even more useful but is more expensive. Better yet, learn how to use a global positioning system (GPS) receiver.

2) **Sun protection (sunglasses and sunscreen).** Ultraviolet light damages your eyes. Always wear UV-blocking glasses when hiking at altitudes above 5000 feet.

3) **Insulation (extra clothing).** Rain and cold weather can develop quickly in the backcountry. Carry raingear and enough extra

Your dog should stay close to you and remain on the trail without harassing wildlife during your hike.

clothing to keep you warm should you become lost or injured.

4) **Illumination (headlamp or flashlight).** Even the best-laid plans can go awry. Should darkness overtake you on a hike, you'll need artificial light to follow the trail. Take a light with good batteries and a strong beam.

5) **First-aid supplies.** Make your own or purchase a prepackaged kit designed for hikers and campers. Bandages, antiseptic, adhesive wrap, and aspirin are essential kit items. Include an emergency space blanket and an instant cold pack as well. Your dog also needs a first-aid kit, described later in this chapter, so you might want to combine the two kits into one all-purpose kit.

6) **Fire (firestarter and matches/lighter).** An emergency campfire provides warmth and a signal if you become lost. Many good commercial fire starters are available, such as tubes of fire-starting ribbon. A candle works too. Pack waterproof matches (they light even when wet) and also carry regular, strike-anywhere matches or a lighter in a waterproof case.

7) **Repair kit and tools (including a knife).** A knife has a multitude of uses in normal hikes and in emergency situations.

Always carry a knife or, better yet, a multitool with a knife blade and accessories such as pliers, wire cutters, and so on.

8) **Nutrition (extra food).** Carry the food you intend to eat on the trail or while camping, plus extra in case of an emergency. A few extra energy bars weigh little but will help if your hike is longer than you think or if you stray from your intended hike.

9) **Hydration (extra water).** Clean drinking water is essential for health. Carry at least 1 liter, and on longer hikes take a purification system so you can drink water from streams safely.

10) **Emergency shelter.** In the backcountry, weather can change and accidents happen. Carry a lightweight emergency shelter—an emergency space blanket or space tent. It weighs only ounces, but it may save your life.

The Ten Canine Essentials

1) **Obedience training.** Before you set foot on a trail, make sure your dog is trained and will obey your commands when faced with other hikers, other dogs, wildlife, and an assortment of strange scents and sights in the backcountry. A dog that can't behave should be left at home.

2) **Doggie backpack.** Dogs can pack their own food, water, and other gear in a doggie backpack. Dogs wear backpacks quite comfortably and specially designed backpacks are widely available. The pack should fit snugly. Don't overload your dog. A general rule is 1 pound in the pack per 20 pounds of dog. If your dog likes to immerse herself in streams, you might want to package everything in her backpack in waterproof plastic bags.

3) **Basic first-aid kit.** Dogs are prone to injury, bee stings, and other traumas. Take a canine first-aid course and read up on canine first aid. Kit contents are listed later in this chapter.

4) **Dog food and trail treats.** You should pack more food than your dog normally consumes, because she (or he!) will be burning more calories than normal. If you have to spend an extra night out there, you need to keep your best friend fed too. Trail treats serve the same purpose for a dog as they do for you, providing quick energy during a strenuous day of hiking. Treats made for dogs usually provide better canine nutrition than human snacks.

5) **Water and water bowl.** Don't count on dog water being available along the trail. Streams are great for keeping Fido cool,

Offer some water periodically during your hike.

but dogs, like humans, are susceptible to giardiasis and other water-borne disease. Give dogs ample water before you begin your hike, and offer water during the trek as well. Having enough drinking water will lower your dog's risk of heatstroke. Pack as much water for your dog as you do for yourself. Carry a bowl, too. Collapsible nylon bowls work well, as do lightweight titanium or plastic bowls.

6) **Leash and harness or collar.** Have a 6-foot leash with you at all times, even if not required by local regulations. Flexible leads are relatively fragile and can tire your arms. For hands-free hiking, run your belt through the leash handle. An inexpensive and versatile alternative to a commercial leash is to buy a length of small-diameter climbing rope and use carabiners to latch one end to your dog's collar (this should be a smaller carabiner) and the other end to your belt. Consider a harness instead of a collar if your dog will be leashed for the entire hike.

7) **Insect repellent.** Be aware that some animals and some people have strong negative reactions to DEET-based repellents. So before leaving home, dab a little DEET-based repellent on a patch of your dog's fur to see if there is a reaction. Look for signs of drowsiness, lethargy, or nausea. Remember to restrict repellent applications to those places the dog can't lick—the shoulders, the back of the neck, and around the ears (staying well clear of the ears and inner ears)—which are also near the most logical places mosquitoes will be looking for exposed skin (at the eyes, nose, and inner ears) to bite.

8) **ID tags, microchips, and picture identification.** Fact: dogs do get lost. Make sure that whoever finds yours can reunite the two of you. Your dog should always wear ID tags that are easily read. A microchip—a small plastic object about the size of a grain of rice implanted just under the skin by a veterinarian—is also recommended. Microchips, which contain the animal's ownership and contact information, never fall off, are inexpensive, and can be read at most animal shelters and clinics. Picture identification is also helpful to have in your pack. If your dog gets lost far from home, you can show the image to local residents and make flyers and handbills to post in the surrounding communities.

9) **Dog booties.** Dog footpads need to toughen to the trail. Dogs who have not hiked much can get sore feet on a long day hike or a backpacking trip. Having a set of booties in the backpack will prepare you to protect your dog's feet from rough ground or harsh vegetation. Booties can also keep bandages secure in case your dog damages his pads. Practice at home at first. And remember that dogs sweat through their feet and can overheat if booties are left on too long.

When the trail is rough for long distances and your dog has tender paws, a set of dog booties can save Fido from a tough and painful hike.

10) **Compact roll of plastic bags and trowel.** Even on a short hike, be prepared to remove or bury dog waste. Carry it out or bury it, according to what is most appropriate to the area.

In addition to the Ten Canine Essentials, you might consider bringing a dog comb or brush on the hike. Periodic brushing during and after a hike can minimize problems from ticks, embedded seeds, and tangled plant materials. Keep toenails trimmed short, too.

If you are planning an overnight trip, make sure that your tent is large enough to accommodate Rover (and you too). A dog appreciates creature comforts as much as humans do, so a sleeping pad just for the dog is another nice touch.

Finally, ensure that your dog has up-to-date and appropriate vaccinations, including a vaccination for giardiasis. Consult your vet. Good health, including preventative vaccines, pest controls for fleas, ticks, and heartworm, and maintaining proper weight, are important for safe traveling and hiking. When traveling, it is also a good idea to carry up-to-date vaccination and health records in case your dog should need veterinary care or an overnight stay in a kennel while you are away from home.

Choosing Trails for Dogs

Hikes in this book were selected for their suitability and safety for dogs. Most hikes in this book meet the selection criteria outlined below. This checklist can be used to determine the suitability of any trail as an appropriate and safe place for adventures with your dog. A trail is a good choice if it has

- Springs, streams, and/or lakes for your dog to take a dip in; dog use must not contaminate a critical human water source
- Shade for much of the hike
- No major roads or vehicular traffic
- Minimal or no contact with livestock or pack stock
- No leash requirement (though a leash should be available at all times)
- No rare, threatened, or endangered species
- Minimal or no poison oak or ivy
- Minimal or no cliffs or other hazards for ambitious and highly energetic or inexperienced dogs
- Few other hikers or small children
- No off-road vehicles, including mountain bikes

- No long rocky stretches—especially over sharp rocks; trails should be easy on paws
- A trailhead that is easily accessible by car

Etiquette and Rules of the Trail

As trails become more crowded, the need for hikers with dogs to be courteous and helpful to others on the trail grows proportionally. There are a few basic guidelines to follow. Ignore them, and the anti-dog forces gain more fodder for complaints. Follow them, and you might win a few for the dogs.

Protect wildlife and sensitive habitats by leashing or controlling your dogs. To keep wildlife (especially young animals) safe, your dog should be leashed at all times in the spring and early summer, from April through July, when deer fawns, elk calves, and nesting and fledgling birds are especially vulnerable. Keep your dog in the tent at night or leashed securely just outside the door. The backcountry at night can be an exciting place for your dog, and it will be exciting for you, too, if Rover encounters a skunk or porcupine during a late night exploration. Defending the camp against nocturnal marauders, whether deer, bear, or raccoons, can result in injury to your dog.

Yield the right of way to other hikers, horse and llama packers, and mountain bikers. Not everyone loves dogs. Some people fear them. No matter how friendly Rover might be, step off the trail with your dog when you meet oncoming hikers and allow them plenty of room. Likewise, yield to horses and llamas. Where possible and safe, step off the trail on the downhill side to be less threatening, and always speak to livestock and make your presence known to them as soon as you see them on the path. This keeps your dog safe, alleviates any sense that she is a threat or is being threatened, and creates a fine impression of dog-owner courtesy.

Ask if it's okay for the dog to approach when you encounter other hikers. The answer is usually an enthusiastic yes, but check first. Other hikers might be allergic to dogs. They might fear dogs. Or they might not want to share their lunch. Make sure

On long hikes where your dog must remain leashed, a harness can ease the neck-snapping strain of a collar. Meesha in harness.

your dog does not rush up to children. No matter how affable your dog's intent, the rapid approach of an unfamiliar dog, especially a big one, can frighten a child. So ask first and keep your dog on a leash and by your side if there are small children in any group you meet.

Clean up and properly dispose of dog waste. You wouldn't leave poop in your yard or on the city sidewalk, so don't leave dog waste along the trail. There are no waste cans in the woods, but there is a giant compost heap just under your feet. You can dispose of your dog's waste by digging a 4-inch-deep hole with your trowel or a stick, placing the poop in it, and covering it with soil. In smaller parks or rest areas, remove dog waste with a plastic bag.

Keeping your dog cool is critical, but consider where you let her take a doggie dip. Don't let her muddy or contaminate water sources that are used by people—or that are important to wildlife.

Go Lightly on the Land

Both you and your dog love a walk in wilderness, but this landscape is shared with an increasing number of other hikers—human and canine. To keep the backcountry as pristine as possible, practice Leave No Trace hiking. The goal of the national, nonprofit Leave No Trace organization (www.lnt.org) is to "avoid or minimize impacts to natural area resources and help ensure a positive recreational experience for all visitors." Following are the basic principles of Leave No Trace.

Plan ahead and prepare. Know the trails you plan to hike and what to expect when you get to your destination. Take what you need so that you don't have to modify or destroy vegetation and other wilderness assets along the way. Take a stove and fuel if you need to cook, rather than building a campfire. Carry a sleeping pad so you don't have to collect pine needles to have a soft bed. Repackage food and other consumables to minimize waste that must be packed out. Know your route and stick to the trail.

Travel and camp on durable surfaces. Use existing campsites rather than disturbing a pristine forest floor or grassland. If there are no pre-hardened sites—or if overused sites are being restored—choose a rocky or sandy area to camp to minimize disturbing plants. If you must camp in a meadow or on top of plant cover, remember that those plants need light and air to survive. Minimize the time your tent covers them. Set up your tent in the evening; take it down in the morning. The grass will thank you for it.

Dogs and humans have been companions on the trail for at least 15,000 years.

Dispose of waste properly. If you pack it in, pack it out. Even seemingly biodegradable items such as orange peels should be packed out with you.

Leave what you find. That nifty stick that you think you might make into a hiking staff when you get back home is better left in the forest where it will someday contribute to forest duff and soils.

Minimize campfire impacts. Take and use a small gas stove if you must cook. Fires are entrancing but leave unsightly charcoal scars, contribute to global warming, and can start a wildfire if not completely extinguished. Put on a good down jacket, cuddle up with Rover, and watch the stars instead. If you crave firelight, consider candles.

Respect wildlife. Take care that your dog does not damage habitat or harass wild animals.

Be considerate of other visitors. Yield to other hikers on trails. Clean up after your pooch.

When to Leave Your Dog at Home

Well-trained and properly socialized dogs are capable of hiking with us anywhere. But in some situations, dogs simply don't belong or cannot go. It is far more humane to leave Rover comfortably and safely at home than to bring him into places or conditions where his health could be endangered or where he is not allowed.

In very hot weather, leave your dog at home or in a kennel if you are away from home. Dogs cannot cool themselves as readily as we can. As a result, dogs are prone to heatstroke and possible death when temperatures rise above 90°F and there is limited shade or water. Dogs who are not acclimated to heat may suffer when temperatures are only in the 70s or 80s. In these conditions, leave your dog at home with shade and water. If you are away from home and the weather turns hot, board your dog at a good local kennel or cancel the day's hike and relax together at a cool, shady streamside instead.

If you plan to hike crowded trails, especially trails with a lot of children, horse packers, or mountain bikers, consider leaving Fido at home. You won't have to worry about your dog's safety and interaction with other hikers. If Fido does accompany you, she should remain on a leash or under close control. Another option is to explore more popular, and thus congested, trails in off-peak seasons and hours.

Keep in mind, too, that some places, such as national parks and Nature Conservancy preserves, do not allow dogs on trails. Not even on a leash. Not even if you carry the dog or zip her into a backpack.

Don't take the dog if you will be hiking where there are sensitive plants, habitats, or endangered or threatened species. Or, if you must take him, keep him leashed. Dogs on the trail are less destructive than reputed, but the fact remains that dogs can't tell the difference between a Shasta daisy (common) and a Columbia Gorge daisy (endangered).

Leave your dog at home or keep him under close control (leashed) when hiking where livestock might be present. Cattle, sheep, and horses often share federal and state lands with hikers. Dogs that harass livestock can be legally shot in Oregon. If there is a herding club in your community, or if you can find a cattle owner who is willing to work with you, train your dog in the presence of livestock to leave the animals alone and respond instantly to your command "Come!"

Likewise, consider leaving your dog at home if there will be unfamiliar dogs (and their unfamiliar owners) in your group. Leaving your dog at home becomes an even better idea if your dog is very submissive or very dominant. If you do take Rover, pay attention to her and the others and be prepared to leave the group if the situation (human or canine) gets tense. Allow dogs to socialize before you set off on a hike. Keep in mind that a dog might believe that he needs to defend you if he is leashed and other dogs are not. The greater the number of unfamiliar dogs on a hike, the more likely it is that trouble will occur.

Preparing Dogs for Hiking

Most hikers maintain a fitness program of sorts, wear hiking boots, pack clothing and other gear to be ready for bad weather, and try to eat the right foods. Even though dogs have a different physiology than humans, they also need to be prepared.

A half-hour of exercise each day will help to keep your dog fit. Ideally, that exercise should include running as well as walking. A half-hour aerobic stroll will build your dog's muscle tone, circulation, and lung capacity, and also begin to toughen her footpads for the trail. A walk that includes some jogging or a chance to chase a ball provides additional canine fitness benefit.

Begin your dog's fitness program slowly. Start with a visit to your veterinarian to ensure there are no hidden health problems, such as hip dysplasia, that might cause trouble on the trail. A walk each day is a good beginning. Along the way, reacquaint Fido with the etiquette of walking on a loose leash, at your pace, and in response to basic commands, including "heel." A dog who pulls on the leash can be a real nuisance on the trail. Quicken your pace as time goes by, and soon you'll both be walking briskly. Teach Fido to swim, too, so he can keep cool on the trail.

Older dogs, like older humans, need patience and special consideration. Dogs reach their prime at about age four, and larger breeds are considered

Dogs of any size make cheerful hiking companions. Suzie on the Angels Rest Trail, Columbia River Gorge.

senior citizens by age seven or eight. Be prepared to go slowly and hike shorter, less-challenging trails if your dog is older, and consult your veterinarian for appropriate, pain-relieving medications or food additives that can help keep joints limber. Older dogs benefit both mentally and physically from time spent on the trail, so if you can adjust your pace and distance, by all means take the dog.

Dogs are sentient and intelligent creatures. Their wild, wolfy ancestors planned hunts, raised families, and maintained a complex, disciplined social hierarchy. Modern dogs need food for thought as well as exercise and a nutritious dinner. Each dog, like each human, has individual aptitudes and interests. Activities that develop discipline, mental agility, and physical fitness—especially activities that appeal to your dog's innate abilities—will also foster a strong bond between you and your dog. Recommended activities include obedience and agility training and participation in search and rescue or animal-assisted therapy, as well as activities that are breed-specific, such as herding, water rescue, field trials, and retrieving.

For a better companion on the trail, interact with your dog at every opportunity. For example, when you watch television you can make commercials a time to practice obedience or learn new tricks. Taking the dog along on a car trip to the store? Take an extra five minutes to go for a short walk down the street to meet and greet people. The more situations you face together, and the more opportunities you provide for learning, the more responsive your dog will be when you are on the trail together.

Essential Commands

Even if your dog never darkens the door of a formal obedience class, Rover should obey basic commands without hesitation on the trail. I have found several commands to be especially useful over the past twenty years of hiking with dogs. Some are obedience class standards. Others are specialized. Three commands—"Come!" "Leave it!" and "Wait!" (or "Stay!")—are helpful for safety. A book on dog training can help you teach your dog these commands if a trainer or class is not an option.

"**Come!**" The most critical command. Make your dog understand that this must be obeyed at all times. Practice "Come!" and other commands at places where there are people, noise, and other distractions. Reward liberally for instant obedience.

"**Leave it!**" Has Fido discovered a most wonderful cow pie to sample for a snack or roll in? Or, more critically, is he about to raid the unknown contents of a bag or plastic wrapper? This command, taught by rewarding the dog for turning away from the questionable object, can save your dog's life. At the very least it will help you avoid a ruined hike and possible veterinarian bills.

"Wait!" This command can stop your dog from advancing into danger—unexpected traffic, a rushing stream, or a turn in the trail that carries her out of your line of sight. "Wait!" is the word I yell instinctively when I see danger ahead. Wait is not the same as "Stay!" It does not freeze your dog in one spot for a prolonged time period or imply that you are going to go someplace else while Rover remains in place. It *does* mean that until you get to Rover and get your mitts on her—or release her from the "Wait!" command—she needs to stop instantly.

I learned to give this command quite by accident: Wolf, a malamute then about a year old, was sauntering toward a road crossing about 20 yards ahead of me. I could hear a car coming and the only thing I could think to shout was "Wait!" Wolf stopped in his tracks. The car missed him. He never forgot that "Wait!" is a command to be obeyed instantly. Since then, I've taught it to all my dogs. Begin by shouting urgently at them to stop when you are close by, and reward them for standing there until you reach them. Gradually increase the distance. Chances are they'll catch on quickly.

"Off trail!" This command tells your dog to move off the trail and sit while other hikers, horses, or bikers pass by. While the majority of hikers seem to like dogs, some are afraid of them or simply prefer not to share the trail with them. Courtesy on the trail includes giving other hikers the right of way. Giving the command "Off trail!" while pointing at the place of direction where you expect your dog to go eliminates risk to your dog and to other hikers—and it usually earns a smile from other hikers.

This command is easy to teach by instructing "Off trail!" while pointing to the spot you want the dog to go. Then reward correct behavior. Research shows that dogs have an instinctive knack for going to a place pointed at by a human. Combining "Off trail!" with "Stay!" will soon have your dog responding to the command by moving to the place you point and then sitting or lying down until you release him. This command is especially useful if you encounter a horse pack string, a flock of mountain bikes, or a thundering herd of off-road vehicles (ORVs).

Hazardous Wildlife

Dogs tend to seek wild animals, so in the backcountry your dog might come face-to-face with a number of risks that a more hazard-savvy human would avoid. Keeping your dog leashed and/or under firm voice control mini-mizes the likelihood of unsavory encounters. Even benign encounters should be controlled. Never allow your dog to disturb, harass, or chase any wildlife. Oregon does have some large and hazardous fauna, however, such as cougars, bears, and rattlesnakes.

Cougars

Cougars are generally solitary and reclusive. Encounters are extremely rare. While their presence should not be taken lightly, cougars are not a great hazard. According to the U.S. Fish and Wildlife Service, in the 112 years between 1890 and 2002, there were only seventy confirmed cou-gar attacks and about one fatality every seven years from a cougar en-counter in the United States. In Oregon there have been no fatalities and only seven documented attacks. To put this in perspective, more than fifty thousand people are killed annually in the United States in auto-mobile accidents, about ninety are killed by lightning strikes, forty by bee stings, and eighty by dog bites. Your likelihood of being attacked by a cougar while you are on the trail is far less than your chances of hav-ing a debilitating or fatal accident driving to the trailhead.

Your chances of a cougar encounter are further reduced if you are hik-ing in a group of adults or if you have a dog. During five years of living along a major cougar corridor on the western flank of the Wallowa Moun-tains, my hikes with or without dogs never knowingly crossed the path of a cougar. We occasionally found cougar tracks. Even more rarely, neigh-bors saw one crossing the road or padding through a field.

The only time I saw a cougar was when invited to accompany a team of wildlife biologists who used hounds to track and tree a female cougar near our house. They needed to capture and sedate her to change the batteries in her radio collar. The treed cougar looked down at us—biologists, dogs, and tourists—with pure malevolence in her eyes. Before the biologists could dart her, she leapt 30 feet to the ground and ran away, a tawny, angry, and fright-ened blur across the snow. She passed within about 10 feet of the aston-ished biologists but never bothered them. We let her go. Two weeks later she was treed again and this time her collar did get new batteries.

Following are some tips developed by the U.S. Fish and Wildlife Ser-vice and the Oregon Department of Fish and Wildlife to minimize your chances of provoking a cougar attack:

- When hiking in cougar habitat, go in groups and make enough noise for your approach to be heard.

- Keep children quiet and physically close to adults, preferably within arm's reach.
- Do not allow children to run far in front of or behind adults. Their high-pitched voices and rapid movements can attract cougars. About half of documented cougar attacks involved children.
- Carry a sturdy walking stick. It can be used as a weapon against a cougar.
- Never approach a cougar. They are unpredictable but will usually avoid a confrontation.
- If you do encounter a cougar, give it an escape route.
- Never approach a dead deer, elk, or other animal. It might be a recent cougar kill, with a cougar nearby guarding it. Partially covered animals are an indicator that a cougar might be in the vicinity, because cougars cover their prey between feedings. Immediately call your dog away from any such "find" and place the dog on leash.
- Keep a clean camp. Reduce odors that can attract small mammals such as raccoons, which in turn attract cougars. Store meat, other foods, pet food, and garbage in double plastic bags.
- Some experts recommend leaving your dog at home when hiking in cougar territory. My preference is to bring a dog, especially if it is a large dog (bigger than 50 pounds), but keep him leashed at all times. This prevents the dog from approaching a cougar or a cougar's kill. A cougar might take you on alone, or it might attack your dog alone—a reason for keeping your dog leashed and close to you when in cougar territory—but a cougar is very unlikely to attack you and a large dog together. Talk to your dog and play with her as you hike. The louder, more boisterous, and more aggressive you appear, the less likely you are to be viewed as vulnerable prey.
- Do not allow your dog to roam at night. Keep your dog inside your tent or shelter. Dogs, especially small dogs, can attract cougars and stand little chance of fighting one off.
- If you do encounter a cougar, do not run. Work to convince the cougar that you are dominant and will put up a fight that the cat might lose. Throw rocks. Yell. Wave sticks. Tell it in no uncertain terms that you will not be easy prey. Keep your dog with you. And lastly, if attacked, fight back.

Bears

The only wild bears in Oregon today are American black bears. These animals tend to be shy and reclusive—with three major exceptions: 1) when they are hungry and you have food; 2) when a mother bear needs to defend her cubs; and 3) when defending themselves against attack.

Dogs usually will know there is a bear in the area long before you do. They might refuse to move forward along the trail or they might run toward the bear with the intent of chasing it. If your dog balks at continuing, you should consider it a fair warning. Make sure your dog is leashed before you proceed farther, and use caution along the trail.

Unleashed dogs might choose to pursue a bear. This confrontation is likely to provoke the intended quarry. Bears usually turn the tables on any dog that tries to chase them. Aggressive dogs that stand and fight will inevitably lose. Dogs that retreat to you for protection can lead an angry, combative bear to you. Preventing either scenario is good reason to keep dogs leashed in the backcountry.

To lessen chances of an unsavory encounter with a bear, watch for bear "sign" along the trail. Look for rocks that have been overturned in a search for grubs and ants, scratch marks on tree trunks, dead trees and snags that have been ripped open recently, berry bushes stripped of leaves and fruit, and bear scat—droppings that look like a very, very large dog has been up the trail. Leash dogs and stay close together if you see any sign of bears. Loud conversation—even if it is just you talking to your dog—alerts bears to your presence and allows them to move away.

The rules of encounter with bears are slightly different than those for cougars.

- **Remain calm.** Talk in a low-pitched, calm manner.
- **Do not look the bear directly in the eyes.** Eye contact can be construed as a challenge and might provoke the bear to attack.
- **Move slowly.** Work your way upwind from the bear so it can smell you and identify you as a human—an animal from which it prefers to retreat. Allow the bear room to escape.
- **Do not run.** During a standoff, a bear might "bluff charge" to see if it can stampede you. If a bear charges, stand your ground and do not run. A bluff charge could turn into the real thing if you run, and your chances of outrunning a bear are small. Black bears can charge at speeds of 35 miles per hour.
- **If you surprise a bear, behave passively.** Keep your dog as calm as possible. Back away or lie down. Allow the bear to leave.

- **As a last resort, fight back.** If the bear sees you and charges from a distance, it likely considers you prey or a threat too serious to ignore. This behavior is rare in black bears, but possible. Fight back by kicking, gouging, and punching. Once it realizes that you are not easy prey, the bear might leave.

Rattlesnakes

The warning buzz of a rattlesnake inspires fear in humans but often incites curiosity in our dogs. Encounters between dogs and snakes are usually one of two kinds: the dog finds a snake in the open and tries to sniff it, or the dog finds a well-fed snake in a vacant gopher or mouse hole. Once again, the best way to avoid these encounters is to keep your dog on a leash. Keep dogs close and under control when hiking in snake territory, which in this guide is mostly the rocky country of southern Oregon.

The effects of a rattlesnake bite include swelling and respiratory distress. There is little to do for a snake-bitten dog except head for a veterinarian and a dose of antivenin as quickly as possible. Immobilize the dog, and place ice or cold packs on the bite areas. Administering a two-tablet (for a 50-pound dog) dose of antihistamine will help keep swelling down. When my malamute was bitten in central Oregon, the veterinarian was a thirty-minute drive away. Given a dose of antivenin less than an hour after being bitten, the dog survived with minimal swelling and respiratory problems. But quick treatment is essential.

Canine First Aid and Prevention

This book and this section are meant to supplement, not take the place of, a comprehensive canine first-aid manual (recommendations are listed in Appendix B). The Oregon Humane Society and other organizations offer canine first-aid courses. It's a good idea to take one.

Poisons

Some common substances and foods that humans relish are directly or indirectly poisonous to dogs. When hiking, pack a separate lunch or separate treats for your dog, even for a day hike. Take only foods that are safe for dogs. If you tend to share your snacks, choose dog-friendly foods, such as soy or oatmeal bars, and avoid anything with chocolate. Here are some foods and substances that are harmful to dogs, along with treatments if they are ingested:

Antifreeze. Antifreeze is a deadly poison that rapidly destroys a dog's kidneys and neurological function. Even miniscule amounts of antifreeze—the amount that leaks into a puddle beneath a car radiator—can kill your dog or cause irreversible kidney damage, especially on a hot day after a long hike when the dog might be dehydrated. Immediate veterinary attention is essential if your thirsty dog ingests even a tiny amount of antifreeze from a radiator puddle. If you cannot get to a vet within minutes to have your dog's stomach pumped or an antidote administered, you can help stave off death or disability until you do get to a vet by inducing vomiting. To do so, place a few tablespoons of hydrogen peroxide or ethyl alcohol deep in his mouth and ensure that the dog swallows it. These measures alone might not save your dog, but they might diminish kidney damage sufficiently that veterinary care can save him.

Acetaminophen (Tylenol™) and ibuprofen (Motrin™, Advil™, Nuprin™). Even small doses (two tablets) of these familiar pain remedies can kill a small dog (less than 15 pounds) and cause significant pathological responses in larger dogs. These drugs provide no pain relief for a dog. Instead, ibuprofen produces bleeding stomach ulcers, kidney damage, and possible death; acetaminophen produces liver failure and damage to red blood cells. Symptoms include vomiting, dehydration, bloody stools, lethargy, and abdominal pain. Veterinary treatment is essential. When hiking with your dog, bring only coated aspirin as your antiinflammatory, pain-control medication. Aspirin can be administered to dogs without harm in small doses of one tablet. Acetaminophen and ibuprofen cannot.

Chocolate. A mere 5 ounces of baking chocolate can kill a 50-pound dog. While for humans, "death by chocolate" is a sort of joke, for dogs it is no laughing matter. Some dogs have ingested a fatal dose of chocolate by eating a pan of brownies or another chocolate dessert, particularly one containing baking chocolate. A 60-pound Labrador died after eating a 1-pound bag of semisweet chocolate pieces. Although dogs might vomit up such excesses and avoid death, they can remain ill for some time. When you hike with your dog, it is best to leave chocolate in any form, including "healthy" snack bars, at home.

Salmon, steelhead, and trout. Ingesting small amounts of undercooked, raw, or dead salmon, steelhead, or trout (salmonid fish) can kill your dog. Prompt veterinary treatment is essential. Loki, my healthy, boisterous 100-pound, two-year old Newfoundland, nearly died from salmon poisoning after he ate a few ounces of freshly caught, barbequed Coho salmon. The tiny piece of fish that Loki ate was from the interior of the fish. It was cooked—but not enough. For two days following the barbeque,

Loki hiked happily with me through the Strawberry Range in eastern Oregon. But on the third day he lagged behind. On the fourth day, he would not leave his bed in camp. By the time I got him to a veterinarian, he could not move and had to be carried from the car into the veterinary clinic. His temperature was 106°F—nearly lethal and verging on brain damage. Loki recovered fully but only after massive doses of antibiotics, intravenous fluids, a week of hospitalization, and a month of diminished activity. If we had arrived at the vet a few hours later, he would have died.

It is not the fish itself that causes canine salmon poisoning but the presence of a bacteria—*Neorickettsia helminthoeca*—that lives in one of the salmon's internal parasites. This parasite, a fluke, travels throughout the fish's circulatory system, invading its muscles as well. When a dog eats uncooked fish, he ingests these flukes—and the pathogenic bacteria they contain. The flukes pass through the dog's intestinal tract, but the lethal bacteria remain behind, causing disease and often death.

The first symptoms are slight fever followed by loss of appetite. The dog's temperature will rise, often to levels high enough to kill it (above 107°F is considered a lethal temperature for a dog). Even if the dog survives this high fever, there are worse effects still to come, which also are often lethal, including severe diarrhea and dehydration. Few dogs survive untreated.

Troublesome Plants

Several plants commonly encountered on hikes in Oregon can cause problems for dogs. Some produce seeds that can invade skin or paws, causing pain and, eventually, a large vet bill. Plants of concern include:

Poison oak/poison ivy. Dogs, like humans, can develop severe reactions to these plants, either on exposed underbelly skin that brushed against the plants or in tissues of the mouth and esophagus if the dog chews the leaves or licks the plant's sap off his fur. Poison oak and poison ivy are common in the dry areas of the Columbia River Basin, where they grow in profusion in moist valley bottoms; in eastern Oregon's Hells Canyon area; on the eastern slopes of the Wallowa Mountains; and in the Rogue River and Kalmiopsis Wilderness of southwest Oregon.

Rhododendrons and azaleas. These seemingly benign plants contain a toxin that affects canine heart rhythm and function. This compound is most concentrated in leaves and flowers, but it is present throughout the plant, including the branches. Avoid using these branches as throwing sticks. Symptoms of this poison include weakness, decreased heart

Expect to encounter more seeds later in the hiking season. A simple pocket comb can quickly remove burrs and sticky seeds from your dog's coat.

rate and blood pressure, and arrhythmia. Other plants that are similarly toxic to dogs include yew and the berries and leaves of most ivy.

Grasses and grass seeds. Some grasses, especially those found in over-grazed or disturbed areas (cheatgrass, ripgut brome, bottlebrush, squirreltail, foxtail, etc.) have seeds with sharp points that can puncture a dog's skin and paws—especially between the toes. If you are hiking where there's grass, trim the hair between your dog's toes before you begin the hike. This makes seeds that invade this vulnerable area easier to spot and remove. Seeds can also lodge in a dog's ears, eyes, nose, and throat, as well as penetrate the fur. As a precaution, brush your dog well after a hike through grass, removing seeds caught in her coat and between her toes before they begin to dig into the skin. If grass seeds become lodged in your dog's nose, she will sneeze repeatedly. If seeds are lodged in the throat, your dog will cough. If you can see the seed, you might be able to pull it out. Otherwise, veterinary attention is essential.

Insects, Pests, and Other Small Animals

Critters to look out for include ticks, bees, giardia, porcupines, and skunks.

Giardia. Most hikers are quite religious about taking water and water filters on any outdoor adventure to avoid acquiring internal parasites. The most notorious of these is *Giardia lamblia,* a tiny flagellated protozoan, often referred to simply as "giardia." Dogs are as susceptible as humans to giardia. But dogs are more likely than humans to drink from streams, ponds, and puddles where giardia awaits.

To help your dog avoid giardiasis and the rampant diarrhea and discomfort it brings, make sure she has plenty of water before your begin your hike and that she drinks frequently from the water you brought with you. Giardiasis can be especially serious in dogs, causing flatulence, weight loss, listlessness, and malaise, and slowing the growth of puppies.

A preventative vaccine is available for dogs. If you hike throughout the year, it should be renewed annually along with your dog's other regular shots. If you are an occasional or summer-only hiker, then be sure that your dog has a giardiasis shot before you begin your summer of traveling and hiking.

Ticks and Lyme disease. When hiking in areas grazed by livestock, you and your dog are likely to pick up ticks. The most common are the brown dog tick (dark red-brown), the American dog tick (slate-gray when engorged), and the deer tick (a light brown tick with dark legs and a dark "shield" on its back). The deer tick is the principal carrier of Lyme disease; the American dog tick is the principal carrier of Rocky Mountain spotted fever. Dogs can get—and die from—both.

Ticks' mouthparts have reverse harpoonlike barbs, designed to penetrate and attach to skin. They secrete a cementlike substance that helps them adhere firmly to the dog (or to you).

Ticks can best be removed by using either tweezers or a tool manufactured for tick removal. Grasp the tick with the tweezers as close to your skin as possible. Do not use fingers, which can squeeze the tick's body, forcing it to regurgitate your blood and any microbes the tick is carrying.

Once you have a firm grasp near the tick's head, lift gently until the surface of your skin puckers. This is enough force to make it difficult for the tick to remain attached. Hold this position until the tick lets go. This can take several seconds, so you might need a bit of patience. Once you have removed the tick, be sure you kill it, but don't touch it with your fingers. My personal preference is to pulverize it with a rock.

Bees. Few dogs can resist snapping at a bee. Fortunately, most dogs are not badly affected by bee stings. The best remedy is to remove the

Brown dog ticks and deer ticks are common in areas where livestock and/or deer forage. Combing around the legs, ears, and belly can remove them before they attach to your dog.

stinger, if it is present, using tweezers, then give your dog an antihistamine tablet and apply a cold pack to the sting. However, as with humans, some dogs react badly to bee stings. If your dog has trouble breathing after a sting, or is stung multiple times, seek veterinary care immediately.

Porcupines. These creatures are yet another reason to keep your venturesome dog leashed in forested backcountry and in your tent at night. The only way to get porcupine quills out of your dog is to pull them out with pliers; needle-nose pliers work best. There is no shortcut and no folk remedy, such as cutting quills to "deflate" them or soaking them to soften them, does any good. Pulling quills is a delicate and painful process, and few dogs will permit more than one or two to be extracted without snapping at you. Seek veterinary attention, so that the quills can be extracted while the dog is under sedation.

Heat and Heatstroke

Heatstroke is one of the gravest dangers to dogs who go hiking in the summer and early fall. It is a life-threatening condition in which your dog's internal temperature exceeds the level compatible with his normal life functions. Put more simply, your dog literally cooks in his own skin.

Dogs are perhaps the least heat-tolerant animals that go hiking. They are engineered to sweat only through their footpads and tongue, a very inefficient cooling mechanism. To help prevent heatstroke, give your dog a drink before you begin your hike, and keep her hydrated throughout the trek.

Dogs can suffer heatstroke on warm, sunny days, especially if traveling through places where there is limited shade and water. Early symptoms include rapid panting, bright red gums, increased heart rate, elevated temperature (above 103°F), and excess salivation. Symptoms of advanced heatstroke include vomiting, diarrhea, and gums that have gone from bright red to pale pink or white as the body goes into shock. Death can quickly follow if the dog's body temperature is not reduced.

Heatstroke can overtake and kill your dog in weather that you find comfortable: temperatures of 70°F and above. A black Labrador retriever died of heatstroke in Portland on a sunny spring day with temperatures in the 70s. The dog had trotted for several miles in the sun with its owner—without a drink, shade, or a swim.

To diagnose heatstroke, use a digital rectal thermometer to take the dog's temperature. Normal dog temperature is between 100°F and 102.5°F.

Heatstroke becomes progressively more severe as your dog's temperature rises. Above 103°F, your dog is at risk of damage to internal organs,

A panting, overheated dog has her bright pink tongue extended more than usual in an effort to cool off. Here, Meesha is resting in a moist, shady spot while her body temperature cools before we continue.

including the brain and brain function. Do what it takes to cool your dog before heatstroke becomes more serious. If your dog appears hot, provide water, seek shade, and, if possible, immerse the dog in cold water or wet its coat for temporary cooling. If water is not available, apply a cold pack to the dog's head while getting the dog to water.

If your dog's temperature exceeds 105°F, it is an emergency situation. Carry the dog to avoid further overheating. Immerse the dog in cold water or spray him with cold water to save his life. If your dog suffers heatstroke on the trail but seems to have recovered, it is still wise to visit a veterinarian for a checkup, especially if the dog's temperature was in the danger zone.

As an aid to canine comfort and safety, most hikes in this book follow shaded streams or provide access to water every half-mile or so. To minimize the chance of heatstroke, keep your dog lean and fit. Carry plenty of water for your dog. Stay in the shade and near cold water when temperatures rise. Get Rover into a stream or a puddle. Slow down when the weather warms, and if Rover decides it is time to dig a hole in cool forest dirt and lie down, stop and rest a bit yourself while he cools off.

You also should acclimate both yourself and your dog to hot weather before attempting backcountry hikes. Remember how warm a 70°F day feels in April—and then how cold the same temperature feels in August after your system has made a seasonal adjustment?

Emergency Care

The general approach to canine emergency first aid is the same as for humans: restraint, bleeding control, wound care, and transportation. It is also a good idea to scope out the location of the closest veterinarians as you travel to a trailhead—just in case you need to find one quickly.

Stretchers. An impromptu dog stretcher can be made from a variety of materials, including your tent fly, jacket, or sleeping pad. An emergency space blanket can serve as a stretcher for dogs that weigh no more than 30 pounds. For larger dogs, consider carrying a 36-by-48-inch piece of lightweight nylon or Kevlar fabric in your backpack as part of a basic first-aid kit.

Muzzles. A muzzle can prevent bites from an injured dog while its wounds are cleaned or bandaged. A lightweight, humane, and effective temporary muzzle can be made from pantyhose. Wrap the wide portion of the pantyhose once around your dog's muzzle, then cross in a figure eight and tie the remaining fabric "legs" around your dog's neck.

Bandages. If your dog gets a cut or other bleeding wound, it is likely you will have to wrap the wound. Wounds should be cleaned, covered with a gauze pad, wrapped with gauze wrap, and then secured with self-adhering veterinary wrap (available in human first-aid kits as the slightly more frail "self-adhering tape"). Be careful not to apply this final elastic layer too tightly.

Treatment for shock. A dog that sustains cuts or other serious injury might need treatment for shock as well as injuries. Signs of shock are pale white gums, shallow breathing, a cool body temperature (below 98°F), and a rapid heartbeat. If these symptoms are present, treatment is essential. Place your dog on his side and extend his head and neck to help breathing. Keep the dog warm by wrapping him in a blanket—an emergency space blanket works well. Do not give him anything to eat or drink. Transport to veterinary care immediately.

Cuts and torn dewclaws. Active dogs can catch long toenails and dewclaws—the toenails on the upper part of front legs—on rocks or brush. A torn dewclaw can bleed profusely but can be pressure-wrapped using a gauze pad, gauze wrap, and self-adhering veterinary wrap until you reach veterinary care. Wounds should be cleaned if possible. Lessen bleeding by applying petroleum jelly (such as Vaseline™) or a triple antibiotic ointment (such as Neosporin™) to the wound before bandaging.

Puncture wounds. Deep wounds such as puncture wounds are potentially life-threatening. Assume that shock will occur and keep your dog warm, with hindquarters slightly elevated. Do not remove any object that has penetrated your dog's body (you might need to apply a light bandage to hold the item in place). Try to find immediate veterinary aid.

Bites. Ragged wounds and shallow puncture wounds such as those that result from bites can bleed profusely. Some bleeding helps cleanse a deep wound, but, if possible, you should clean the wound with water, then apply pressure using a gauze pad. Apply rolled gauze and self-adhering veterinary wrap. Be careful not to wrap the wound so tightly that you create a tourniquet. If the wound is on a dog's leg, you can slow bleeding by applying pressure to arterial pressure points. On the front legs, grasp the leg just above the elbow and apply pressure between your thumb on the outside and your fingers on the inside. On a rear leg, you can find the large artery on the inside of the dog's leg just below the groin. You might wish to rewrap the wound after bleeding has stopped. Seek veterinary care.

Removing fishhooks. Dogs are attracted to fishy smells. As they explore these attractive scents along a stream, they can pick up fishhooks in paws, gums, or noses. You should first restrain and muzzle your dog before attempting to remove a fishhook. If the barbed end of the hook is visible, cut if off with wire-cutters and gingerly pull the rest of the hook out. If the barb is not visible, use pliers to push the barbed end through the skin, then cut it off and pull the rest of the hook out. Clean the wound.

Inducing vomiting. If your dog has eaten raw salmon or steelhead, or other potentially lethal material, you can induce vomiting by administering hydrogen peroxide. The dosage is approximately three tablespoons for a 70-pound dog. Hold the dog's mouth closed to ensure he swallows the peroxide. If vomiting does not occur in about 5 minutes, repeat the dosage.

Performing CPR. Cardiopulmonary resuscitation (CPR) can be administered when your dog has no heartbeat or is not breathing, as might be the case in the event of a near-drowning or a traumatic injury. Canine CPR is similar to human CPR. Clear your dog's airways and pull his tongue forward. Hold his mouth closed, place your mouth over his nose, and breathe into his nose at the rate of ten to twenty exhalations per minute. Perform heart massage by placing the dog on its right side, positioning your hands on the chest just behind the dog's elbow, and pressing down strongly and abruptly, repeating at the rate of one and a half compressions per second (one hundred per minute). Alternate heart massage for 15 seconds and breathing for 10 seconds alternately.

Basic Canine First-Aid Kit

Humans need a first-aid kit; dogs need one too. Here's a list of items you need to carry when you hike with your dog. Most of this kit fits nicely into a small nylon sack.

- Tweezers
- Multifunction pocket tool (should include scissors, wire-cutter, and knife)
- Plastic digital rectal thermometer
- Pantyhose/nylon for muzzle or other restraint
- Gloves (heavy enough to avoid being bitten when handling an injured dog)
- Benedryl or other antihistamine
- Betadine
- Entric-coated aspirin (aspirin only; no ibuprofen or acetaminophen)
- Hydrogen peroxide
- Petroleum jelly and/or antibiotic ointment
- Gauze bandage
- Veterinary wrap or other semielastic, self-sticking outer bandage
- Emergency space blanket
- Chemical cold pack

Your canine first-aid kit might also include:

- An oversized dog booty or a soft vinyl camera lens bag (available in the used bins of camera stores for a dollar or two) to cover an injured paw
- An 8-foot soft nylon rope to use as spare leash
- Lightweight, nylon fabric for use as stretcher or shade/shelter
- A handkerchief for washing wounds

How to Use This Book

An information block at the beginning of each hike is an at-a-glance overview of the hike length, difficulty rating, and other important elements. Information in these blocks is defined as follows:

The hike's total mileage is given as a **round trip** or **one-way trip**. Most round-trip hikes are out and back from a single trailhead. For one-way trips, hikers can either turn around and retrace their steps or arrange for a shuttle or pick-up from the far end of the hike. Several hikes offer options for shortening or lengthening a hike.

Elevation range is the hike's lowest and highest elevation, in feet. Commonly, the trailhead is the lowest elevation and the destination is the highest. Where the trailhead is highest and the trail heads downhill, the higher elevation is provided first. Elevations were determined from United States Geological Survey (USGS) topographic maps and a GPS receiver.

Difficulty ranking evaluates the hike's length, steepness, and trail conditions. It is a subjective judgment based on how quickly one works up a sweat or how slowly one must go to navigate challenging terrain. Steep, rough trails that might require crossing fallen trees, include pitches of greater than 6 percent grade, or skirt a cliff for a short distance were judged difficult. Broad, flat trails were judged easy. Most hikes are classified as moderate, though virtually all vary in difficulty from start to finish.

Hiking time assumes that Fido will want to take a break from time to time, will want to explore a bit and sniff a lot, and that in between doggie dips and sniffing stations you both maintain an average hiking pace of

Conditioning and obedience training will prepare you and your dog for the challenges you'll face on the trail.

about 2 miles per hour on a moderate-to-easy trail. These are relatively leisurely hikes with more time allotted than for human-only hikes. Rover is in no big hurry.

Best canine hiking season is determined by seasonal trail accessibility, the need for dogs to keep cool, and your need to return to the car with a dog that is relatively clean.

Regulations regard parking permits and leash requirements. All National Forest parking areas require a daily or annual Northwest Forest Pass ($5 and $30 in 2003).

Most Oregon State Parks require a daily or annual State Parks parking permit ($3 and $25 in 2003). Many county facilities also charge a parking fee. Portland and Multnomah County Parks offer free parking.

Parking permits are widely available at Forest Service offices, visitor centers, and private retailers, or by depositing a fee in a drop box. Travel into the wilderness requires that you fill out a free wilderness permit at a kiosk near the trailhead specifying how many dogs or livestock are going along.

Dogs must be on a 6-foot leash at all times in Oregon State Parks. This rule also applies to many Forest Service interpretive and recreational trails and to about half the hikes in this book. Dogs are banned on all national park trails in Oregon, though leashed dogs are permitted in Crater Lake National Park on the park's segment of the Pacific Crest Trail.

Maps are from the United States Geological Survey (USGS) 7.5-minute quadrangle series. These maps are available in many bookstores, sporting goods stores, and other retailers, online, by phone, and at ranger stations and information centers.

Information provides the name and telephone number of the agency responsible for the hiking area.

Getting there provides driving directions to the trailhead from a nearby town.

A Note About Safety

Safety is an important concern in all outdoor activities. No guidebook can alert you to every hazard or anticipate the limitations of every reader. Therefore, the descriptions of roads, trails, routes, and natural features in this book are not representations that a particular place or excursion will be safe for your party. When you follow any of the routes described in this book, you assume responsibility for your own safety. Under normal conditions, such excursions require the usual attention to traffic, road and trail conditions, weather, terrain, the capabilities of your party, and other factors. Because many of the lands in this book are subject to development and/or change of ownership, conditions may have changed since this book was written that make your use of some of these routes unwise. Always check for current conditions, obey posted private property signs, and avoid confrontations with property owners or managers. Keeping informed on current conditions and exercising common sense are the keys to a safe, enjoyable outing.

The Mountaineers Books

PART 2

The Trails

*All knowledge,
the totality of all questions
and all answers,
is contained in the dog.*

— *Franz Kafka (Investigations of a Dog)*

WILLAMETTE VALLEY AND PORTLAND AREA

1. Tryon Creek State Park

Round trip: 3.8 miles
Elevation range: 115–260 feet
Difficulty: Easy
Hiking time: 1.5 hours
Best canine hiking season: Year-round
Regulations: Dogs must be on leash
Map: USGS Lake Oswego 7.5′ quadrangle
Information: Tryon Creek State Park, (503) 636-9886, or Oregon State
   Parks, (800) 551-6949

Getting there: From Interstate 5 in Portland, take exit 297 (Terwilliger Boulevard). Turn east onto Terwilliger Boulevard and go 2.3 miles to the entrance to Tryon Creek State Park on the right. Follow the entry road 0.1 mile to the parking area. Trailheads are west of the parking lot near the Nature Center.

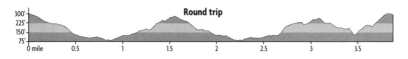

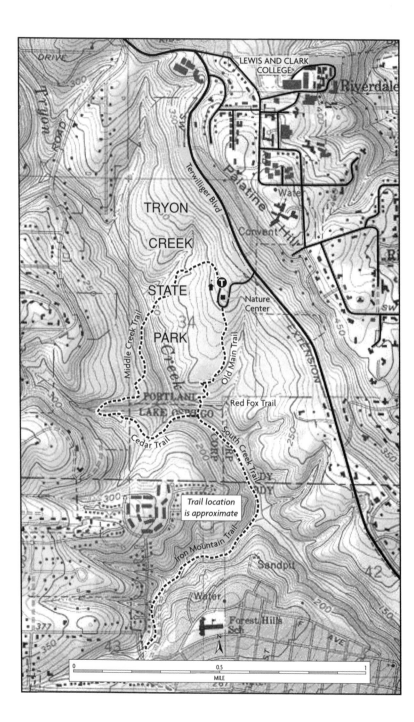

DRIVE

Tryon Road

300

LEWIS AND CLARK
COLLEGE

Riverdale

Terwilliger Blvd

SW

Palatine Hill

Water

Convent Hill

TRYON

CREEK

STATE

34

PARK

Middle Creek Trail

Creek

Old Main Trail

Nature
Center

EXTENSION

450

SW

PORTLAND
LAKE OSWEGO

Red Fox Trail

250

Cedar Trail

South Creek Trail

DY

RP
LOOP

200

*Trail location
is approximate*

300

Iron Mountain Trail

Sandpit

42

350

Water

200

150

377

Forest Hills
Sch

AVE

350

43

MILE

0   0.5   1

This 645-acre state park is tucked away in the southern hills of Portland, just north of Lake Oswego. It offers a variety of rolling trails through forest. Don't expect solitude here. You'll share the trails with hikers, horses, and, on some paths, mountain bikers. It is green and quiet, however, and a quick getaway at the edge of the city. This is a state park, so dogs must be on a leash no more than 6 feet long.

The hike begins at the Nature Center. Turn left (south) on the Old Main Trail—a relatively broad, flat thoroughfare. The path strides through a largely alder and bigleaf maple forest that replaced the conifer forest logged in the late 1800s. The path forks in 0.2 mile. Turn left heading down the winding, switchbacking Red Fox Trail as it scoots into the canyon of Tryon Creek. Here's a good place for a quick doggie dip—on leash, of course.

Michelle and her golden retriever, Dasha, hike a shaded trail in Tryon Creek State Park.

Cross the sturdy bridge here and turn left onto the South Creek Trail. This leads to an out-and-back hike of 2 miles. Follow the South Creek Trail along the ivy-festooned alder and Douglas fir forest of Tryon Creek for 0.4 mile to its junction with the Iron Mountain Trail at a bridge. Both Chinook salmon and steelhead spawn in Tryon Creek. Keep an eye out for fish here in the fall and winter and don't let your dog sample any of the spawned-out adults.

At the bridge, turn right and continue uphill on the Iron Mountain Trail another 0.6 mile to the trail's end on Iron Mountain Boulevard. Turn around here to return the way you came to the junction with the Red Fox Trail. Jog left at the junction to join the Cedar

Trail—a path that clings to the steep canyon slope, ducking beneath cedars and Douglas fir.

The Cedar Trail crosses a small creek in 0.4 mile and contours northward to find Tryon Creek again. Continue north along the creek to High Bridge. Cross this bridge and follow the meandering Middle Creek Trail 0.3 mile upslope back to the parking area and Nature Center.

2. Forest Park Wildwood Trail

One-way trip: 21 miles
Elevation range: 240–820 feet
Difficulty: Moderate
Hiking time: All day
Best canine hiking season: Year-round
Regulations: Dogs must be on leash
Map: USGS Portland 7.5' quadrangle
Information: Portland Department of Parks and Recreation,
(503) 823-7529

Getting there: To reach the south trailhead (Pittock Mansion) where this hike starts, from downtown Portland follow West Burnside Avenue 2.7 miles west from the Burnside Bridge or 1.3 miles west from Northwest 23rd Avenue. Turn right (north) onto Northwest Barnes Road, go 0.7 mile, and then right at the relatively obscure entry sign for Pittock Mansion. Follow the entrance road about 0.2 mile to the visitor parking lot. The trailhead is on the north side of the parking lot.

To reach the north trailhead (Germantown Road) where you will park a second car, from Portland take Interstate 405 west to its merger with U.S. Highway 30. Follow US 30 west for 5 miles. Continue another 0.2 mile past the Saint Johns Bridge. Turn left onto Northwest Bridge Avenue and in 0.24 mile make a sharp right onto Northwest Germantown Road. Follow Northwest Germantown Road 1.2 miles to a small pullout on the left and the north trailhead for the Wildwood Trail.

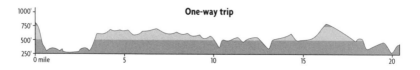

Even though it is within the city of Portland, the Wildwood Trail in Forest Park is a worthy wilderness hike. Many Portlanders drive for hours to access trails that are not much wilder than what they have in their own backyard. This 21-mile segment of the 24.6-mile Wildwood Trail crosses several streams and avoids the portions of the path with the most foot traffic. Road crossings along the way provide turnaround points for more moderate hikes.

Expect plenty of people along this trail, including runners and cyclists. Dogs must remain leashed in this enormous—more than 5000 acres—city park, which is the largest in the United States. Carry plenty of dog water in the summer.

Before you plunge into the forest at Pittock Mansion, take a moment to walk east, past the mansion, to take in the vista of Portland and Mount Hood. It's one of the few views on the entire hike. Although you'll be hiking along the top of the Tualatin Mountains—also known as Portland's West Hills—trees obscure the landscape. The forest here is mostly second-growth fir interspersed with alder and bigleaf maple, though you'll also find cedars and western hemlock along the way.

From the Pittock Mansion trailhead, the path plunges into a dense woodland as it heads north. The trail is broad and meanders downhill here, reaching Northwest Cornell Road and an Audubon Society reserve in about 2 miles. This first mile or two can be fairly congested, but the crowds thin once you get beyond Cornell Road. You can find water for a doggie dip at Balch Creek 3.5 miles from the Pittock trailhead.

All along the trail, the forest varies in its density of Douglas fir, incense cedar, hemlock, alder, and bigleaf maple. Look for the scraggly Pacific yew in moist, heavily shaded spots. Sword ferns dominate the forest floor with salal running a close second. Watch for a few rhododendrons to show off in the spring. The trail contours along the intricate topography, sometimes dropping slightly to avoid steep slopes, sometimes rising gently to cross divides.

At 5.3 miles from the Pittock Mansion, the trail crosses Northwest 53rd Avenue—a point for easy automobile access if needed. The path then returns to its meandering through the trees. Watch for anachronisms along the hike. For example, you'll find fire hydrants tucked in the underbrush—what more could any dog ask for? Many are relics of efforts to develop the park in the early twentieth century. The broad character of the Wildwood Trail belies its origin as a roadway for both development and logging. Look for white mileage posts marked ORRC—artifacts of the

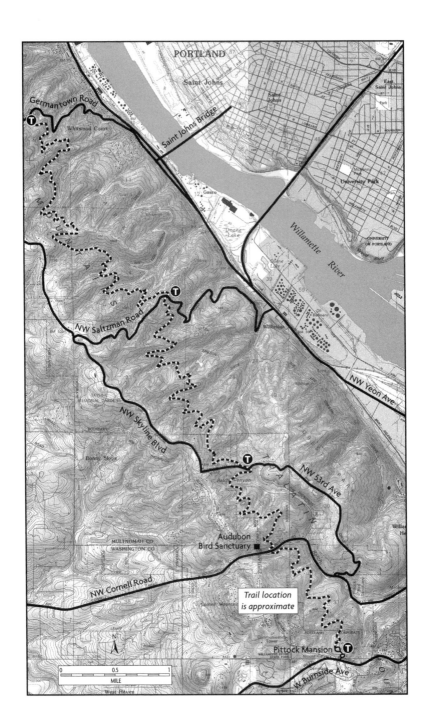

The trail in Forest Park offers solitude, mile-markers, and shade.

Oregon Road Runners Club.

At 12 miles from the Pittock Mansion, the path descends into the broad canyon of Saltzman Creek and intersects Northwest Saltzman Road. This road is a good destination for a day hike—consider it as a drop point if you wish to hike the 8 miles from this road to Germantown Road, the next easy access point. Parking is available in a small four-car area.

Your best bets for doggie dips along the Wildwood Trail include nameless creeks at about 7, 9, and 10 miles into the hike, as well as Saltzman Creek at mile 12. However, the trail tours the upper portion of these drainages, so the water is usually gone by midsummer.

Look for glimpses of Mount Hood about 16 miles into the hike. As it gradually descends to Germantown Road, the trail teases you with views of the Willamette River industrial parks. The sound of traffic presages your return to civilization about 0.2 mile before you reach the Germantown trailhead.

3. Powell Butte

Round trip: 4 miles
Elevation range: 450–630 feet
Difficulty: Easy
Hiking time: 1.5 hours
Best canine hiking season: Year-round
Regulations: Dogs must be on leash; access hours vary and generally correspond to seasonal daylight hours
Maps: USGS Gladstone and Damascus 7.5' quadrangles
Information: Portland Bureau of Environmental Services, (503) 823-7740

Getting there: From Interstate 205 east of Portland, take the Powell Boulevard exit. Drive east on Powell Boulevard 3.4 miles to SE 162nd

On the south and west sides of Powell Butte, fern-lined trails explore cedar and fir forest.

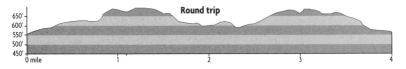

Avenue. Turn right (south) onto 162nd Avenue, and drive 0.7 mile to the parking area. The main trail begins near a visitor's information kiosk on the south side of the parking area.

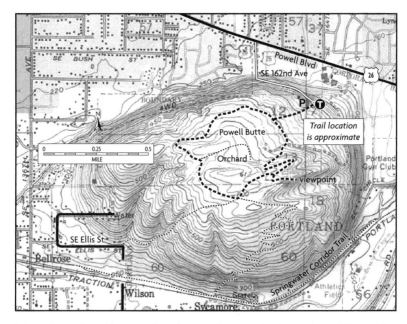

Many formal and informal paths wind across the huge Powell Butte Nature Park on an extinct volcano. Much of Powell Butte is open meadowland—a relic of a time when dairy cows were pastured here. Expect to meet mountain bikers, horses, and plenty of other people and dogs; take water to keep your dog cool and happy.

From the trailhead, the paved Mountain View Trail leads south through grassland then turns east and climbs 0.6 mile to the top of the butte. There are benches to rest on along the way and at the top a "mountaintop finder" helps identify the five Cascade peaks that can be seen from here. Redtailed hawks and kestrels like to hunt the grass slopes atop Powell Butte.

Take the trail to the butte top, continuing past a path that splits to the right immediately after the trailhead. At the top of the grade in 0.2 mile, continue straight, then turn right for a short downhill stretch, and then turn quickly left again, all in less than 0.3 mile from the trailhead. The dirt trail to the left is longer and accommodates hikers and horses. The graveled path is shorter and accommodates mountain bikers and hikers. Opt for the unnamed but well-developed dirt path here. In 0.6 mile it circles into a Douglas fir and cedar forest and then meets a junction of four trails at a complex intersection.

Cross the creek here and then bear left. This path continues through forest, turning downslope and meeting an upbound trail from Southeast Ellis Street at 1.8 miles from the hike's beginning. Continue right along the main trail here. In 0.8 mile it meets a trail to the right. Continue straight to maximize the length of your hike. From this junction, the trail continues about 1.4 miles along the north side of Powell Butte to return to the trailhead 4 miles from the beginning.

4. Sauvie Island: Warrior Rock Trail

Round trip: 5.8 miles
Elevation range: Flat
Difficulty: Easy
Hiking time: 3 hours
Best canine hiking season: September–March
Regulations: Daily or annual parking permit required to park at or near trailhead (applies to all Oregon Department of Fish and Wildlife trailheads on the island). Permits are available at the Cracker Barrel Store on Sauvie Island Road, the 7-Eleven store in Linnton, and at G.I. Joe's stores in Portland. Dogs must be on leash.
Map: USGS Sauvie Island 7.5' quadrangle
Information: Oregon Department of Fish and Wildlife, (503) 621-3488

Getting there: From Portland, take U.S. Highway 30 6 miles west through the town of Linnton. Four miles west of Linnton, turn right to cross the Sauvie Island Bridge. Continue west (left) on Sauvie Island Road and at 3.2 miles, turn right onto Reeder Road. In another 8 miles, Reeder Road changes to a wide gravel road and continues as gravel for 3.4 miles to the trailhead at the road's end 14.6 miles from the Sauvie Island Bridge.

This 2.9-mile hike to Warrior Rock weaves along the Columbia River through cottonwood groves and grassy glades to a lighthouse and rocky point where Multnomah tribal members greeted Captain William Broughton and his ship in 1792. Broughton commanded one of the

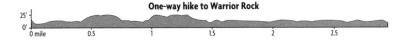
One-way hike to Warrior Rock

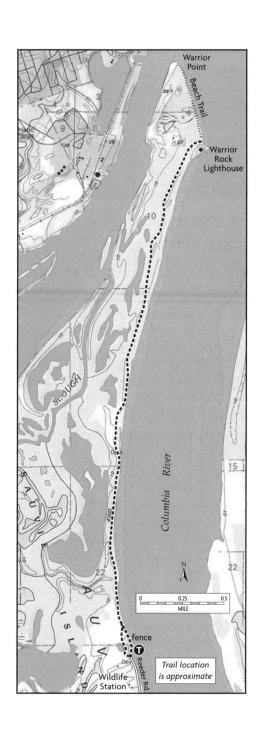

Warrior
Point

Beach Trail

Warrior
Rock
Lighthouse

10

SLOUGH

Columbia River

15

22

N

0   0.25   0.5
MILE

fence

Ⓣ

Reeder Rd

Trail location
is approximate

Wildlife
Station

ships in the expedition with Captain George Vancouver, the first European to explore the Columbia River tidewater.

Sauvie Island is a wildlife refuge and a pasture, and dogs must remain leashed on this hike. Migratory waterfowl and songbirds, as well as residents like great blue heron abound here. You might encounter cattle grazing in the pasture adjacent to the trailhead and along the first portion of the trail from the parking lot, so be doubly sure that your dog is under control as you begin your hike. Despite the proximity of the Columbia River, there's no potable dog water along the way, so carry extra for four-legged hiking companions.

From the parking area, the unmarked Warrior Rock Trail follows a narrow path through a wooden gate and then minces between a cow pasture and Columbia beaches that

The lighthouse at the north end of Sauvie Island overlooks the Columbia River near Warrior Rock.

often host anglers or families on a summer outing. Just beyond the cow pasture, a blue stock gate offers an easy entrance to a grassy field. The narrow path leads through this gate to a service road. Alternatively, you can follow a path along the shoreline that joins the service road in 0.2 mile. This route thrashes its way through blackberries and crosses a partly downed barbed wire fence.

The main path leads through cottonwoods on a level grade. This path to the lighthouse is a double-track road that consistently bears to the right (toward the river) wherever it junctions with other trails. Two open areas are noteworthy. The first, encountered about 0.75 mile into the hike, flirts with the open sky for about 100 yards, then ducks back under trees. At 2 miles into the hike, another grassy open area of about 200 yards length opens up. The main trail reaches the northern tip of Sauvie Island at 2.9 miles. The lighthouse is to the right of the trail.

Use caution in letting dogs swim at the lighthouse. The Columbia River currents can be treacherous here, and it is an abrupt plunge from rocks into deep water. Better swimming can be found to the left where the beaches are sandy and the water is less turbulent.

During times where the Columbia's flow and the tides permit, you can return by walking along the beach on the Columbia side. If you choose this route, be ready to wade in a few places and be wary of oily flotsam and dead fish. Even a single taste of a dead salmon can kill a dog. This route offers the advantages of an open view of the river and its oversized cargo vessel traffic, as well as the Ridgefield and Bachelor Island wildlife refuges and of the mouth of the Lewis River across the Columbia.

5. Silver Falls State Park: Smith Creek Trail

Round trip: 6.4 miles
Elevation range: 1020–1980 feet
Difficulty: Moderate
Hiking time: 3.5 hours
Best canine hiking seasons: Spring, fall
Regulations: Oregon State Parks parking permit; dogs must be on leash
Maps: USGS Drake Crossing and Stout Mountain 7.5' quadrangles
Information: Silver Falls State Park, (503) 873-8681

Getting there: From Salem, take Interstate 5 to eastbound Oregon Route 22 (Santiam Highway). Drive 11.8 miles on ORE 22 and turn north onto Oregon Route 214, marked for Silver Falls State Park. Follow ORE 214 15 miles to the park boundary, then look for the trailhead (214 Trail) on the right (east) side of the road.

Silver Falls State Park showcases four waterfalls more than 80 feet in height and offers several great backcountry hikes for dogs; however, dogs are prohibited from the most popular human hikes that visit the major waterfalls, including the Rim Trail—a hazardous and steep, stair-stepped trail.

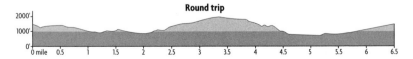

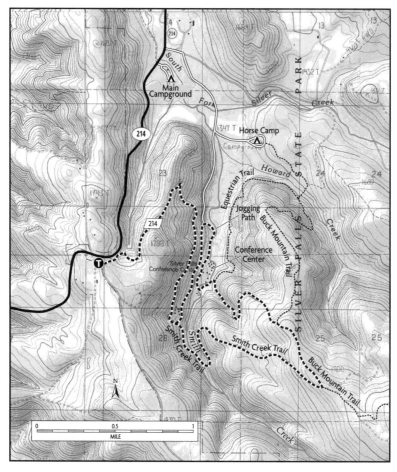

Leashed dogs are allowed on the 15-mile Perimeter Trail and most of the Canyon Trail.

Of all the paths in the park, the Smith Creek Trail is perhaps the most dog-friendly and most varied. It leads through a diverse western Cascade forest, touring second- and third-growth Douglas fir and hemlock stands and riparian areas replete with cedar, alder, and bigleaf maple. Part of the trail is shared with horses. Keep dogs leashed at all times in this Oregon State Park.

From the trailhead adjacent to ORE 214, the 214 Trail descends into Smith Creek canyon in a long, elegant switchback, hanging well above the stream and the Silver Falls Conference Center and remaining sequestered in second-growth Douglas fir for most of its trip to the creek. The

Many trails in Silver Falls State Park, including the Smith Creek loop,
provide for multiple uses.

first 0.7 mile of the hike is on an access trail shared with plenty of horses.
You then reach a junction with the quieter Smith Creek Trail (which
horses also share). Turn right onto Smith Creek Trail. This path meanders through the forest for 1.2 miles, crossing two drainages and slipping
past the conference center. At 1.9 miles from the trailhead, the path
emerges briefly onto a gravel drive and parking area before scooting back
into the woods and meeting Smith Creek in another 0.2 mile. A sturdy
wooden bridge escorts hikers across the creek and through a diverse riparian forest of bigleaf maple, cedar, and spruce. Smith Creek is the last
canine-cooling water for the next 2.4 miles. Once over the bridge, the
path follows Smith Creek for 0.3 mile, then makes an abrupt turn and
begins a climb of about 1000 feet over the next mile, rising through
Douglas fir, hemlock, and alder second-growth forest. The understory here
is lush, mostly comprised of sword ferns and salal.

At the hilltop junction with the much broader Buck Mountain Trail,
turn left (north), following the two-track Buck Mountain Trail through
old-growth Douglas fir and hemlock along a ridge top. Some of these trees
are jaw-dropping, neck-stretching 5-foot-diameter monarchs. The big

trees stand out in cleared areas and among brushy young trees as the Buck Mountain Trail drops gradually toward its next junction.

At 0.4 mile from the hilltop, look for a trail to the left—the "cutoff trail." This path begins with an easy downward grade, but in 0.4 mile it begins to drop more quickly into a small canyon and becomes quite cobbly and rough. At the bottom of this segment you'll reach a grassy field at the Silver Falls Conference Center. Turn right to reach the main driveway, and then turn right again into a parking area just before the road that leads out of the conference area. At the far (north) end of this parking area, you'll find a soft, shady, inviting trail—the "jogging loop"—that heads back into woods. For most of its 0.8 mile, this path toggles between Smith Creek's riparian area and the road, even taking to the road's shoulder at one point. A little farther beyond its shoulder stint, the loop trail intersects the 214 Trail.

Turn left (west) onto the broader, horse-tracked 214 Trail, following it across the park roadway and back into the forest. The trail rises up the ridge in a meandering route that leads back to the trailhead in 1.7 miles.

6. Howard Buford County Recreation Area: Mount Pisgah

Round trip: 7.8 miles
Elevation range: 510–1561 feet
Difficulty: Moderate
Hiking time: 2.5 hours
Best canine hiking seasons: Spring, fall, winter
Regulations: Leashes recommended
Map: USGS Springfield 7.5' quadrangle
Information: Lane County Parks, Mount Pisgah Arboretum,
    (541) 741-4110

Getting there: From Interstate 5 at Eugene, take exit 188, Oregon Route 58/Willamette Highway. Almost immediately after exiting I-5 (virtually at the end of the exit ramp) turn left (north) onto Seavy Loop Road

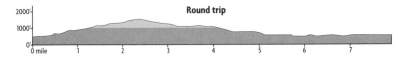

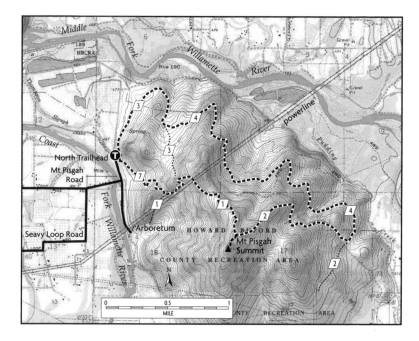

marked for Buford Park. Follow Seavy Loop Road 1.8 miles to a T intersection, and then turn right (north) onto Seavy Way to cross a bridge over the Coast Fork of the Willamette River. Once across the bridge, turn left into a large parking area. The trailhead is at the west end of the parking area.

Whether you are looking for a short, scenic hike or an all-day outing, Mount Pisgah in the Howard Buford County Recreation Area is an excellent place for hikers and their dogs. This Lane County park features 2300 acres of an almost-native Willamette Valley hilltop oak savannah balanced between the Middle and South Forks of the Willamette River. Park rules require that you keep dogs leashed on the main trail to the summit and under immediate control on other trails, that dogs do not harass wildlife (there are plenty of squirrels here and chasing squirrels is a definite no-no), and that you clean up dog waste.

The most popular hike in the huge Buford Recreation Area starts on Trail 7, the Bridge Bowl Trail, from the North Trailhead about 0.6 mile west of the arboretum and winds its way to the summit in 7.8 miles. At a trail junction just past an entry gate to the trail, bear to the right. The trail meanders upward. Its mild switchbacks and curves make the walk interesting. At 0.7 mile, the trail merges with Trail 1, Beistel's West Summit Trail. This hike explores a tiny remnant of the Willamette Valley's native oak woodland, though there are also plenty of tall Douglas firs here, mostly on more moist and sheltered slopes. The firs provide a welcome, deeper shade on summer hikes, but the gnarly countenance of the white oaks makes Mount Pisgah a special place. The landscape is being slowly restored from grazing. Watch for poison oak along the trail on sunny, open slopes and in oak glades.

The path navigates mostly oak savannah, providing exquisite views of the valley to the south as it climbs. The first 2 miles cross several small drainages that can provide a doggie dip in winter, but they are dry most of the year so be sure to carry plenty of water for your dog, especially on sunny days, as much of the hike crosses open savannah. The main summit trail tours stands of Douglas fir about halfway to the summit, then remains on open ground for the rest of the trudge to the 1561-foot summit. From the top, Mount Pisgah provides a superior view of the Willamette Valley, the Cascades, and even hints at the Klamath Mountains to the southwest.

Trails on Mount Pisgah provide a hike through forest and native oak savannah, as well as a view of the surrounding Willamette valley.

Take Trail 2, Beistel's East Summit Trail, to descend. This path is narrower, rockier, steeper, and rougher than the veritable freeway that leads to the summit. It tours grassland and oak savannah. It also boasts considerable poison oak along the path, so it's best to take this trail during the winter when poison oak is not in leaf.

Leading steeply down from the Mount Pisgah summit, Trail 2 meanders less than the main summit trail and reaches the East Trailhead on the Middle Fork of the Willamette in 2 miles. Before that, turn left onto Trail 4, the West Boundary Trail. The path wobbles toward the west, connecting with Trail 3, the West Slope Trail (a short loop hike around a small butte just west of Pisgah) at about 0.5 mile. It ducks under cover of fir trees as it swings west around the base of the mountain and turns toward the first trailhead. The path returns to the trailhead parking area 4 miles from the summit.

Five More Great Dog Hikes in the Willamette Valley and Portland Area

1) Springwater Corridor, Hogan Road to Powell Butte, 5.5 miles one-way. Portland Bureau of Parks and Recreation, (503) 823-2223 or (503) 823-7529.

2) Marine Drive bike and hiking path, 12 miles along the Columbia River beginning at 33rd Avenue and Marine Drive. Portland Bureau of Parks and Recreation, (503) 823-2223 or (503) 823-7529.

3) Milo McIver State Park, Clackamas River, 4.3-mile loop. Milo McIver State Park, (800) 551-6949.

4) Sandy River Delta, between Interstate 84 and the Columbia River beginning at exit 18. Many miles of hiking trails in a 1400-acre U.S. Forest Service reserve. Columbia River Gorge National Scenic Area, (541) 386-2333.

5) Perimeter Trail, Silver Falls State Park, 7 miles one-way. Passes through old-growth forest, and the first half of the trail is horse-free. Silver Falls State Park, (503) 873-8681.

COLUMBIA RIVER GORGE

7. Larch Mountain (almost) to Multnomah Falls

Round trip: 12 miles
Elevation range: 150–4056 feet
Difficulty: Moderate
Hiking time: 4 hours
Best canine hiking seasons: Spring, summer, fall
Regulations: Keep dogs leashed in Larch Mountain picnic areas and near Multnomah Falls
Maps: USGS Bridal Veil and Multnomah Falls 7.5' quadrangles
Information: Mount Hood National Forest Headquarters, (503) 668-1771; Columbia River Gorge National Scenic Area, (541) 386-2333

Getting there: To reach the Larch Mountain trailhead, from Portland follow Interstate 84 east to exit 22, Corbett. Turn right and follow the curving road 2 miles to a junction with Columbia River Gorge Highway (US 30). Turn left (east) onto the Columbia River Gorge Highway and drive 2 miles to Larch Mountain Road at a Y intersection. Follow Larch Mountain Road (Forest Road 15) 10 miles to the trailhead at the road's end.

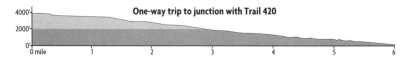

While gazillions of people mob Multnomah Falls, and millions hike the first mile of switchbacking Forest Service Trail 441 to the top of the falls, practically no one hikes the other end of this well-maintained and easy

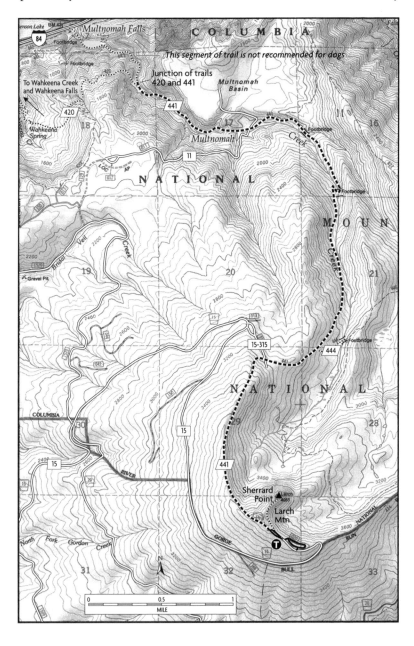

trail at Larch Mountain. Though the full length of the trail is 7 miles, it is recommended that you turn around at mile 6 during the high-volume summer months. If you must make this a through-hike from Larch Mountain all the way to Multnomah Falls, your dog will be a lot happier if you hike it in the spring or on a weekday when the trail is less crowded—otherwise, the last mile of trail can be a lot like waiting in line for concert tickets while taking a shower in the falls overspray.

Trail 441 departs from the from Larch Mountain picnic area just west of the parking area. Before you head out, be sure to take the short walk to Sherrard Point, which has a spectacular view of the Portland Basin and Columbia River. Trail 441 leads along a ridge crest at an even and level pace through a dark forest of small Douglas fir, western hemlock, and grand fir that provides shade and a sense of privacy. Listen for the flute-like song of hermit thrush here early in the summer.

At 1.3 miles, the path and forest change. The trail turns more steeply downhill, crossing a road and entering an old-growth forest dominated by Douglas fir. At 1.8 miles, Trail 444 turns east and drops even more steeply downhill. If you are looking for a doggie dip, a short stroll downhill on this trail will bring you to Multnomah Creek. Return to Trail 441 and continue toward Multnomah Falls. At 2.5 miles, the trail touches the creek, then follows it for the remainder of the hike, crossing the water on sturdy footbridges at 3 miles and 3.5 miles and returning again to water at 4 miles just after crossing a gravel road.

From this point, Multnomah Creek gets very serious as it gears up for the falls. Its channel steepens and the creek enters a real canyon. Between 4 and 5.5 miles, the trail edges along the creek, sometimes on the brink of sheer and quite slippery cliffs. The final 1.5 miles largely spirals downhill, crossing the bridge across the falls, and landing amongst the outdoor vendors at Multnomah Lodge. Return as you came.

8. Angels Rest

Round trip: 4.6 miles
Elevation range: 170–1590 feet
Difficulty: Moderate
Hiking time: 3 hours
Best canine hiking season: Year-round
Regulations: Dogs must be on leash
Map: USGS Bridal Veil 7.5' quadrangle
Information: Columbia River Gorge National Scenic Area,
    (541) 386-2333

Getting there: From Portland, drive east on Interstate 84 to exit 28, Bridal Veil. Turn right at the end of the exit ramp and continue 0.2 mile to a stop sign. Turn right at the stop sign and immediately turn right again into a large trailhead parking lot. An overflow parking area another 0.1 mile down the road provides more shade. The trailhead is across the road from the main parking lot. A spur trail connects to the overflow lot.

This relatively short hike leading to a spectacular view is one of the most popular trails in the Columbia River Gorge—and in Oregon. Expect to meet many other dogs and hikers no matter what season or time of day. There's one reliable stream for a doggie dip, but the summit is devoid of shade, so carry plenty of water on hot days.

From the trailhead, the Angels Rest Trail heads into a forest dominated by bigleaf maple and a few Douglas firs. Look for white trillium blossoms on spring hikes. In the first half-mile, the path leads uphill at a moderate pace, providing an overview of Coopey Falls and then crossing Coopey Creek. This is a great place to cool off your dog before the remaining 0.9-mile assault on the summit.

From the wooden bridge across Coopey Creek, the trail rises through a mixed forest, offering one more pause to peer into the moist canyon.

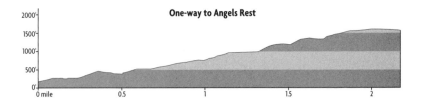

One-way to Angels Rest

The path then climbs more steeply, touring the stark, skeletal remains of a 1991 forest fire at 1.4 miles. Most of this area has healed into a sea of salal and ceanothus, and alder now replaces the burned Douglas fir. Shade is rare along the upper half of the hike.

At 2 miles into the hike, the path crosses rough, gray talus and, after a detour around rocky outcrops, arrives at Angels Rest in 2.3 miles from the trailhead. The views from the rocky bluffs are spectacular—to the west you can view the Portland Basin, to the east, Vista House and Beacon Rock.

Dana and Scout near the trailhead on their return from Angels Rest.

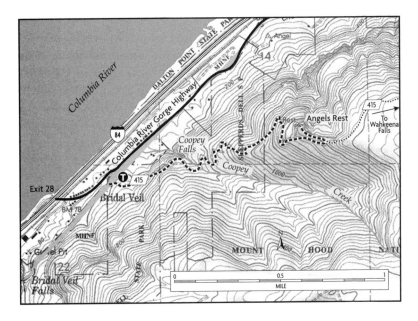

Most hikers elect to return to the trailhead directly from Angels Rest—a satisfying day hike. However, you can extend your hike past Angels Rest by continuing east along the ridge top, rather than returning to the Angels Rest trailhead. This path leads to Wahkeena Spring in 2.5 miles, and reaches Wahkeena Falls 4.2 miles from Angels Rest.

9. Latourell Falls: Upper Trail

Round trip: 1.6 miles
Elevation range: 170–750 feet
Difficulty: Moderate
Hiking time: 1 hour
Best canine hiking season: Summer
Regulations: Dogs must be on leash
Map: USGS Bridal Veil 7.5' quadrangle
Information: Columbia River Gorge National Scenic Area,
(541) 386-2333

Getting there: From Portland, drive east on Interstate 84 to exit 31. Turn right onto the Columbia River Gorge Highway, and follow it 6 miles to the well-marked Latourell Falls parking lot on the left. The trail to the upper falls heads upslope directly from the parking area.

Although Latourell Falls is one of the more popular attractions in the Columbia Gorge, few people use the trail to the upper falls. The path inches around precipitous cliffs just above the main (lower) falls, so be sure to keep venturesome dogs on a short leash here.

From the parking lot, the trail to the upper falls edges along the canyon of Latourell Creek, providing screened views of the picturesque lower falls. At 0.3 mile into the hike, the path navigates along the cliffs almost directly above the falls.

Meesha mooches a handout from Dick at Upper Latourell Falls.

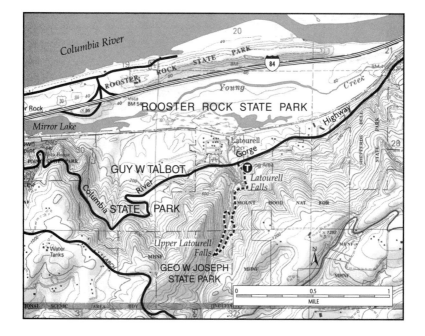

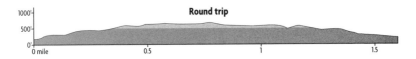

Then, 0.4 mile into the hike, the trail splits. Take the left trail to approach the smaller falls. This path remains remote from the creek until it reaches the falls. Along the way it provides close-up views of rock outcroppings and some gnarled Douglas fir.

At the falls, there are opportunities for doggie dips and a bridge leads across the creek. The return path stays closer to water. You can hear the creek chuckling as it heads for its next acrobatic feat—the 120-foot leap at the lower falls. However, vegetation screens you from most views and access to this upper portion of the creek. At 0.4 mile from the falls, the path rejoins the trail you hiked up. Return as you came.

10. Oneonta Gorge: Triple Falls

Round trip: 7.4 miles
Elevation range: 120–1430 feet
Difficulty: Moderate
Hiking time: 3.5 hours
Best canine hiking season: Year-round
Regulations: Dogs must be on leash
Map: USGS Multnomah Falls 7.5′ quadrangle
Information: Columbia River Gorge National Scenic Area, (541) 386-2333

Getting there: From Portland, drive east on Interstate 84 to exit 28, Bridal Veil. Take this exit and turn left (east) onto the Columbia River Gorge Highway (US 30). Drive 3.5 miles to a parking area on the right with a poorly marked trailhead. If you cross Oneonta Creek, you've gone about 0.4 mile too far.

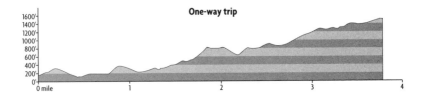

Most hikers to Triple Falls begin at Horsetail Falls, about 1.5 miles east of this trailhead. By starting at the less popular trailhead, you avoid crowds, a few slippery jaunts behind two waterfalls, and the botanically sensitive areas of Oneonta Gorge. There are some steep drop-offs and cliffs along the way, so keep dogs leashed.

The trail begins with a long, gentle ascent through a forest of Douglas fir and vine maple. At 1.1 miles the path enters Oneonta Gorge and turns

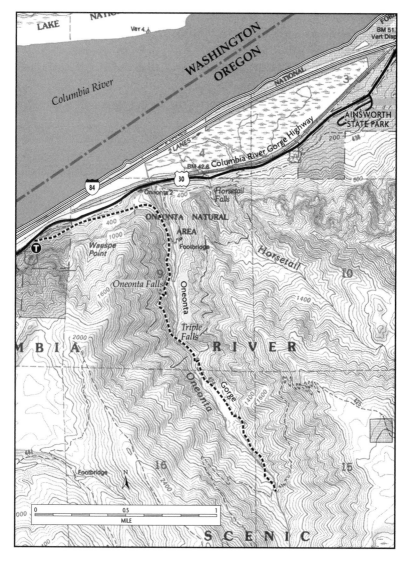

Tara, a seven-year-old Labrador mix, keeps a watchful eye on lunch below the bridge across Oneonta Creek.

to the south. There are several good views into the steep canyon, but for the most part, trees screen and soften the steepest trailside drops. At 1.8 miles, the official Oneonta Falls Trail merges from the left. Continue straight ahead.

This portion of the route also hugs the canyon rim. The path is relatively flat and allows ample room for passing others. At 2.5 miles into the hike, the trail reaches a broad rock rim, providing a view of Triple Falls—a place where the creek divides into three separate plumes as it dives over a rock bench and enters Oneonta Gorge. From the overview (not a good place to hang out with dogs), the path leads down to a bridge across the creek. From this point, the nearly level trail follows the creek closely. The trail beyond the creek crossing is little used and, for dogs, is the best part of the hike. It continues through spectacular old-growth forest for another 1.2 miles before it begins to climb away from the creek. Turn around where the trail begins its ascent away from water and return as you came.

11. Wahclella Falls

Round trip: 1.8 miles
Elevation range: 500–800 feet
Difficulty: Easy
Hiking time: 1 hour
Best canine hiking season: Year-round
Regulations: Dogs must be on leash
Map: USGS Tanner Butte 7.5' quadrangle
Information: Columbia River Gorge National Scenic Area,
    (541) 386-2333

Getting there: From Portland, drive east on Interstate 84 to exit 40, Bonneville Dam. At the end of the exit ramp, turn right (south) and continue to a parking area at the end of the roadway.

This short hike dead-ends at a spectacular, 120-foot double falls. The trail is an easy grade, water is accessible, and use is fairly light for a Gorge trail. From the parking area, the path skirts along Tanner Creek, keeping the creek within easy sight. The trail rises over several groups of creek-smoothed boulders and tours a forest of mostly Douglas fir. Side trails invite contemplative visits to Tanner Creek.

At 0.7 mile, the canyon opens up, providing a view of a huge, moss-covered cliff on the west. In winter and early summer, a misty waterfall plunges over this wall of rock. You can hear the roar of Wahclella Falls before you see it. At 0.9 mile, the trail rises a bit, providing a view of the

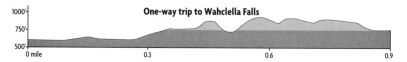

The double cataract at Wahclella Falls is scenic.

double falls. The path scampers downslope for a more intimate view, and crosses an arching wooden bridge just downstream. The bridge leads to a rock-strewn slope below the misty falls. This is a great place for dogs to explore and unwind before the trip back to the car. Return as you came.

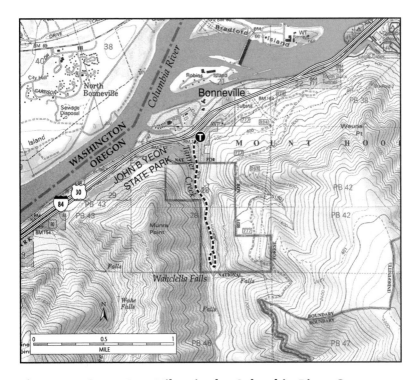

Five More Great Dog Hikes in the Columbia River Gorge

1) Wyeth Campground to North Lake and Rainy Lake (Trail 411), 4 miles to North Lake, 6.5 miles to Rainy Lake. Columbia River Gorge National Scenic Area, (541) 386-2333.

2) Herman Creek Trail to Wahtum Lake (Trail 406), 11 miles. Columbia River Gorge National Scenic Area, (541) 386-2333.

3) Starvation Creek to Warren Lake (Trail 414), 5 miles one-way with hard initial climb. Columbia River Gorge National Scenic Area, (541) 386-2333.

4) Old Columbia River Gorge Highway Trail, 7 miles. Old highway with a lot of bikes. Trail access near Mosier. Columbia River Gorge National Scenic Area, (541) 386-2333.

5) Lower Deschutes River Trail, 17 miles along the Deschutes River from its confluence with the Columbia. Deschutes River State Recreation Area, (541) 739-2322.

COAST AND COAST RANGE

12. Banks–Vernonia State Trail: Vernonia to Braun

One-way trip: 5.5 miles
Elevation range: 660–750 feet
Difficulty: Easy
Hiking time: 2.5 hours
Best canine hiking seasons: Fall, winter
Regulations: Oregon State Parks parking permit; dogs must be on leash
Map: USGS Vernonia 7.5' quadrangle
Information: Oregon State Parks, (503) 324-0606

Getting there: From Portland, take U.S. Highway 26 west about 30 miles to the junction with Oregon Route 47. Turn right (north) onto ORE 47 and drive 14 miles to Vernonia. Turn right onto Weed Street and right again into the trailhead parking area.

To leave a second vehicle at the Beaver Creek trailhead, return to ORE 47, the Nehalem Highway, and follow it about 4.4 miles south to a bridge over Beaver Creek.

The ambitious, 20-mile Banks–Vernonia Trail was the first "rails-to-trails" park in Oregon. It follows a narrow-gauge rail line built in the 1920s that carried lumber and logs from a mill in Vernonia and passengers from nearby Keasey to Portland. When the mill closed in 1957, the line was

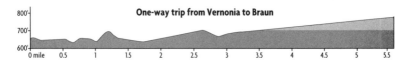

One-way trip from Vernonia to Braun

800'

700'

600'

0 mile   0.5   1   1.5   2   2.5   3   3.5   4   4.5   5   5.5

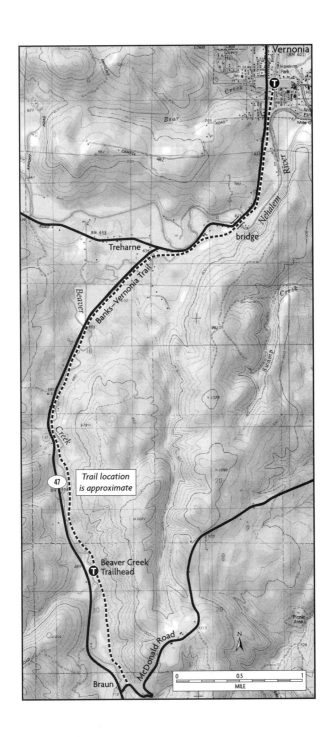

Trail location
is approximate

converted to accommodate steam excursion train use. The last train ran in 1965 and the line was abandoned in 1973. The right-of-way has been an Oregon State Park since 1990. Horses, bikes, bladers, and families with small children are abundant on the trail near Vernonia. Dogs must remain on a 6-foot leash throughout this park. Pavement offers dry-footed winter hiking.

From Vernonia, the pathway heads generally south, paralleling Beaver Creek, but staying well away from the water. In 1 mile it crosses the Nehalem River, and in the next mile encounters a small tributary stream, a road, and Beaver Creek. The path never strays far from the Nehalem Highway (ORE 47), and there is no fence to restrain dogs from traffic. Much of the first 2 miles crosses open meadows and summer shade is limited. After the first crossing of Beaver Creek, there is no water access for the next mile.

At 2.5 miles into the hike, the trail again crosses Beaver Creek. Now the path runs between highway and creek, with the road on your right and creek on the left. After another mile, the path crosses Beaver Creek yet again, then hugs the creekbank most of the way to a toilet and trailhead at mile 4.3. This is the Beaver Creek trailhead, a popular hiking objective and turn-around point—or a place to drop a second vehicle for use as a shuttle.

The paved segment of the trail continues another 2.5 miles. This segment is less popular. It is also more remote from water throughout its length. However, for winter hikes, it makes a fine, more private walk than the first segment of the paved trail. At the end of the paved path, you can return as you came, or continue on a rough railroad grade to the Tophill trailhead, 8 miles from Vernonia (see Hike 13).

A rustic picnic table awaits hikers at Beaver Creek's bridge.

13. Banks–Vernonia State Trail: Tophill to Buxton

One-way trip: 5 miles
Elevation range: 360–1040 feet
Difficulty: Moderate
Hiking time: 3 hours
Best canine hiking seasons: Spring, fall
Regulations: Oregon State Parks parking permit; dogs must be on leash
Maps: USGS Vernonia and Buxton 7.5' quadrangles
Information: Oregon State Parks, (503) 324-0606

Getting there: From Portland, take U.S. Highway 26 west about 30 miles to the junction with Oregon Route 47. Turn right (north) onto ORE 47 toward Vernonia. At mile 14, turn left into trailhead parking area—you'll drive beneath a huge trestle just before the turn into the Tophill trailhead parking area.

To leave a second vehicle or arrange for a pickup at the Buxton trailhead, from the town of Buxton take Bacona Road about 1 mile north to the large parking area.

This portion of the Banks–Vernonia Trail is more primitive and less developed than other parts. It is remote from roads, offering a good opportunity for solitude. There's no potable water at the trailheads, so be sure to bring plenty for you and your dog. And as this is an Oregon State Park, dogs must remain on a leash throughout your hike.

From the Tophill trailhead, the old railroad grade turns west toward Beaver Creek, then swings south, climbing steadily to the summit 1 mile from the trailhead, then dropping to cross Nowakoski Road. It turns again, continuing its descent through woods cluttered with oak and maple, reaching ORE 47 in 0.3 mile. The path plunges across the road and crosses the West Fork of Dairy Creek on a footbridge. From here it passes through the wetland headwaters of a tributary and then climbs gradually once again.

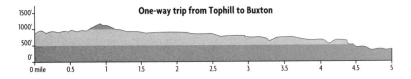

One-way trip from Tophill to Buxton

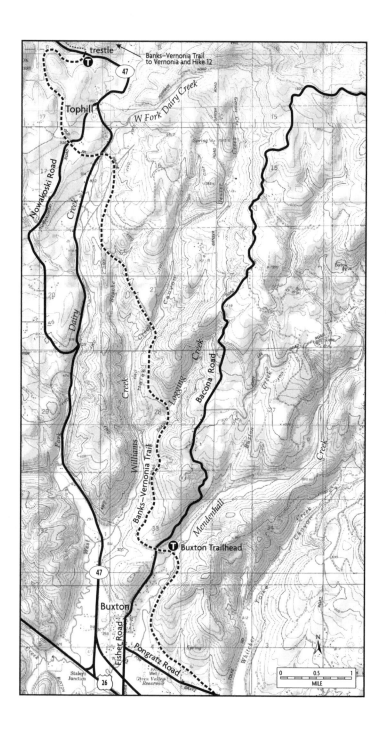

The next 3 miles are the most remote and rugged on the trail. Brooke Creek is crossed in another mile. The trail then rises slightly before dropping into the valley of Williams Creek. These woods offer a variety of bigleaf maple, white oak, and vine maple with an understory of ferns. Deer abound, so be doubly certain that dogs are leashed at all times on spring and summer hikes. (On fall hikes, unleashed dogs risk being mistaken for deer by hunters, so it's always best to heed park rules and keep leashes on your pet.)

Most of the Banks–Vernonia trail is graveled or paved.

Four miles from the Tophill trailhead, the trail finds the valley of Mendenhall Creek and winds downhill until it reaches and crosses Bacona Road and then Mendenhall Creek. Here, the Buxton trestle towers above the Buxton trailhead 5 miles from the beginning.

You can arrange for a pickup here on Bacona Road or choose to continue as the trail crosses the road and continues along a slope for another 1.5 miles to the Banks–Vernonia State Park headquarters just off ORE 47.

14. Harts Cove at Cascade Head

Round trip: 5.8 miles
Elevation range: 200–1010 feet
Difficulty: Moderate
Hiking time: 3–4 hours
Best canine hiking season: Year-round
Regulations: Northwest Forest Pass required
Map: USGS Neskowin 7.5' quadrangle
Information: U. S. Forest Service Pacific Northwest Research Station, (503) 808-2592

Getting there: From Lincoln City, drive 7 miles north on U.S. Highway 101 to Forest Road 186, located at the top of a grade through the Cascade Crest Natural Research Area. Turn left (west) onto FR 1861 and drive 3.7 miles to the road's end and a parking area. The trail leaves from the far end of the parking lot.

From the trailhead, the path plunges into a sparse forest of young hemlock, swinging downward at an easy gait. On my last visit, the trail had been recently widened and improved, leaving a number of springs and muddy spots. At 0.7 mile, the trail crosses Cliff Creek on a sturdy wooden bridge. Although creek access is difficult for humans, this is a good opportunity for a quick doggie dip.

Beyond the creek, the trail flattens, leading past huge Sitka spruce

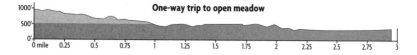

One-way trip to open meadow

and Douglas fir, and through sword fern–lined grottos. In another 0.5 mile, it rises and turns a corner into the Chitwood Creek drainage. If your canine companion has been acting a bit wary, the reason should be apparent here: you can hear the calls of sea lions. The inaccessible, cliff-bounded coves at the Chitwood Creek outlet are home to a large sea lion colony. Their barks will be audible—and puzzling—to your dog long before you can hear them.

In 2.9 miles from the trailhead,

Dundee checks out the view and the barks of sea lions from the hills above Harts Cove.

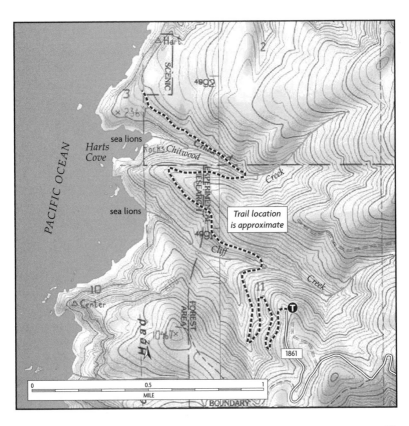

the path reaches an open meadow with a view of the shoreline—Cape Kiwanda and Two Arches to the south and the craggy cliffs where sea lions live. You can hike around a bit and follow informal trails to a hilltop to the north where there's a view of Cape Lookout. Return as you came.

15. Cascade Head Trail

One-way trip: 6.5 miles
Elevation range: 100–1380 feet
Difficulty: Moderate
Hiking time: 3–4 hours
Best canine hiking season: Year-round
Regulations: Northwest Forest Pass required
Map: USGS Neskowin 7.5' quadrangle
Information: U. S. Forest Service Pacific Northwest Research Station, (503) 808-2592

Getting there: To reach the south trailhead where this hike starts, drive north from Lincoln City on U.S. Highway 101 for 4.5 miles to Three Rocks Road. Turn left (west) on Three Rocks Road and immediately turn right into the south trailhead parking area.

If you want to reach the north trailhead from the road, in order to leave a second car or arrange a shuttle, drive north out of Lincoln City on US 101 for 9 miles, passing Three Rocks Road and the top of Cascade Head. Head down to a very small parking area on the left (west) side of the road.

The Cascade Head Trail explores a cross section of the 11,890-acre Cascade Head Experimental Forest. Established in 1934, the reserve of Sitka spruce and western hemlock is typical of forests found along the Oregon coast. The forest stands at Cascade Head have been used for long-term studies, experimentation, and ecosystem research. A Nature Conservancy preserve

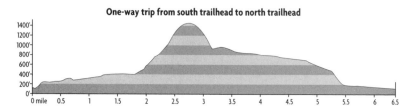

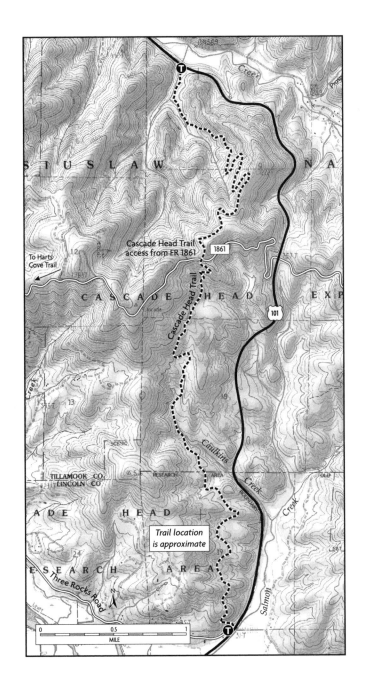

SIUSLAW NA

Creek

To Harts
Cove Trail

Cascade Head Trail
access from FR 1861

1861

CASCADE HEAD EXP

101

Cascade Head Trail

Caulkins

SCENIC

TILLAMOOK CO.
LINCOLN CO.

RESEARCH AREA

ADE HEAD

Trail location
is approximate

ESEARCH AREA

Three Rocks Road

Salmon Creek

Creek

OLD

0   0.5   1
MILE

on Cascade Head is off-limits to dogs and is not included in this hike.

From the south trailhead, the trail navigates a narrow corridor through alder thickets and a spruce and alder–dimpled wetland for the first mile. The path then rounds a bend and drops into a wetland area along Caulkins Creek. The marsh is replete with false hellebore, oxalis, and cattails. Here, the path would be an impassible morass without the lengthy and well-constructed boardwalk that traverses the wettest portion. Alaska red cedar flourishes here. Once past the bogs and safely across the headwaters of Caulkins Creek, the trail rises through an awe-inspiring old-growth forest of Douglas fir and Sitka spruce. This forest is more open, and the trees are truly huge.

At 2 miles from the trailhead, the path begins a steady climb through an open forest of huge spruce. Occasional stumps, snags, and trunks bear scars from a stand-replacement fire that burned much of the northern Coast Range in the 1840s.

The trail crosses Forest Road 1861 about 2.5 miles from the trailhead. After a brief stroll along the ridge crest, the path drops gradually through a somewhat denser stand of fir, spruce, and bigleaf maple, reaching an unnamed stream in a little less than 1 mile. Huge spruce and impressive firs again punctuate the hike. The path follows the unnamed creek closely for the last half-mile of the hike, then emerges at the skimpy trailhead pull-off on the main highway, 6.5 miles from its start.

16. Cape Lookout: South Trail

Round trip: 2.6 miles
Elevation range: Sea level–890 feet
Difficulty: Moderate
Hiking time: 3–4 hours
Best canine hiking season: Year-round
Regulations: Oregon State Parks parking permit; dogs must be on leash
Map: USGS Sand Lake 7.5' quadrangle
Information: Cape Lookout State Park, (503) 842-4981

Getting there: From Tillamook, drive south 11 miles on U.S. Highway 101. Turn right (west) onto County Road 871. Continue 4.2 miles and turn right (north) onto Cape Lookout Road (Forest Road 11). The large parking area is 3 miles farther on your left (west) at the crest of a long hill.

One-way trip to beach

The Cape Lookout Trail to the western tip of Cape Lookout is the most popular of the hikes that tour the cape. It is also the least suitable for dogs, with steep cliffs and places where there is no room to allow other hikers to pass easily. The South Trail, described here, and the North Trail (Hike 17) are better alternatives and both have the added advantage of beach access, as well as views every bit as good as the view from the west end of the cape.

From the east end of the parking area, start down the Cape Lookout Trail toward Cape Lookout. About 200 feet from the trailhead, turn sharply left and downhill on a spur trail that is poorly marked and ap-

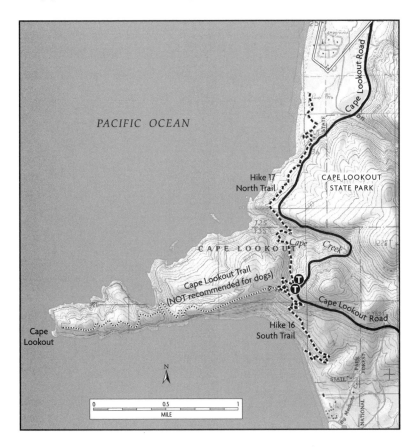

The South Trail at Cape Lookout leads to a cobbled beach and a good view of the cape's basalt cliffs.

pears to lead in the opposite direction. This path is the South Trail. It heads downhill in a straight line for the first 0.3 mile, then begins a series of elongated switchbacks.

The forest near the trailhead is mostly Douglas fir and western hemlock. Sword ferns and salal form a riotous understory. In late summer, the salal berries turn blue-black. They are plump and quite edible by both humans and dogs. If your dog has learned to eat huckleberries, chances are that he'll also enjoy the slightly chewier salal.

The trail's switchbacks become shorter as it winds downhill. In 0.9 mile it crosses a small stream with enough water to cool canine feet. This water seeps from the base of a huge Sitka spruce, giving the spot a sort of fairy tale feeling.

Beyond the spring, the trail spirals downward more tightly, offering a view of Cape Lookout's cliff-lined south side and its outstanding columnar joints. The last 0.5 mile of the trail tours moist thickets of salal, then plunges to the log-laden beach. Depending on the previous season's storms, the last few yards to the beach can be perilous. From here, you can hike south toward Cape Kiwanda. At low tides, it can be fun to examine the base of Cape Lookout. Return as you came.

17. Cape Lookout: North Trail

Round trip: 5.2 miles
Elevation range: Sea level–890 feet
Difficulty: Moderate
Hiking time: 2–3 hours
Best canine hiking season: Year-round
Regulations: Oregon State Parks parking permit; dogs must be on leash
Map: USGS Sand Lake 7.5' quadrangle
Information: Cape Lookout State Park, (503) 842-4981
See Hike 16 for map

Getting there: From Tillamook, drive south 11 miles on U.S. Highway 101. Turn right (west) onto County Road 871. Continue 4.2 miles and turn right (north) onto Cape Lookout Road (Forest Road 11). The large parking area is 3 miles farther on your left (west) at the crest of a long hill.

From the parking area, the North Trail down the north side of Cape Lookout leads to the beach and Cape Lookout State Park in 2.6 miles. Along the way, there are views of the Netarts Spit to the north, as well as a nice stream for cooling off. The trailhead on the northwest side of the parking area is separate from the trailhead to Cape Lookout's western point.

From the trailhead, the path ambles through a forest sprinkled with mammoth Sitka spruce to reach Cape Creek in 0.9 mile. From the creek, the path climbs across a long and ingenious set of steps, then flattens and crosses a ridge where it offers a tantalizing view of the Pacific Ocean. From this spot 1.5 miles into the hike, the trail begins dropping. It edges briefly along the top of cliffs—the drop-offs are screened and cushioned by salal and shore pine. Occasional gaps in the salal fringe permit glimpses of the beach below.

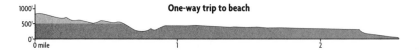

One-way trip to beach

Cape Lookout's north trail travels through a shady forest.

At 2.2 miles, the trail begins an earnest, switchbacking descent to Cape Lookout Campground. Before it enters the campground, the path crosses an inviting creek, offering another dog-cooling opportunity. Once on the beach, you can follow the beach northward past the camping area and along Netarts Spit. Return as you came.

18. Cape Perpetua: Cummins Ridge to Gwynn Creek

Round trip: 7.8 miles
Elevation range: 430–1350 feet
Difficulty: Moderate
Hiking time: 5 hours
Best canine hiking season: Year-round
Regulations: Northwest Forest Pass required
Map: USGS Yachats 7.5' quadrangle
Information: Waldport Ranger District, Siuslaw National Forest, (541) 563-3211

Getting there: Starting from the Cape Perpetua Visitor Center located 11 miles south of Waldport on U.S. Highway 101, continue south on US 101 for 1.1 miles. Turn left (east) onto Forest Road 1050. Continue 0.3 mile to the trailhead and a small parking area on the right (south) side of the road.

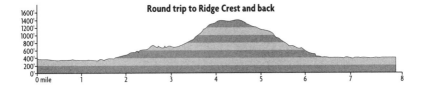

Round trip to Ridge Crest and back

The Cummins Creek Trail tours the watershed of Cummins Creek, climbing through recovering logged areas that are now alder-laced forest, and arriving at a ridge top to provide a nice view of the Pacific coast. Carry water for Fido, as parts of the trail are in the open with limited water after the first 0.3 mile.

From the trailhead, Trail 1382 enters the riparian environment along Cummins Creek, following the stream closely for the first 0.3 mile. The hike follows an abandoned logging road that rises above Cummins Creek, and then turns north, weaving through alder and young Douglas fir. The path maintains an even grade through the alder. Salal and blackberries line the trailside.

The coastal forest of mostly cedar and spruce provides ample shade along Cummins Creek.

After 2 miles of easy walking, the path begins a steeper climb through more recent clear-cuts. The trail up the south-facing slopes can be sunny and hot in the summer, but it makes an ideal spring or winter hike. At 2.4 miles, the Cummins Creek Trail turns left, while a spur trail (also an abandoned road) continues straight to dead end after 0.6 mile. Bear left here, climbing through a landscape of more recent clear-cuts. In time, alder and fir will obscure the view here (and also provide more summer shade), but there are plenty of places along this rising trail segment where you can glimpse the coastline to the south.

At 3.4 miles, the Cooks Ridge/ Gwynn Creek Trail bears to the left. Turn left onto this trail to return to

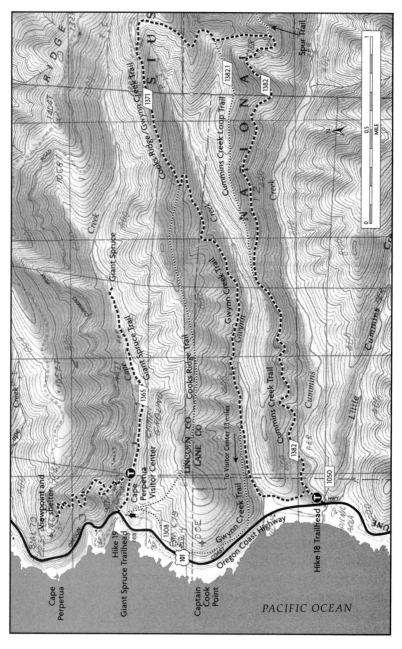

the trailhead via old-growth forest and a moist creek bottom. The Cooks Ridge/Gwynn Creek Trail turns west to follow the ridge crest for about a mile, dropping gradually and finding deeper shade. You reach a trail junction at 0.9 mile from the ridge crest. The trail straight ahead leads to the Cape Perpetua Visitor Center. To return to your vehicle, turn sharply left onto the Gwynn Creek Trail (Trail 1371). This path makes a long, single switchback, descending into the old-growth forest of Sitka spruce, hemlock, and diminishing numbers of Douglas fir. After a steady downhill track of about 2 miles, a path heads to the left (south), while the Gwynn Creek Trail continues straight toward the Cape Perpetua Visitor Center. To return to the trailhead, turn left (south) here, crossing Gwynn Creek in 0.1 mile—a welcome place for a refreshing doggie dip. Beyond Gwynn Creek, continue 0.5 mile to FR 1050, then follow the road 0.2 mile back to the trailhead and your car.

19. Cape Perpetua: Giant Spruce Trail

Round trip: 4.6 miles including side trip
Elevation range: 160–800 feet
Difficulty: Moderate
Hiking time: 3.5 hours
Best canine hiking seasons: Winter, spring
Regulations: Northwest Forest Pass required
Map: USGS Yachats 7.5′ quadrangle
Information: Waldport Ranger District, Siuslaw National Forest, (541) 563-3211
See Hike 18 for map

Getting there: From Waldport, drive 11 miles south on U.S. Highway 101 to the Cape Perpetua Visitor Center. Turn left (east) at the visitor center entrance, and drive 0.2 mile to the Giant Spruce trailhead on the right.

Aptly named, the Giant Spruce Trail leads through spectacular old-growth forest. This is a popular path, especially in summer. You should keep Rover

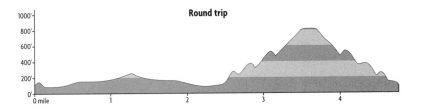

leashed. Hike during off-peak tourist seasons—in the winter or spring—for the easiest excursion with your dog. The trail follows Cape Creek, and intersects several tributary streams, so cooling water is readily available. However, as always, carry drinking water for your dog.

From the trailhead, the path to the Giant Spruce plunges into coastal forest. Salal and a variety of berries, including salmonberry, thimbleberry, and huckleberry, line the trail. Massive Sitka spruce and a few hemlock and alder provide a rich canopy.

The relatively flat trail follows Cape Creek through a forest of huge spruce. The grandmother of them all is the Giant Spruce at 0.5 mile. The Giant Spruce is more than 6 feet in diameter and ringed by the path, benches, and an interpretive sign.

As you return along the same path that brought you, look for a side trail to the north marked for the cape viewpoint. In its 1.3-mile length, the Saint Perpetua Trail (Trail 1365.1) crosses Cape Creek and rises out of the forest to visit Cape Perpetua's windswept brow, then bears left to a rock shelter and an overlook. The overlook offers a compelling view of the coastline, as well as a good binocular-based whale-watching post during the spring and fall migrations of gray whales. Return to the visitor center trailhead as you came.

The Saint Perpetua Trail to a viewpoint atop Cape Perpetua branches off the main trail to the Giant Spruce.

20. Humbug Mountain State Park: Summit Trail

Round trip: 4.7 miles
Elevation range: 40–1730 feet
Difficulty: Moderate
Hiking time: 3–4 hours
Best canine hiking season: Year-round
Regulations: Oregon State Parks parking permit; dogs must be on leash
Map: USGS Port Orford 7.5' quadrangle
Information: Humbug Mountain State Park, (541) 332-6774

Getting there: Take U.S. Highway 101 5.5 miles south of Port Orford to Humbug Mountain State Park. The parking lot is on the west side of the highway just past where the road swings away from the beach.

The 2.9 mile walk to the top of Humbug Mountain (1756 feet) is more a pilgrimage than a hike. One of the most-climbed summits on Oregon's coast, Humbug Mountain proffers a memorable climb through a vigorous coastal forest, along with a feeling of accomplishment when you reach the summit. But don't expect great views. Except for a tunneled glimpse of the coast to the south, and a few rare, tree-obscured views to the north in the first mile of hiking, on this hike you mostly see the trees, the forest, a few other hikers, and their dogs.

For dogs, the path provides several crossings of a small unnamed stream, so there are opportunities for canine cooling. But carry water, because there is no water on the upper portion of the mountain, and in summer and fall the streams could be dry or inadequate to keep your dog cool. This is an Oregon State Park, so keep dogs leashed at all times.

The Humbug Mountain Summit trailhead can be reached from a tunnel in the campground between the A and B Loops roadways, or from a roadside parking lot along US 101, 5.5 miles south of Port Orford in Humbug Mountain State Park. The trail leads into a forest of bigleaf maple, Douglas fir, and myrtle trees, rising at a rapid-but-hikeable rate,

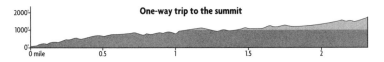

switchbacking past a stream and a number of old-growth Douglas fir that sport scars from a fire that burned much of this coastal area almost a century ago. The first half-mile is the steepest part of the trail—a climb of 420 feet. The trail crosses the stream twice, first at 0.7 mile (at about the 550-foot elevation), and later, on a higher switchback, at 0.9 mile. Wildflowers, including Columbia lily, adorn the trailside along with maidenhair ferns.

Just before the 1-mile marker, the trail splits. Here, you'll also find a bench for planning the next phase of your ascent. Both paths lead to the summit, but take the path to the east (left), which tracks through the drier side of Humbug Mountain and is slightly less steep than the alternative route, to reach the summit in 2 more miles. The path leads

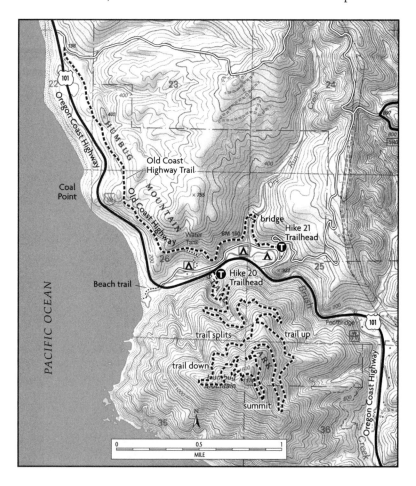

Bloodhound Oma and her master on the trail to the top of Humbug Mountain.

through groves of small-diameter tanoak trees. Wild rhododendrons share the forest with an understory of salal and sword ferns. The summit area is a small meadow with several rock outcroppings and a limited view of Cape Sebastian and Gold Beach to the south.

Dogs, even dogs that are in good condition and provided with adequate drinking water, can become overheated on this climb. If your dog asks for a break to cool off, pay attention to her needs—even if you haven't "summited" and the top is tantalizingly close.

To return to the trailhead, take the steeper, west trail down. This path is somewhat rockier that the upbound route. It switchbacks downward, exploring a more dense forest on the wetter, western slopes of Humbug Mountain where Douglas fir and Port Orford cedar—including some large second-growth trees and a few old-growth giants—far outnumber tanoak. Rock outcroppings are noticeable along the upper 0.5 mile of the trail. After a quick, steeply switchbacked drop, the western trail hits a saddle and sashays through a brighter forest where salal and vanilla leaf form the understory. The forest here is relatively open for good reason. In 1962, Oregon's infamous Columbus Day storm uprooted and blew down so many trees here that this portion of the trail was closed and did not re-open for more than twenty years. The western loop rejoins the main Summit Trail in 0.9 mile from the summit.

21. Humbug Mountain State Park: Old Coast Highway

Round trip: 4.6 miles
Elevation range: 70–300 feet
Difficulty: Easy
Hiking time: 2 hours
Best canine hiking seasons: Winter, spring
Regulations: Oregon State Parks parking permit; dogs must be on leash
Map: USGS Port Orford 7.5' quadrangle
Information: Humbug Mountain State Park, (541) 332-6774
See Hike 20 for map

Getting there: Take U.S. Highway 101 6 miles south of Port Orford to Humbug Mountain State Park. Turn left (north) into the park entrance, and drive 0.25 mile to a trailhead on the right where the Old Coast Highway is gated and before entering a campground

This broad, gentle path follows the abandoned Old Coast Highway from Humbug Mountain north toward Port Orford. For those who are used to

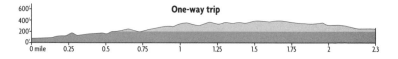

Humbug Mountain is one of the Oregon coast's more distinctive features.

hiking in the wilderness, this trail can seem rather civilized—portions of the old road's pavement remains and the route crosses vintage concrete highway bridges rather than the quaint wooden structures familiar to hikers. Cyclists are attracted by the fact that this trail is a former road, so watch for zippy mountain and road bikes. Yet the route does offer seclusion from crowds, as well as beautiful views of the south-curving reach of shoreline below and Humbug Mountain serving as an exclamation point in the distance.

There is no water along this hike after the first 0.2 mile from the trailhead, so, as always, carry extra for your dog. The stretches of remnant pavement can be very hot on dog paws, so provide opportunities for occasional shady rest stops if you hike this trail on a sunny day.

From the trailhead, the Old Coast Highway heads gently uphill into a cool, leafy tunnel of bigleaf maple, alder, and spruce, passing once barren road cuts now bristling with mosses and sword ferns. The pavement here is intact, right down to the fading centerline. The path remains at least partly pavement throughout the hike. Gravel appears periodically where erosion or other forces have removed the asphalt. In about 0.5 mile, the old highway crosses a creek on an impressive old bridge. This is the last reliable chance for a doggie dip before the path climbs a bit more steeply through the shade of maples and spruce.

In about 0.7 mile from the start, a spur trail from the campground amphitheater joins the path just as the old highway breaks out of the trees and into the open. At 1 mile, the path rounds a bend and offers a nice beach view complete with a bench to sit on. From here, the route turns north and remains high above the existing highway. You can catch glimpses of the shore through the wind-sculpted fir and spruce. This path continues for about 2 miles, alternating between open and shady stretches, until it merges with U.S. Highway 101. Watch for poison oak along the edges of the trail where the path is open to the sun. The old road follows a powerline for much of its journey above and parallel to the newer coast highway. The Old Coast Highway Trail ends where it meets the new highway 2.3 miles from the trailhead. Return as you came.

22. Floras Lake State Park: Blacklock Point

Round trip: 7–9 miles
Elevation range: Sea level–200 feet
Difficulty: Easy to moderate
Hiking time: 4–5 hours
Best canine hiking seasons: Fall, winter
Fees: Curry County fee for trailhead parking area
Map: USGS Floras Lake 7.5' quadrangle
Information: Curry County Parks, (541) 247-7011

Getting there: Drive 7 miles north of Port Orford on U.S. Highway 101 past the entrance to Cape Blanco Park, and turn left (west) onto Curry County Road 190 (Airport Road). Drive 2.9 miles west on this road to a dead end at Cape Blanco Airport and a sign for Blacklock Point, Floras Lake Coast Trail. A large parking area is down a gravel road to the left.

This delightful 9-mile shoreline hike offers some of the most diverse landscape on the coast, introducing you to shore pine groves, wetlands, dunes,

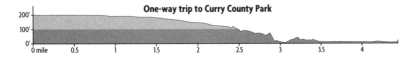

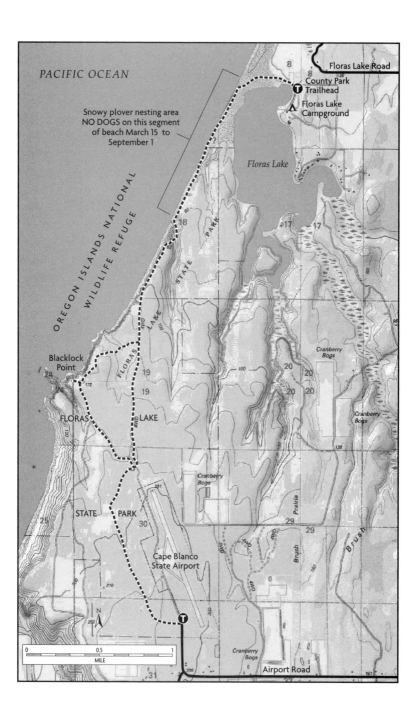

PACIFIC OCEAN

Snowy plover nesting area
NO DOGS on this segment
of beach March 15 to
September 1

Floras Lake Road

County Park
Trailhead

Floras Lake
Campground

Floras Lake

OREGON ISLANDS NATIONAL
WILDLIFE REFUGE

18

STATE PARK

17

Cranberry
Bogs

Blacklock
Point

FLORAS LAKE

19

20

20

20

Cranberry
Bogs

FLORAS LAKE

Cranberry
Bogs

STATE PARK

30

29

29

Cape Blanco
State Airport

Brush Prairie

Brush

N

Cranberry
Bogs

31

Airport Road

0   0.5   1
MILE

Meesha ponders the trail along the route to Floras Lake.

freshwater lakes, beaches with fantastic rock outcroppings, and bold views of the coast from high atop coastal headlands. There is one major caution. The north portion of the hike leads along beaches and dunes that are critical habitat for the endangered snowy plover. Only about 100 snowy plovers have been documented in Oregon, and there are only nine nesting sites, this being one of them. As such it is strictly off limits to dogs, even dogs on leash, from March 15 to September 1. During those months, you can still take a shorter hike of 7 miles.

Make sure you carry extra water for dogs. Even though there is fresh-water in wetlands and a small stream at about 2.5 miles, active dogs can work up quite a thirst along this scent-filled trail.

From its beginning at the airport trailhead, the broad trail leads boldly through continuous thickets of pygmy shore pine. This area also includes Sitka spruce and many native shrubs, including evergreen huckleberry, black twinberry, rhododendron, Sitka alder, wax myrtle, black crowberry, and juniper. Wild azalea, salal, and a few wild iris occupy shady or wet areas. The trail drops subtly. At 0.2 mile there is an unmarked fork. Take the right trail, and after a half-mile stroll along a relatively straight path, the trail splits again at a fork marked for Blacklock Point to the left and Floras Lake to the right. From this point, Floras Lake is 2 miles farther along a mostly well-groomed trail—plus a beach hike that skirts cliffs for another 0.7 mile. This segment is best done at low tide, so plan your day accordingly.

The Floras Lake segment marches straight through the salal and aza-lea bushes for another mile on a broad thoroughfare, and then splits again. Left leads to Blacklock Point; you will turn here to visit Blacklock Point on the return loop. For now, bear right and continue toward Flo-ras Lake. The trail ducks into a spruce grove, occasionally weaving around fallen trees. There are high beach cliffs just west of the trail, so keep energetic dogs under control. At 2.4 miles, the trail spills down a slope into a wide coastal ravine and bifurcates into several paths, each of which leads across the creek here. Trails join on the west side of the clearing and lead to a wonderful beach of coarse sand and tall yellow sandstone sea stacks.

At this point, the coast trail turns into a beach trail. Follow the beach 0.7 mile north, passing more sculpted sandstone cliffs. This section is best done at low tide. North of these cliffs, you will find soft, low dunes. Here you enter snowy plover habitat. Do not continue north, even with dogs leashed, during nesting season, which is March 15 to September 1. A coast trail marker is 0.3 mile beyond the cliffs. From here the trail leads around Floras Lake to the end of the hike at a bridge and parking area for Curry County Park.

When you return, follow the beach back to the coast trail, and then follow the trail back to the second Blacklock Point marker passed earlier. Turn right along a broad path that tunnels through pines, spruce, and salal. This tail crosses three small bridges in 0.6 mile to another marked intersection. Continue on the right-hand trail here, and in 0.3 mile you reach Blacklock Point. A grassy meadow area along the point beckons, while the views, especially to the south, entice you closer to the cliffs. Keep dogs leashed here for their safety. It is a long, steep fall to the beach. Informal trails lead southward to the beach, which, from the top of the headland, seems much farther than its actual 0.2 mile.

From the top of the headlands, return 0.3 mile to the trail marker, then turn right onto the trail you didn't take before. In 0.5 mile you will find yourself back at the intersection with the trail you started on. Turn right here and follow the trail back to airport and parking lot.

23. Samuel H. Boardman State Scenic Corridor

Round trip: 12 miles
Elevation range: Sea level–400 feet
Difficulty: Easy to moderate
Hiking time: 7 hours
Best canine hiking season: Year-round
Regulations: Oregon State Parks parking permit; dogs must be on leash
Maps: USGS Brookings and Carpenterville 7.5' quadrangles
Information: Oregon State Parks, (800) 551-6949

Getting there: From Bandon, drive 12 miles on U.S. Highway 101 to the trailhead at Lone Ranch State Wayside. The unmarked trailhead is at the north end of the picnic area.

The Coast Trail is a 300-mile-long, mostly informal network of trails and beach hikes that navigate Oregon's coastline from Astoria to Brookings.

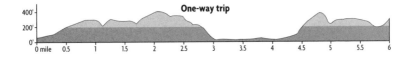

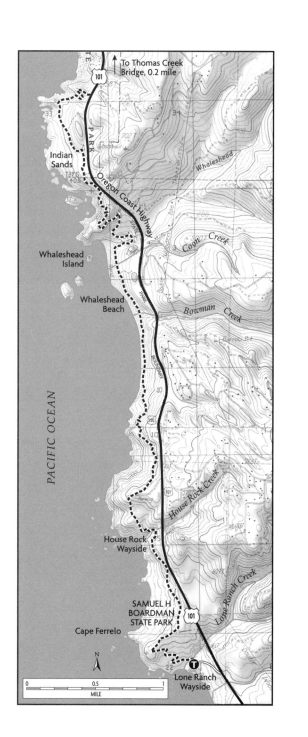

To Thomas Creek
Bridge, 0.2 mile

101

PARK

Indian
Sands

Oregon Coast Highway

Coon   Creek

Whaleshead
Island

Whaleshead
Beach

Bowman   Creek

PACIFIC OCEAN

10

101

House Rock Creek

House Rock
Wayside

Lone Ranch Creek

SAMUEL H
BOARDMAN
STATE PARK

101

Cape Ferrelo

N

T

Lone Ranch
Wayside

0   0.5   1
MILE

One of the network's best—and newest—segments is in southern Oregon. Expect to find relatively tame deer and other wildlife on the grassy slopes of the Lone Ranch Wayside and in park areas farther along the path, so keep dogs leashed. There is no reliable water along this hike, so be sure you carry plenty for your dog.

Begin at the unmarked trailhead at the north end of Lone Ranch State Wayside picnic area. Follow the paved path past the pit toilets, and instead of continuing west (left) to the beach, bear straight ahead along a mowed path that seems to lead into the riparian brush. This is where a dog is especially helpful. Chances are that your four-footed friend can easily find the tunnel through the brush and the informal ford of Lone Ranch Creek, as well as the path that leads out of the dense thicket on the other side.

On my last trip across this creek an informal bridge constructed with a railroad tie provided a way over the water. In most seasons, this is adequate to allow you to cross the stream with minimal wading. After the

Deva, a five-year-old American Stafforshire terrier, leads the way along the foggy Coast Trail above Lone Ranch Creek.

creek, the trail bears left through the dense willow thicket, emerging onto a grassy slope, and winding uphill across this hummocky and open land-scape at the west end of Cape Ferrelo. Numerous trails lead all over the slope—the Coast Trail peters out here like an unraveled rope. Choose trails that mostly head upward and you will ultimately merge with the main Coast Trail near the top of the slope.

The trail leads through thickets of salal and thimbleberry to a park-ing area, then plunges into the underbrush again on the north side of the lot. From this point, the trail follows the top of cliffs, balancing between beach and road and ultimately emerging from salal thickets to views of the beach far below. About 0.5 mile from the top of Cape Ferrelo watch for a spur trail that descends to the beach. This path seems like a difficult route down, but in the end it proves quite dog-worthy and hiker-friendly.

To continue the hike, you'll have to scramble back up to the main trail and follow it through a thickening forest dominated by Sitka spruce. These trees are huge, and their gnarly roots look like something out of the *Wizard of Oz*. This segment of the path emerges into the House Rock Wayside parking area to take a breather before diving back into salal thick-ets as it continues north.

From the House Rock Wayside parking area, the trail moves closer to the highway, then meanders downslope, reaching Whaleshead Beach in about 1.5 miles. From here, it's a 1.5-mile walk along the beach to reach the Whaleshead Beach picnic area and entrance road. Follow the entry road back toward US 101, and look for the trail's resumption just before you reach the highway. The path ducks back into Sitka spruce forest, lopes west to a slight hilltop, wobbles briefly back to the highway, and then heads west again to the dunes of Indian Sands about 1.7 miles from the Whaleshead Beach picnic area. Watch for wooden signposts for the Coast Trail to be sure you are on the right track here. A spur trail to the right at about 1.9 miles from the picnic area leads to the Indian Sands trailhead and parking.

From Indian Sands, you can continue along the trail to the Thomas Creek Bridge in another mile. This portion of the trail follows the high-way shoulder closely for almost 0.3 mile, making the last stretch a less than great place for dogs. Turn around either at Indian Sands or, if your dog is accustomed to traffic, at the Thomas Creek Bridge, which, at 345 feet above Thomas Creek, is the highest span on the Pacific coast north of San Francisco. Return as you came.

24. Francis Shrader Old Growth Trail

Round trip: 1.5 miles
Elevation range: 1800–2100 feet
Difficulty: Moderate
Hiking time: 1 hour
Best canine hiking seasons: Summer, fall
Regulations: Northwest Forest Pass required; dogs must be on leash
Map: USGS Signal Buttes 7.5' quadrangle
Information: Gold Beach Ranger Station, Siskiyou National Forest,
(541) 247-3600

Getting there: From the town of Gold Beach, drive 0.5 mile south on U.S. Highway 101, cross the Rogue River, and turn left onto Jerrys Flat Road. Continue up the Rogue River 9.8 miles. Turn right onto paved, single-lane Forest Road 090 just before the Lobster Creek Bridge and Campground. Drive 2.1 miles to find a parking lot on the left and a trailhead on the right.

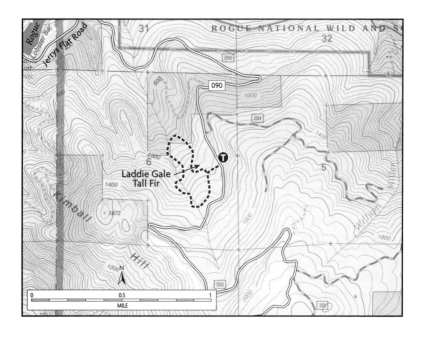

Fallen cedars cross the Frances Schrader Old Growth Trail.

This is an interpretive hike through a multistoried old-growth coastal forest where huge cedar and Douglas fir intermingle with deciduous tanoak. Rhododendron form a radiant spring understory. Your drive here will include road signs warning of logging trucks on the road and a clear-cut converted to a plantation of Douglas fir—visual reminders of why there are not many hikes like this left. Yes, it's a short hike. But take time to savor it.

From the road, the looping Francis Shrader Old Growth Trail dives down into the forest, then splits. Take the path on the left to follow numbered interpretive sites in consecutive order. This is a very moist forest

and there are plenty of mosquitoes looking for lunch, so you might want to protect yourself and Fido with insect repellent or long sleeves.

Crossing a small creek five times on sturdy bridges, allowing plenty of soggy doggie dips, the trail loops through an astonishingly complex, multi-storied old-growth stand that includes deep forest duff; a huge variety of lichens, ferns, and mosses; and riparian areas that bustle. In spring, the rhododendrons are astonishing. Interpreted sites include nurse logs, riparian areas, and evidence of a devastating fire about a century ago.

An off-trail picnic area marks the midpoint of the hike. From the midpoint, the path rises to the Laddie Gale Tall Fir, a towering Douglas fir named for the star of the 1939 University of Oregon NCAA champion basketball team, and returns you to your car for only the price of a few donations to the mosquito blood bank.

Five More Great Dogs Hikes on Oregon's Coast and Coast Range

1) Gales Creek, Tillamook State Forest, 11 miles. Follows creek through peaceful second-growth forest. Tillamook State Forest, (503) 357-2191.

2) North Fork Smith River, 8 miles. Hike along river to 100-foot falls; trail is off Forest Road 23 and has some steep climbs, cliffs. Oregon Dunes National Recreation Area, Siuslaw National Forest, (541) 271-3611.

3) Sweet Creek Trail, 3.5 miles. Hike along creek with eleven waterfalls. Mapleton Ranger District, Siuslaw National Forest, (541) 902-8526.

4) Mount Hebo Pioneer Trail, Mount Hebo summit, 8 miles. Two lakes at the roof of the Coast Range. Hebo Ranger District, Siuslaw National Forest, (503) 392-3161.

5) Horse Creek Trail, Drift Creek Wilderness, 3.5 miles. Waldport Ranger District, Siuslaw National Forest, (541) 563-3211.

CASCADE MOUNTAINS

25. Wildwood Recreation Area and Salmon-Huckleberry Wilderness

Round trip: 3–9.4 miles
Elevation range: 1150–4250 feet
Difficulty: Easy–difficult
Hiking time: 1–6 hours
Best canine hiking seasons: Summer, fall
Regulations: Northwest Forest Pass required
Maps: USGS Wildcat Mountain and Rhododendron 7.5′ quadrangles
Information: Mount Hood National Forest Information Center, (503) 622-7674

Getting there: From Portland, drive east on U.S. Highway 26 about 39 miles. The entrance to Wildwood Recreation Area/Cascade Stream Watch is on the right (south) side of the highway just east of milepost 39 and 0.9 mile west of Wemme. Turn right (south) onto the entrance road and continue 0.3 mile to the trailheads at the parking lot.

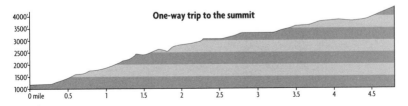

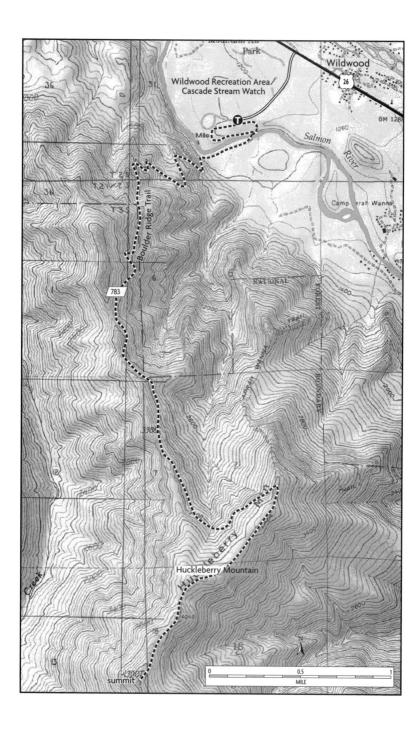

Park

Wildwood

Wildwood Recreation Area/
Cascade Stream Watch

26

BM 128

Mile
1260

Salmon

River

Camp Arrah Wanna

36

31

36

T 2 S

T 3 S

Boulder Ridge Trail

783

NATIONAL

2000

TRAIL

1400

BOUNDARY

2200

3600

3800

2000

12

7

Huckleberry Mtn.

TRAIL

BOUNDARY

2600

2800

Huckleberry Mountain

Creek

4045

13

18

4005T
summit

18

N

2600

0   0.5   1
MILE

The first portion of this hike follows well-manicured, civilized interpretive trails that are part of Cascade Stream Watch, a collaborative, environmental education project. An extensive boardwalk leads through wetlands and a riparian forest, allowing occasional glimpses of the surrounding forested peaks. The nearly flat trail system here tours the 600 acres of the Stream Watch program.

Two paths diverge from the trailhead. The path to the right (south) is a broad gravel trail that begins an inviting loop through a riparian old-growth

Meesha takes a stroll on a boardwalk above a wetland in the Cascadia-Wildwood Trail on the way to Wildwood-Boulder Ridge: Salmon-Huckleberry Wilderness.

forest of cedar and fir, meandering back and forth across a small secondary channel of the Salmon River. Bear right at the loop's start to find an underwater viewing area where you and your dog can watch fish migrating upstream or just hanging out in a small pool. The path into the viewing area slants down, allowing you to witness the stream bottom through a window placed at eye level.

Beyond the viewing area, the path crosses the side channel on a sturdy bridge and then parallels the bank of the Salmon River, offering opportunities for on-leash doggie dunks. Watch for families with picnic lunches sequestered at off-trail tables along this path.

In 0.4 mile, the trail turns away from the river and joins a gravel path that leads back to the parking lot in another 0.1 mile.

To find the wetlands boardwalk trail, follow a path from the north side of the parking area. It leads across an arching suspension bridge spanning the Salmon. To protect fragile plants and habitat, dogs should be prevented access to the wetlands along this 1-mile boardwalk, but the subtle aromas of strange creatures and decaying plants should keep them enthralled with the hike.

The wetlands trail meets Sixes Creek and the Boulder Ridge Trail at 0.5 mile. This is a good location to let your dog off leash before venturing up the steep and rocky path into the Salmon-Huckleberry Wilderness. For a short day hike, you can finish the wetlands loop and return to the trailhead.

As you continue into the Salmon-Huckleberry Wilderness, you face a demanding climb of almost 3000 feet in about 3.5 miles of hiking to Huckleberry Mountain's open, brushy summit (4250 feet). There is no water along this trail, and lots of exercise, so it's especially important to carry sufficient dog water.

From Sixes Creek, the trail leads past a sign announcing your impending entry to the Salmon-Huckleberry Wilderness on Forest Service Trail 783, the Boulder Ridge Trail. Once across the small side creek, Trail 783 continues past huge cedars and cedar stumps. The trail rises steeply, switchbacking into the wilderness area through a forest that teeters on the steep, north-facing slopes of Huckleberry Mountain. Watch for a variety of mosses and lichens here, especially on winter or spring hikes. For the first 1.3 miles, this trail weaves up the slope, passing through a forest of small-diameter, pistol-butted Douglas fir that hint at the forest floor's inherent instability. A few giant trunks, victims of fire in the early 20th century, or logging soon thereafter, pepper the slope.

Then, at an elevation of about 2100 feet, a thousand feet above the beginning of the climb, the path straightens, angling up the north face of the ridge. This portion of the trail reveals a few springs in early summer. Its cooler air is welcome on warm days. At about 2 miles into the hike, the trail rounds raggedy, vegetated rock outcroppings and reaches the brushy ridge top. The trail remains on the cool, north slope of Huckleberry Mountain then, at 3 miles, swings north across the head of a drainage, and climbs into the open. It achieves a false summit at 3850 feet about 4 miles from the trailhead and the real thing in another 0.75 mile after dipping across a saddle. Huckleberry Mountain gets its name honestly—from the profusion of blue-berried bushes at its summit. The berries are at their best in late August and the views, if you are tall enough to poke your head above the brush, are a reward all by themselves. Return as you came.

26. Burnt Lake

Round trip: 5.4 miles to Burnt Lake; 7 miles to Zigzag Mountain
Elevation range: 2650–4970 feet
Difficulty: Moderate to Burnt Lake; difficult to Zigzag Mountain
Hiking time: 5–7 hours
Best canine hiking seasons: Summer, fall
Regulations: Northwest Forest Pass required
Map: USGS Government Camp 7.5' quadrangle
Information: Mount Hood National Forest Information Center, (503) 622-7674

Getting there: From Zigzag on U.S. Highway 26, turn north onto Forest Road 18, marked for Lolo Pass. Drive 4 miles and bear right onto FR 1825, and continue 3.3 miles to a parking area and trailhead, about 1.5 miles past Lost Creek Campground.

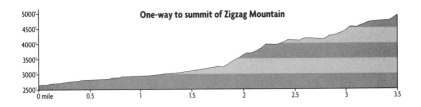

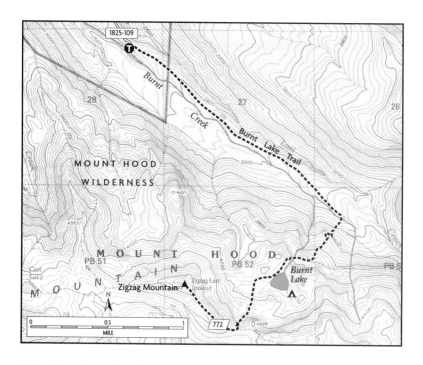

This 3.5-mile walk to Burnt Lake and the summit of Zigzag Mountain provides both water and scenery, as well as a lesson in forest history in an eerie but inviting woodland where the giant, charcoaled stumps of a vanished cedar forest hide among moss-draped younger trees. Although a popular trail, there are fewer hikers here than on the nearby Ramona Falls Trail. Water is accessible on the first part of the hike in Burnt Creek and at Burnt Lake.

From the trailhead parking area, the Burnt Lake Trail squeezes through a livestock-restricting gateway and edges along the rim of Burnt Creek's small canyon. You might take a moment to admire the huge cedar trees here and at the edge of the parking lot. These trees all bear large fire scars. They are among the few trees that survived a devastating, human-caused forest fire in 1910 that exterminated much of the old-growth cedar forest here.

In 0.3 mile, just past the wilderness registration ledger, the path enters a darker forest of medium-size Douglas fir and hemlock. Scattered across this relatively flat forest floor for the next 2 miles of the hike are the stumps and cut logs of huge cedar. A close look reveals deep fire scars. Some standing trees have been completely hollowed by fire. Dogs and small children take great delight in climbing over and peering into these charcoal-lined trees. It's worth venturing off the trail and into the open forest here just to explore this burned forest and its fire-sculpted remnants. Burnt Creek is easily accessible just west of the trail.

When this portion of the forest burned, most cedars—a species with relatively thin bark that is not especially adapted to fire—burned. Only tall, charcoaled trunks were left. Believing that these naked tree boles would act as lightning rods, starting yet another fire, the Forest Service sent in crews to cut down the burned trees—and the result is the stumps and cut logs still found here.

After 1.8 miles of a gentle uphill stroll through this altered forest, the trail crosses a small branch of Burnt Creek where a huge hollow cedar greets you; meanders through a marshy area where a number of younger, post-fire cedars are prospering; and then turns and begins a serious ascent to Burnt Lake. The switchbacking trail rises past some old-growth cedars that survived the fire and are probably the progenitors of the younger trees below.

Meesha and Leigh take a break along the Burnt Lake Trail.

The trail reaches Burnt Lake in another mile. There are a number of good campsites here—if you arrive early enough. Burnt Lake occupies a small glacial basin. The post-fire forest obscures what might be a magnificent view of Mount Hood. To catch a great view of the surrounding landscape, continue past Burnt Lake to the summit of Zigzag Mountain, adding another short mile and about 800 feet in elevation to the hike. The rocky promontory supports salal, huckleberry, and a few rhododendron. Once you've absorbed the view, return as you came.

27. Ramona Falls

Round trip: 7.2 miles via the Portage Trail both ways; 6.7 miles via the Portage Trail and returning on the Sandy River Trail
Elevation range: 2400–3550 feet
Difficulty: Easy
Hiking time: 4 hours
Best canine hiking seasons: Summer, fall
Regulations: Northwest Forest Pass required
Map: USGS Bull Run Lake 7.5′ quadrangle
Information: Mount Hood National Forest Information Center, (503) 622-7674

Getting there: From Zigzag on U.S. Highway 26, turn north onto Forest Road 18, marked for Lolo Pass. Drive 4 miles and bear right onto FR 1825, and in 1.8 miles, just before the Lost Creek Campground, bear left onto Spur Road 1825-100. Continue 0.7 mile to a gigantic parking area and trailhead.

The hike to Ramona Falls is one of the most popular in the Mount Hood area. For dogs, it provides bounteous water and shade as well as the chance to meet other dogs and dog-friendly hikers. The trails are generally broad

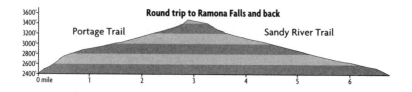

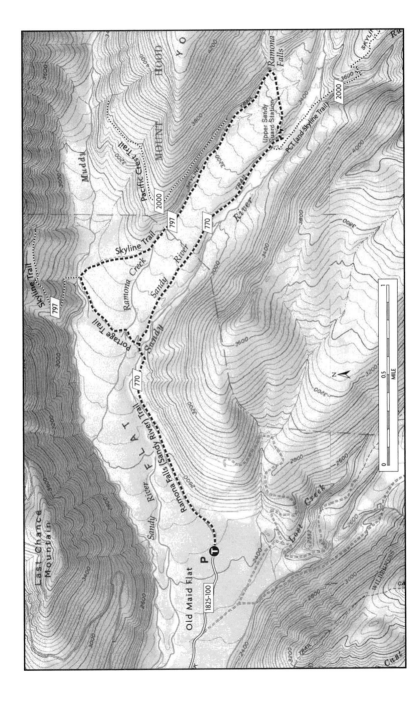

and gentle. The forest is varied. And there is scarcely a prettier waterfall in Oregon.

Most of the hike—and the drive along narrow forest roads to the huge trailhead parking lot—crosses the deposits of Mount Hood's last major temper tantrum, the eruption of 1781. En route to your Ramona Falls hike you can pause at Lost Creek Campground and nature trail to view the remains of trees buried by thick debris flows from the 1781 eruption. You will be hiking atop the very same mudflows—which likely contain a forest buried beneath them—on your way to view Ramona Falls.

Tyler and family at a trail junction on the Ramona Falls Loop.

From the trailhead parking lot, the broad Sandy River Trail follows an abandoned roadway for 1.3 miles to the Sandy River crossing. It is a broad path that winds through the mossy lodgepole pines. These trees specialize in colonizing dry and disturbed sites—including volcanic mudflows and debris flows such as here. Some of these tiny lodgepole pines only 5 or 6 inches in diameter could be 100 years old. They represent the first conifers to colonize this young mudflow.

In 1.3 miles the trail minces across the Sandy River on a small log bridge. This structure is placed across the stream in the early summer and taken away by helicopter after the main hiking season closes in the fall to protect it from early spring torrents. From this point, the trail takes you farther into the lodgepole thickets, reaching a trail junction and wilderness registration station in about 0.2 mile.

Both trails lead to Ramona Falls on a loop route, but the best route to Ramona Falls and back for hikers with dogs is the trail to the left. The Portage Trail to the left follows Ramona Creek through well-shaded forest, offering plenty of water and cooling opportunities. The more popular Sandy River Trail on the right is a dry, sunny, sandy path that offers no water and little shade. If you were a dog, which route would you choose?

The path to the left, Portage Trail, fords Ramona Creek in another 0.2 mile, then digresses a bit west toward the Muddy Fork. To reach Ramona Falls, bear right at the junction with Muddy Fork, following Ramona Creek on the Skyline Trail. Along the trail, huge lichen-covered gray andesite cliffs form a colorful tapestry. Ramona Creek is easily accessible to dogs for much of the hike, and the tawny cliffs offer texture and geology to admire. A trail that leads left and upward to connect with the Timberline Trail and Yokum Ridge appears at 3.4 miles—just before Ramona Falls. Ramona Falls appears 3.6 miles from the trailhead, plummeting down a huge, dark, mossy cliff. A sturdy wooden bridge spans the creek at the foot of the cascade, offering a great vantage point as well as a dry-footed creek crossing. Dogs will likely prefer a more watery route.

There are no restrictions on dogs at the falls, but you should keep your canine companion on a leash here and under control, as the falls area is often crowded, or at least shared with picnicking families. Return as you came, especially in warm weather. On cool days, the Sandy River Trail portion of the loop, which tours the edges of the Sandy River canyon, becomes a feasible option for dogs. It leads without interruption back to the trail junction and the Sandy River crossing in 1.8 miles.

28. Mirror Lake and Tom, Dick, and Harry Mountain

Round trip: 6.5 miles
Elevation range: 3425–4970 feet
Difficulty: Easy
Hiking time: 4 hours
Best canine hiking seasons: Summer, fall
Regulations: Northwest Forest Pass required
Map: USGS Government Camp 7.5' quadrangle
Information: Mount Hood National Forest Information Center, (503) 622-7674

Getting there: From Portland, take Interstate 205 to the exit for Division Street and U.S. Highway 26. Drive east 45 miles on US 26 through the communities of Sandy, Zigzag, and Rhododendron. The trailhead is on the right at a nondescript but often car-choked pull-off approximately 0.6 mile east of the Laurel Hill historic marker and 2 miles west of Government Camp.

This hike to Mirror Lake and the top of Tom, Dick, and Harry Mountain is one of the most popular in Oregon—for good reason. It's a comparatively short and easy stroll to a pretty lake with an astounding view. Expect a lot of other people, dogs, and children on this hike, especially on the length of trail to Mirror Lake. You'll find every mode of humanity here, from exuberant children to the frail and hesitant elderly. It's essential that you keep your dog leashed and yield the right of way to other hikers.

From the trailhead, the Mirror Lake Trail saunters across a small bridge and into the woods. Look for huge stumps here—the heritage of logging in the early 1900s. Note also that there's ample evidence of fire, because many stumps and old trees bear charcoal scars.

The trail meanders through the forest—look for rhododendrons

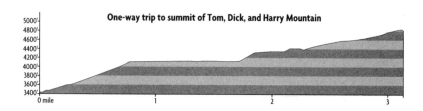

One-way trip to summit of Tom, Dick, and Harry Mountain

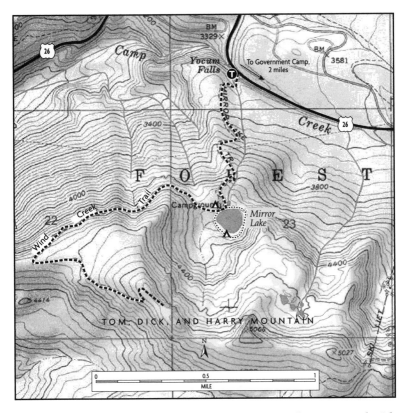

blooming in late May, a few yew trees, and a forest floor carpeted with sword ferns and salal. At 0.8 mile, the trail makes a single switchbacking turn, crossing a talus slope and climbing past some of Mount Hood's older volcanic outcrops. This area of jumbled rock offers a brief glimpse of the Sandy River Valley to the west of Mount Hood.

The trail climbs more seriously above the talus slope, offering more switchbacks and handrails for the weary. While this is an easy hike for experienced hikers, many folks on this trail need occasional rests and welcome the added reassurance and civilized touch of a handrail. The path reaches a junction at 1.2 miles. Continue straight to reach Mirror Lake. A well-worn path circumnavigates the small lake.

As you emerge into the sunshine at the lakeshore, watch for a path that spurts off to the right. This is the Wind Creek Trail to the summit of Tom, Dick, and Harry Mountain, taking a long 2 miles to reach the top. The Wind Creek Trail has little shade and no water, so if you plan to continue past the lake, be sure you take plenty of water for your dog.

A light muzzle is a good idea if your dog is unused to hiking on busy trails.

The trail to the ridge summit strikes off into a wilderness of alder and willows—trees that grew after a fire demolished much of the forest on the west slopes of this ridge in the 1960s. Conifers are slowly reasserting themselves. The path climbs to the top in a long switchback—the curve between straight stretches occurs about 1 mile from Mirror Lake and marks the approximate midpoint of your ascent. Once atop the ridge, you are rewarded with views of Mount Hood and Cascade peaks to the north, including Mount Rainier on a clear day. Two ridge-top summits to the east beckon, but they are restricted from hikers during peregrine falcon nesting season May through August. Check with the Mount Hood Information Center to determine whether restrictions are in effect at the time you visit. Return as you came.

29. Badger Creek Trail

Round trip: 22 miles
Elevation range: 2160–4475 feet
Difficulty: Moderate to difficult
Hiking time: 2 days
Best canine hiking season: Summer
Regulations: Northwest Forest Pass required
Maps: USGS Badger Lake and Flag Point 7.5′ quadrangles
Information: Dufur Ranger Station, Mount Hood National Forest, (541) 467-2291

Getting there: From Government Camp on U.S. Highway 26, drive east 3 miles to the junction with Oregon Route 35. Continue east on ORE 35 for 4.3 miles to Forest Road 48 just beyond the White River. Turn right (south) onto paved FR 48, and follow it 25 miles, continuing past Rock Creek Reservoir, to FR 4810. Turn left (north) and follow FR 4810

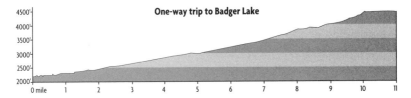

2 miles to FR 4811. Turn left (east) onto FR 4811 and follow it 1.2 miles to FR 2710. Turn sharply right onto FR 2710 and continue 2 miles to Bonney Crossing Campground. The trailhead and parking area are on FR 2710 just past the entrance to the tiny and informal campground.

Even if you don't complete the 11-mile trek to Badger Lake, the trail is worthy of any amount of effort you invest here. The route traverses an ecologically diverse landscape that shifts from pine and oak savannah at the trailhead to Douglas fir, hemlock, lodgepole pine, and spruce in Badger Lake's glacier-carved basin. Water is abundant in early and midsummer, especially in the lower 5 miles, and, because the trailhead is far from the madding crowd, your hike will be relatively solitary. Be on the lookout for horseback riders, however, as this has become a fairly popular equine trail.

The Badger Creek Trail begins in a landscape laced with oak trees and attendant poison oak. The trail and creek are inseparable for the first 3 miles. This is also the flattest portion of the hike. With 3000 feet to climb in its long journey to the lake, the path diverts from Badger Creek at about mile 3.2, where it begins a switchbacking ascent through grassy, oak-shaded slopes. With elevation, oaks yield to ponderosa pine, juniper, and Douglas fir, providing somewhat more shade. The trail returns to the creek at 4 miles, following it closely for the next 2 miles.

At 7 miles, the trail swings away from contact with the creek. The path straightens and also loses both sight and sound of the water. For the next 4 miles you'll rely on side drainages for cooling your dog. These occur every mile or so for the remainder of the hike. They can be dry in times of drought or low precipitation, but they are reliable in spring and early summer.

With increasing elevation, the canyon becomes more tree-bound, and forest composition shifts to ponderosa and lodgepole pine, mountain hemlock, and Douglas fir. Portions of the upper trail can be dusty in late summer, and there are occasional horse-churned rocky places to negotiate. At 11 miles, Badger Lake, situated in a tree-lined glacial bowl, offers

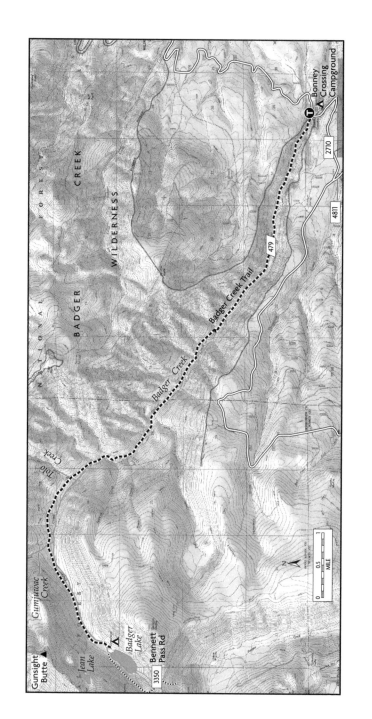

a great overnight spot, with abundant camping sites and plenty of shade. Return as you came.

30. Olallie Lake Scenic Area: Red Lake Trail

Round trip: 11.5 miles
Elevation range: 3670–5370 feet
Difficulty: Moderate
Hiking time: 6 hours
Best canine hiking seasons: Summer, fall
Regulations: Northwest Forest Pass required
Map: USGS Olallie Butte 7.5′ quadrangle
Information: Estacada-Clackamas Ranger District, Mount Hood
National Forest, (503) 630-6861

Getting there: From Salem, follow Oregon Route 22 about 35 miles east to Detroit. Turn left (north) on Breitenbush Road (Forest Road 46). Follow this paved road for 18 miles. Near the top of a hill, turn right onto Forest Road 46-380, marked for the Red Lake Trail. Follow this gravel road for 0.9 miles to the Red Lake trailhead on the left and a skimpy parking area on the right.

Alternatively, you may begin this hike from the Lower Lake Campground near Olallie Lake. (The road to this trailhead was closed and under construction at the time this book went to press.) Follow FR 46 for 5 miles past the turn-off to the Red Lake Trail. Turn right on Forest Road 4690, marked for Olallie Lake. In 7 miles, turn right on Forest Road 4220 and follow it for 5 miles to Lower Lake Campground. The trailhead is at the far end of the campground loop.

The forested area at the western foot of Olallie Butte is sprinkled with lakes, many of which are small, private, and secluded. The forest here verges on subalpine: lodgepole pines and hemlock line lakeshores, and rocky buttes support small fir. There's water aplenty to keep dogs cool once you are on the trail. As you approach Olallie Lake you may encounter more hikers outbound from the Olallie resort area, but especially when you start at the Red Lake Trailhead, this is a quiet and secluded place. A few mountain bikers share the trails here occasionally.

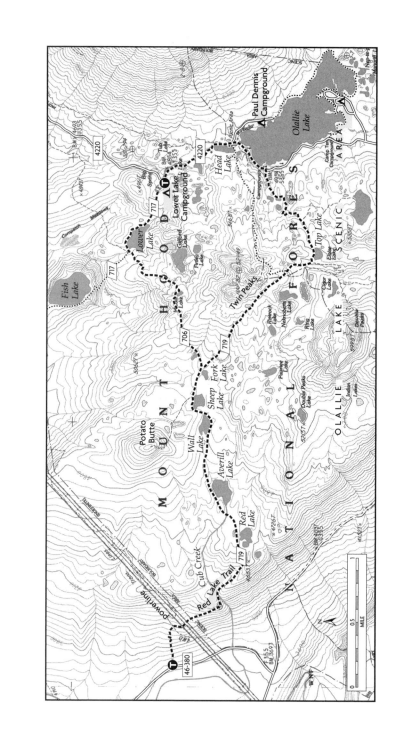

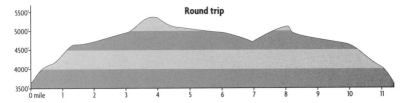

From the trailhead, Red Lake Trail 719 navigates the young trees of a recent clear-cut, then dives into shaded forest. It moves steadily uphill, jogging slightly to the left across a rough two-track road at 0.3 miles, then crossing beneath powerlines from Detroit Dam.

Once past these outposts of civilization, the trail returns to the hemlock–Douglas fir forest, moderating its uphill pace. At 1 mile from the trailhead you encounter Cub Creek, the outlet for Averill Lake and other small upland ponds. It's a great spot for cooling off your dog. After another 0.4 miles of gradual, forested uphill progress, the path side-swipes Red Lake, an inviting pond just south of the trail, and then continues to cross Cub Creek a second time. At 2 miles, the path begins a climb past Averill Lake. Both these lakes make great places for dogs to relax.

End of the hike, Red Lake Trailhead.

At 2.5 miles, the trail levels again as it reaches the multilaked Olallie Lake basin. Here Wall Lake, Sheep Lake, and Fork Lake emerge from lodgepole pines to greet you. At 2.7 miles, a trail to Potato Butte angles left. Continue straight here. The trail forks just past Fork Lake, 3 miles into the hike. The trail to Lower Lake (706) bears left. To reach Olallie Lake, bear right on Trail 719 and continue 1.2 miles to Top Lake, the next large pond along this trail. The trail skirts the west side of Twin Peaks and drops abruptly to find Top Lake in 1.3 miles from the junction with Trail 706. Turn left (east) here. This trail rises and falls over a multitude of small ridges and divides between lakes. It tours through a lodgepole pine forest, finding a small creek and several ponds along the way, and reaches Olallie Lake 5.3 miles from the Red Lake Trailhead.

To make this a loop hike back to the trailhead, follow the gravel road (FS 4220) to the right (north) along Olallie Lake to the Lower Lake Campground. (Keep dogs leashed along this portion of the hike, as there is traffic and plenty of people on summer weekends.)

From the campground, follow the path (Trail 717) northwest toward Lower Lake. You'll reach the lakeshore quickly, in about 0.25 miles. At the far end of the lake, the path meets Trail 706. You may continue straight on Trail 717 to reach Fish Lake 0.4 mile ahead—and 400 feet lower.

To return to Red Lake, turn left on Trail 706. In the next mile, this path climbs over a ridge (400 feet in elevation gain) and visits several diminutive lakes. Where the path forks again, continue straight and follow the trail to reach the junction with Trail 719 at Fork Lake in 1.2 miles. Return as you came to the Red Lake Trail trailhead.

31. Three Sisters Wilderness: Matthieu Lakes and Collier Cone

Round trip: 14.4 miles
Elevation range: 5310–7020 feet
Difficulty: Moderate
Hiking time: 8 hours or overnight
Best canine hiking seasons: Summer, early fall
Regulations: Northwest Forest Pass required; register for wilderness entry
Maps: USGS Mount Washington, North Sister, Black Crater, and
    Trout Creek Butte 7.5' quadrangles
Information: Sisters Ranger District, Deschutes National Forest,
    (541) 549-7700

Getting there: From the Central Oregon town of Sisters on U.S. Highway 20, drive 14 miles west on Oregon Route 242, the McKenzie Pass Highway, toward McKenzie Pass. Turn left (south) onto a rough, red-cinder road marked for Lava Camp. Follow this road 0.3 mile, then bear right and continue 0.1 mile to the far end of this small and relatively undeveloped, waterless campground. The trailhead is at the end of this looped road.

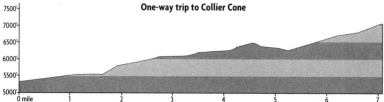

This hike is among the most beautiful in Oregon's High Cascades—a region chock-full of scenic hikes. It provides two lakes, close encounters with one of the youngest lava flows in the Cascades (including a short stretch of the hike where booties are in order if your dog is tender-footed), and provides an intimate view of one of the Cascades' longest glaciers—or at least, the moraine-rimmed valley where Collier Glacier used to be. All this in a 7-mile walk on well-maintained and easy-to-follow trails where there are no lung-numbing climbs. What hiker and dog could ask for more?

As always, you'll need to take a few aspects of this hike under advisement. Carry extra dog water. Although you'll visit two large lakes and a reliable spring, there are long open stretches in the last two-thirds of the hike—some that cross dark cinders or lava—that can be hot, dry going for your canine friends. Not surprisingly, this is a popular route, so expect other hikers, as well as llama trekkers and horseback riders.

The hike to Matthieu Lakes and Collier Cone begins on a short path that leads generally south from the parking area to the Pacific Crest Trail (PCT), which is the main thoroughfare for the hike. Signs point the way to the PCT. At about 0.3 mile the path encounters a dark, crumpled lava flow—and the PCT.

Turn left (south) onto the main PCT. Almost immediately, the path veers away from the rugged lava, entering a cool forest of lichen-draped fir and hemlock. It passes through inviting wetlands—these can be dry in the late summer and fall but usually can provide a good doggie soaking in June and July. At 1 mile from the trailhead, the PCT reaches a well-marked junction. There's a small pond just north of this junction, though it is hard to see among the trees. At the junction, the inviting trail to North Matthieu Lake points straight ahead; the less-traveled PCT turns left to detour around this first lake. If it were up to your dog, chances are she would choose the path straight ahead into darker and wetter woodland.

This is a good choice. Take the trail to North Matthieu Lake straight ahead. It leads through shady forest, crawling over outcrops and rocks, then tracks along the edge of the lava flow, encountering a tiny forest pond and

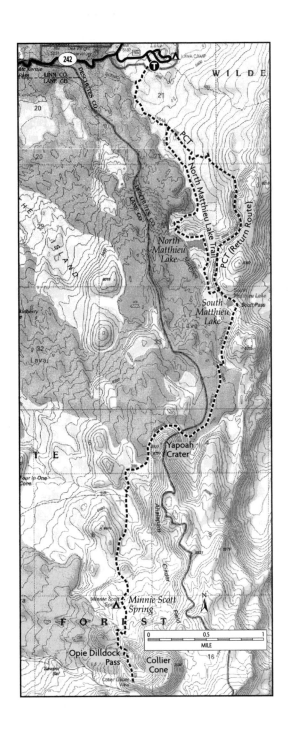

Collier Cone in the Three Sisters Wilderness is a starkly barren landscape, but at 7000 feet in elevation, it's usually cool and breezy.

wetland in a half-mile, and then switchbacking up to forest-lined North Matthieu Lake 2.2 miles from the beginning of the hike.

The trail tours along the lakeshore, passing a number of designated camping sites. Then it begins a quick, 0.6-mile ascent to South Matthieu Lake. The difference between the settings of the two lakes is stark. North Matthieu Lake, at 5795 feet, is surrounded by forest; the much smaller South Matthieu Lake, elevation 6040, sits in a rock-lined subalpine basin offering a view of North Sister and Collier Cone ahead.

Once past South Matthieu Lake, there are few reliable, dog-friendly water sources, especially late in the summer. Be sure you have adequate dog water for the next 4 miles (8 miles round trip) to Collier Cone.

At South Matthieu Lake, a trail leads east to connect with Green Lakes Basin between Broken Top and South Sister. However, for this hike, you should keep straight ahead toward Collier Cone and North Sister on the PCT.

From South Matthieu Lake, the PCT navigates across a lava flow for about 0.7 mile, then steps off into a meadow along the barren side of Yapoah Crater and tiptoes over the top of the very vent that, about 2500 years ago, produced the lava that today clogs McKenzie Pass. From the vent, the path leads downslope to a verdant meadow and another side trail that leads northwest toward Four-in-One Cone about a mile to the west.

Follow the PCT south. At 6 miles from the trailhead, and 0.5 mile from the Four-in-One intersection, the trail reaches Minnie Scott Spring, usually a reliable source of backpacker water and really no place for a dog. It's fine for Fido to romp and roll in the marshy grass downstream from the spring itself, but keep dogs away from the spot where water emerges and most backpackers dip their (filtered) water bottles. In late summer, this spring may go dry, so plan accordingly.

From the spring, the trail rounds a bend and heads for Collier Cone. About 7 miles into the hike, the PCT climbs to Opie Dilldock Pass on the north flank of Collier Cone. This is an inviting place to explore the varied sculptures that lava and cinders can produce. A short climb to the top or south side of Collier Cone's red cinders provides a view of the rapidly shrinking Collier Glacier and the huge gravel moraines it has left behind.

Return as you came, or for variety, at South Matthieu Lake, continue straight on the PCT rather than dropping to North Matthieu Lake. Here the PCT follows the side of a volcanic cinder cone, providing great views and cooler air (but more sun) than the route past North Matthieu Lake. In 2.1 miles from South Matthieu Lake, the PCT meets the North Matthieu Lake Trail. Continue along the PCT, returning as you came to the trailhead.

32. Metolius River Trail

Round trip: 12 miles
Elevation range: 2730–2880 feet
Difficulty: Easy
Hiking time: 6 hours
Best canine hiking seasons: Spring, summer, fall
Regulations: Northwest Forest Pass required
Maps: USGS Candle Creek and Prairie Farm Spring 7.5' quadrangles
Information: Sisters Ranger District, Deschutes National Forest, (541) 549-7700

Getting there: From Sisters, drive 9 miles west to milepost 91 on U.S. Highway 20/Oregon Route 126. Turn right (north) onto Forest Road 14 and continue 5 miles, past the Metolius River headwaters parking area,

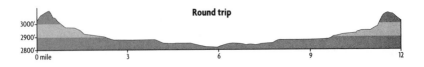

Round trip

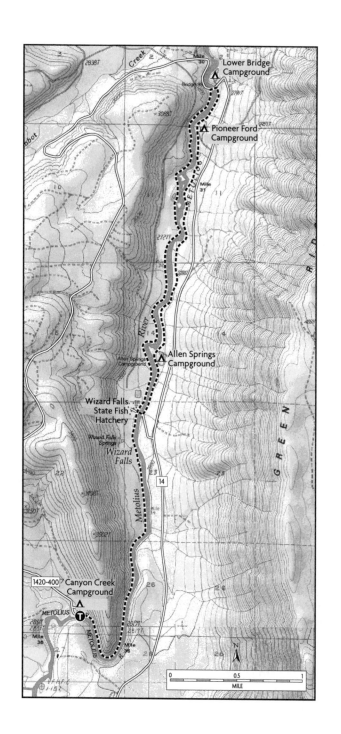

to FR 1420, marked CAMPGROUNDS. Bear left onto FR 1420, following it 2.9 miles to the Canyon Creek Campground entry road, FR 400. Drive 0.8 mile to the trailhead at the far end of the looped road, and park in the designated trailhead parking area. There is no trail connection, unfortunately, to the Metolius River headwaters.

The Metolius River emerges from springs at the base of Black Butte, a symmetrical volcanic cone that is more than a million years in age and one of the oldest mountains of the High Cascades. The riverbank trails here are practically flat by any hiking measure. Mountain bikes, horses, and many other distractions are banned.

The trails along the river follow the clear, cold water (average temperature is below 50°F), tempting humans and their dogs with its placid appearance. A swim in this frigid, fast river is hazardous, however, so keep Fido out of the deep, swift water.

The trail from the lower part of the Canyon Creek Campground closely follows the west bank of the Metolius. It parallels the river around a sharp meander. At about 0.5 mile down the path, several highly productive springs gush water into the river on the opposite (west) bank, creating small waterfalls. From here, the well-worn trail threads along the bank through a narrowing gorge, while the stream frolics through a set of riffles and small rapids and rushes past several small islands at 1.7 miles into the hike. The river's histrionics culminate in 3-foot-high Wizard Falls 2.5 miles downstream from the trailhead.

The trail encounters springs and small wetland areas that provide cooling breaks along the stretch just below the falls where the river is not very accessible. In another 0.2 mile, the path enters the Wizard Falls State Fish Hatchery parking area. While the hatchery offers

A shady rest stop along the Metolius River Trail.

an interesting tour, it is better to continue your hike, returning to tour when you don't have to take the dog along.

For a short hike, you can turn around here. To continue, cross the river at the hatchery to follow the east bank trail for another 3.2 miles. The east trail also follows the river closely, though vine maple and small conifers often obscure the stream—a quick plunge through the vegetation will generally bring you to streamside for a scenic break. At 3.5 miles from its start, the east trail moves away from the river to veer around a piece of private property and across the neck of a meander loop. In another 0.5 mile, the path returns to the riverbank.

At Lower Bridge, 3.2 miles from the Wizard Falls Hatchery, cross the river back to the west side and return along the west bank. The landscape is more open on this trail, and the ponderosa pines are perhaps more in their element of flat-sloped, dry-footed, and sunny ground. Back at Wizard Falls, cross back over the river and continue as you came to the trailhead where your vehicle awaits.

33. South Breitenbush River National Recreational Trail

One-way trip: 4.5 miles
Elevation range: 2440–3080 feet
Difficulty: Easy
Hiking time: 2.5 hours
Best canine hiking seasons: Summer, fall
Regulations: Northwest Forest Pass required
Map: USGS Breitenbush Hot Springs 7.5′ quadrangle
Information: Detroit Ranger District, Willamette National Forest, (503) 854-3366

Getting there: From Salem, follow Oregon Route 22 about 35 miles east to Detroit. Turn left (north) on Breitenbush Road (Forest Road 46). Drive

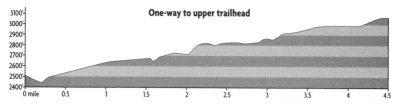

10.7 miles, and turn right onto Forest Road 4685. Drive 0.5 miles to a small trailhead parking area on the right.

To reach the upper trailhead and leave a shuttle vehicle there, continue 4.5 miles on FR 4685 to a large parking area on the right. The

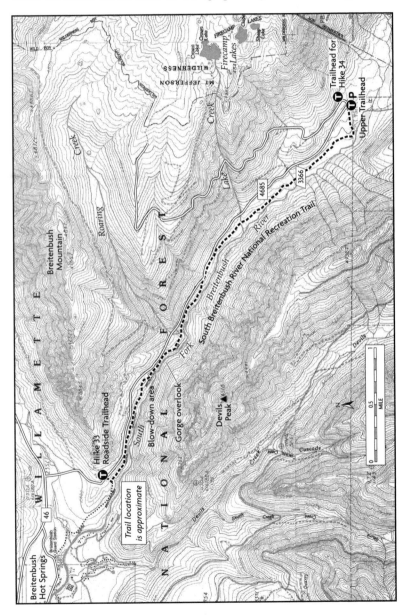

Steps were hewn into giant logs where the South Breitenbush River Trail navigates a blow-down area.

trailhead for the South Breitenbush River Gorge National Recreation Trail (Trail 3366), marked by a sign, is on the west side of the parking area.

From the roadside trailhead, the path travels about a hundred yards south to connect with the main trail. Officially named the South Breitenbush River Gorge National Recreation Trail, the trail is more informally called the South Breitenbush River NRT, especially on signs. Turn right for a 1-mile walk to Breitenbush Hot Springs. But the better dog hike is to the left: a 4-mile stroll through old-growth Douglas fir with a few cedar and hemlock to add diversity. In about 0.6 mile, the path plows past gigantic, blown-down trees felled by a 1990 windstorm— conveniently cut for your passage and a reminder that Mother Nature can be a bit heavy-handed at times. In August, ripe huckleberries make this a favorite trail segment.

At 1.5 miles, a well-marked side trail to the left follows a wooden walkway to a slippery overlook of the South Breitenbush's tempestuous gorge. Return to the main trail to continue the hike.

The remainder of the hike weaves through scenic old-growth forest.

At 2.4 miles, a path leads to the left and back to FR 4685 at an intermediate trailhead. If you wish to continue on the longer, one-way hike, the trail is less traveled but well maintained. Although this trail is never far from the road, it seems remote and provides several informal side paths for access to the river. Alternatively, crossings of Rogue Creek at 2.5 miles and White Creek at 3.8 miles provide doggie water. Even in late summer, seeps and springs along the path provide additional doggie cooling spots. Look for towering Douglas fir that are more than 5 feet in diameter. In June the rhododendrons along the trail put on a spectacular show. At 4.5 miles you reach the upper trailhead.

34. Jefferson Park via South Breitenbush Trail

Round trip: 13 miles
Elevation range: 3200–6040 feet
Difficulty: Difficult
Hiking time: 10 hours
Best canine hiking seasons: Summer, fall
Regulations: Northwest Forest Pass required. Campsites are regulated in this very popular area; call ahead to determine whether entry permits are required.
Maps: USGS Mount Bruno and Mount Jefferson 7.5′ quadrangles
Information: Detroit Ranger District, Willamette National Forest, (503) 854-3366

Getting there: From Salem, follow Oregon Route 22 about 35 miles east to Detroit. Turn left (north) on Breitenbush Road (Forest Road 46). Drive 10.7 miles, and turn right on Forest Road 4685. Drive 4.5 miles and turn left into the huge trailhead parking area. To find the beginning of the hike to Jefferson Park, walk 0.2 mile farther (east) along FR 4685 to the South Breitenbush Trail (Trail 3375).

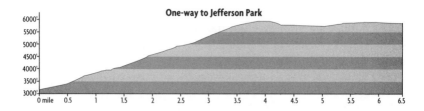

One-way to Jefferson Park

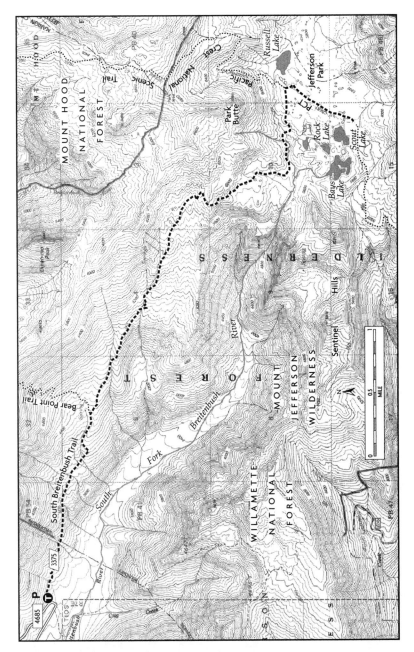

The hike to Jefferson Park, one of the High Cascades' most scenic spots, is deservedly popular. Lakes and water abound in the alpine landscape. Expect to meet other hikers and dogs, even in nonpeak times. Much of the area is in recovery from past overuse, and campfires are banned. So here, especially, go lightly on the land.

From the trailhead, the South Breitenbush Trail (Trail 3375) begins an unrepentant but even-gaited climb. The forest is mostly 50- to 100-year-old Douglas fir and hemlock, replacements for the Douglas fir–cedar forest that was consumed in a forest fire here almost a century ago. Charcoal-encrusted snags still loom along the trail. In the first 3 miles, the path encounters four small streams that provide cool water for warm paws. In addition, the trail crosses several smaller, seasonal streams and seeps, but late in the season, these smaller water sources may dry up.

At 1.6 miles, the Bear Point Trail turns left. This path provides a tempting climb along a less popular trail. It leads to Bear Lake in another 1.6 miles of uphill. It makes a tempting side trip in cooler weather. However, the lack of shade and water for most of the climb advises against it on hot days, especially for dogs not in great condition.

To reach the alpine lakes of Jefferson Park, bear right on the South

From the South Breitenbush Trail, Mount Jefferson rises above Jefferson Park.

Breitenbush Trail at its junction with the Bear Point Trail. Look for western white pine along with azalea and rhododendron as the forest opens. The path leads through a mile of young trees growing where the older forest was burned away several decades ago. You can catch glimpses of Mount Jefferson from the trail, or saunter a few hundred feet off the trail to better viewpoints along the rim of Breitenbush Canyon. As you reach 5000 feet near the base of Park Butte, the forest closes in again. Look for young Western red cedar trees in trailside wetlands.

The trail makes a quick plunge into a small, forested basin and tiny lake, then climbs out again to find the Pacific Crest Trail (PCT) and Russell Lake at the base of Mount Jefferson 5.5 miles from the trailhead. This is the portal to Jefferson Park. Subalpine firs grow on rock-clad islands amid spongy alpine meadows. Fido will exult in the soft, spongy footing but may not fully appreciate the views of Whitewater Glacier and Jefferson's craggy summit. Turn right at the PCT and follow it about a half-mile to Scout Lake at the south edge of Jefferson Park. Return as you came.

35. Mount Washington Wilderness: Patjens Lakes

Round trip: 6.1 miles
Elevation range: 4550–4810 feet
Difficulty: Easy
Hiking time: 4 hours
Best canine hiking seasons: Spring, summer
Regulations: Northwest Forest Pass required
Maps: USGS Mount Washington, Clear Lake, Santiam Junction, and Three Fingered Jack 7.5' quadrangles
Information: Sisters Ranger District, Deschutes National Forest, (541) 549-7700

Getting there: From Sisters, drive west on U.S. Highway 20/Oregon Route 126 about 13 miles. Turn left (south) onto Forest Road 2690, just west of Santiam Pass. Continue on this road for 3.2 miles, passing the Hoodoo Ski Area. The trailhead and parking area are on the right just before the second Big Lake Campground, which lines the shore of Big Lake here. The trailhead is almost directly south of Hoodoo Ski Area.

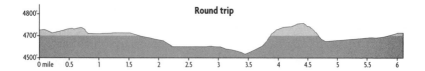

This hike is an almost flat 6.1-mile loop through lodgepole pine and Douglas fir. For dogs, there are woodland smells aplenty and four small shallow lakes (three in a dry summer) to play in. These small lakes are shallow depressions in the thick deposits of volcanic ash north of Belknap Crater. The lakes are named for a Sherman County sheep rancher, Henry Patjens, who grazed livestock here around 1900. With its abundant water, this secluded lake basin—called Hidden Valley for good reason—is a haven for does and fawns in spring and early summer.

From the trailhead, the Patjens Lakes Trail saunters into a lodgepole pine forest of small trees. In about 100 yards, the path splits to begin the loop. Take the trail to the left, which leads more quickly to the lakes—the hike's main attractions.

This trail bypasses the road and campground, then turns into the forest, crossing a small stream—the first of many opportunities for a doggie dunking—and climbing a small hill that offers a nice view of

Dundee and Meesha in the tall grass at Patjens Lakes, Mount Washington Wilderness.

Mount Washington (virtually the only nice view of the Cascades you will see on this mostly forested hike). The path skirts the Douglas fir forests and bigger trees, finding the south shore of Big Lake at 1 mile. While the trail stays back from the lakeshore, it's an easy jaunt through the underbrush to the water for dogs. There is a trail junction at 1.2 miles. The trail to Patjens Lakes turns right, entering lodgepole-dominated forest again.

About 2.6 miles from the trailhead and 1.6 miles after the trail leaves Big Lake behind, the trail sideswipes the first of the four little lakes without approaching it directly. You'll find it when you will notice an open area to the north (right) of the trail. This is one of the largest of the Patjens Lakes—a body of shallow water about the size of a football field surrounded by tall bunchgrasses and reeds. Dogs will find a welcome place for a roll or a game of "Chase me." In late fall, the lakes are too

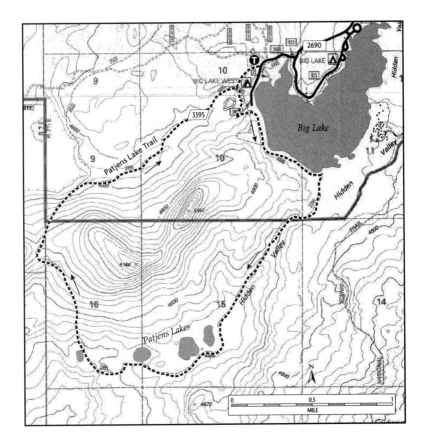

shallow for dog paddling, but there is plenty of wading to be had. A low, unnamed butte can be seen on the opposite side of the lake.

From this lake, the trail continues through woods to the second lake. As with the first, the trail bypasses the lakeshore, giving you and your dog an opportunity to sniff a way through the forest on informal trails to find the lake in a few hundred feet. It is a short jaunt from this lake along the trail to the third, much smaller lake, also hidden in the pines though visible from the trail. A number of paths lead to the lakeshore. The fourth lake, which is smaller yet and often converts into a boggy flat area by midsummer, lies along the trail in another 0.6 mile, or 3.6 miles from the trailhead.

From the fourth lake it takes another 2.5 miles of hiking to complete the loop. The trail rises for 0.8 mile, crossing a low saddle. It then drops more steeply, continuing through what begins to seem like an endless lodgepole forest. At 0.4 mile from the saddle, there is a junction with Trail 3522. Bear right here to return to the trailhead, which is about a mile ahead. The last mile is almost flat, but there is no water from the last lake to the trailhead, so carry ample water for your dog to drink in this last half of the hike. Alternatively, you could skip this section and instead turn around at the fourth lake, pausing at the other lakes for a canine-cooling dip as you return the way you came.

36. Deschutes River

One-way trip: 8.5 miles
Elevation range: 3850–4290 feet
Difficulty: Easy
Hiking time: 5 hours
Best canine hiking seasons: Spring, summer, fall
Regulations: Northwest Forest Pass required; dogs must be on leash
Maps: USGS Benham Falls and Shevlin Park 7.5′ quadrangles
Information: Bend/Fort Rock Ranger District, Deschutes National
Forest, (541) 383-4000

Getting there: To reach the start of this hike at the Benham Falls trailhead, drive west from Bend on Century Drive, which becomes the Cascade Lakes Highway and then Forest Road 46. Approximately 6 miles from downtown Bend, turn left (south) onto Forest Road 4600-100.

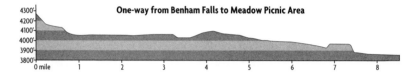

Continue past the Meadow Picnic Area on FR 4600-100 for another 2 miles toward Mount Bachelor. Turn left (south) onto Forest Road 41, marked for Benham Falls. Drive 2.6 miles, then turn left (east) onto Forest Road 4120 and continue for 0.5 mile. Bear right onto Forest Road 4120-100 and follow the washboarded gravel road 3.1 miles to a parking area and the trailhead.

The Benham Falls trailhead can also be reached from Interstate 97. To use this route, drive 9 miles south from Bend on I-97. Turn right (west) at Lava Butte, and then almost immediately turn left onto Forest Road 9702, marked for Benham Falls. Drive 4 miles to a picnic area and parking (crossing a set of railroad tracks at 3.2 miles). Cross the Deschutes River on the bridge at the west end of the picnic area, and follow the well-developed riverside trail 0.7 mile to Benham Falls and a connection with the Deschutes River Trail 0.2 mile past the falls.

To leave a second vehicle at Meadow Picnic Area, where this hike ends, exit the Benham Falls Trailhead and return to FR 4600-100. You will reach the trailhead at Meadow Picnic Area in about 2.1 miles. There also is trail access at five other points along the Deschutes, all of them reachable from FR 41.

The trail along the Deschutes River is really three trails—one that is dedicated to horses, another that is dedicated to mountain bikers, and a third, the one closest to the river, for hikers. The three paths often overlap, however. Generally, as long as you follow the river, it's hard to get lost.

This is a popular trail, so watch for other hikers and dogs, and also mountain bikes. Bend is a mecca for mountain bikers, the Deschutes River Trail is a favorite ride, and some riders stray from the mountain bike route. In the spring, you are likely to find deer—especially does and young fawns near the trail—or if you don't, your dog will. Forest Service guidelines require that dogs be leashed, and it's best to heed the rules here.

The hike begins at the Benham Falls trailhead, a manicured, civilized path replete with handrails, mesh fences, and wooden benches. The trail

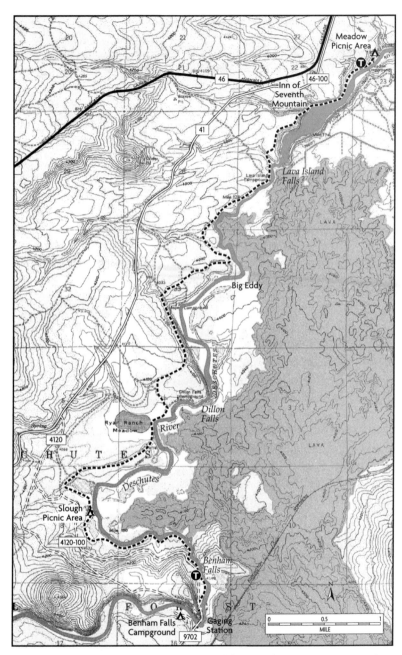

switchbacks down to an overlook of the falls and the narrow canyon that the unruly river has chopped through a lava flow belched out of Lava Butte about 6200 years ago. The river plays tag with the flow for most of the hike. It was this eruption that pushed the river channel west to its present location. The Deschutes is only now fighting its way back to its former channel closer to Lava Butte.

From the overlook area, a gravel path leads down to the river and the start of the 8.5-mile Deschutes River Trail. The path is broad for virtually all of its length as it weaves from the river's edge for views of desolate lava flows and back into forest dominated by ponderosa pine. Shootingstars and lupine color the early summer forest floor. Bitterbrush and rabbit brush fringe the rocks at the river's edge.

Cody and Donna take a break along the Deschutes River Trail.

The first segment of the trail, Benham Falls to the slough (a sluggish, abandoned river meander), is 1.5 miles long. It hugs the water's edge, rising and falling gently along an undulating forest floor, allowing relatively easy river access at numerous places with a short scramble. This segment, like most of the trail, is popular for fishing, so be wary of lost hooks and other gear, as well as discarded fish. (Trout can carry the same parasites that produce salmon poisoning.)

At 1.5 miles, the trail moves away from the riverbank, crossing the Slough Picnic Area (accessible by car from FR 41), then tours the edge of a large, lily-filled pond and wetland (the slough). This is a good place to practice good canine citizenship and avoid disruption of the wetland and slough while dogs cool off.

In about 0.3 mile, the path returns to the Deschutes, again following a low bank with easy access to water before it swings away from the river to shortcut through bunchgrass meadows.

At Dillon Falls, 3.8 miles downstream from Benham Falls, there is another automotive access point. Here, the river enters a deeper, narrower gorge, remaining inaccessible for about the next 1.2 miles. Be sure to carry extra dog water for this segment on hot days. The trail occasionally teeters toward the gorge rimrock, then meanders back under cover of ponderosa pine. The path is relatively level here and provides views of the lava field across the river. At 4.3 miles from the trailhead, a side trail leads to a nice view of Dillon Falls, a 15-foot-high cataract, and the Class IV rapids below it.

From Dillon Falls, the trail generally parallels the river, but the stream remains inaccessible for another mile. Here the water becomes more accessible in a few places, but access requires some adroit climbing over rocks. At 5.7 miles from Benham Falls, the path reaches the flat terrain of Big Eddy access point, a calm river stretch where lodgepole pines, bitterbrush, and bunchgrass are the dominant vegetation.

Beyond Big Eddy, the path returns to more familiar ponderosa pine and tracks along low, friendly riverbanks for about a mile before winding through more rocky terrain above the canyon that encloses Lava Island Falls. Six-thousand-year-old human artifacts have been found in small caves near this small cataract, indicating probable human occupation of the area within several hundred years of Lava Butte's eruption.

At Lava Island Falls, the trail detours away from the river for the last 1.2 miles before reaching the Meadows Picnic Area and your shuttle car waiting at the end of the trail.

37. Three Sisters Wilderness: Green Lakes to Soda Creek

Round trip: 12 miles
Elevation range: 5460–6750 feet
Difficulty: Moderate
Hiking time: 7 hours
Best canine hiking seasons: Summer, fall
Regulations: Northwest Forest Pass required
Map: USGS Broken Top 7.5' quadrangle
Information: Bend/Fort Rock Ranger District, Deschutes National
Forest, (541) 383-4000

Getting there: From Bend, drive 27 miles east on Cascade Lakes Highway (Forest Road 46). Turn right (north) into the Green Lakes Trail parking area just before Sparks Lake.

This extremely popular trail follows Fall Creek about 4 miles to alpine meadows and spectacular views of Broken Top and South Sister. The stream is aptly named. Waterfalls are abundant along its channel, ranging from scenic, 25-foot plunges to short, bubbly cascades. Dogs and people can access the stream in a number of places, which means plenty of opportunities for cooling dips along the hike. The first and last portions are well shaded; the middle portion of the hike in Green Lake Basin and along the south shoulder of Broken Top crosses alpine meadows where a profusion of lupines and paintbrush await in the summer. As an added bonus, the trail also skirts some of Oregon's youngest volcanic rocks—the glassy, obsidian-like lava flows of the Devils Chain, about 1200 to 2600 years in age.

The hike begins from a huge (and likely full) trailhead parking lot. Follow the Green Lakes Trail that heads due north. It accompanies Fall Creek

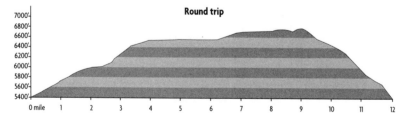

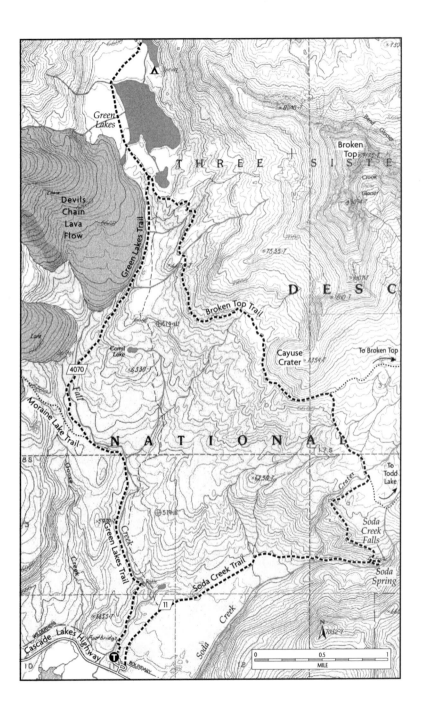

across meadows thick with sedge and into a forest of fir, lodgepole pines, and a few errant ponderosa pines. Beyond the meadows, numerous waterfalls plunge over rocky ledges in 4- to 25-foot leaps, providing calm and often accessible pools at their feet for a cooling wade. The trail rises at a steady and very hikeable pace—one reason for its popularity, aside from the spectacular scenery.

In the first mile, the trail shies away from Fall Creek. It meets a spur trail on the right that leads downhill and east toward Broken Top, then rejoins Fall Creek, providing views into the creek's small canyon. At 1.9 miles, a trail to Moraine Lake spurts to the left. Continue straight ahead on the Green Lakes Trail.

At 2.5 miles, the path flattens as the trail reaches the lower end of Green Lakes Basin. Here, Fall Creek is a calm, meandering alpine stream. Alpine fir is an increasingly common forest component. To the west, you can catch glimpses of South Sister and a huge wall of rugged, glassy volcanic rock that is part of Devils Chain. Then the path weaves away from the rocks and climbs into forest again before returning to Fall Creek and following the stream along the base of another jagged lava dome. The trail follows the base of the Devils Chain flows for another 0.6 mile, then emerges into the Green Lakes basin. There are better views of South Sister as the basin opens, revealing the largest of the Green Lakes (elevation 6160 feet) ahead. The path touches the shore of Green Lake at 4.5 miles.

The Green Lakes basin is beginning to recover from years of overuse. Many areas along the shoreline are cordoned off for recovery. Camping is restricted to designated sites that change from year to year.

At the south shore of this lake, 4.4 miles into the hike, a four-way trail junction appears. If you wish to explore the Green Lakes basin further, continue straight ahead to cross a series of alpine meadows along the west side of the lake and reach a smaller lake in 1.2 miles. This smaller lake has more secluded campsites. Beyond this lake, the trail climbs abruptly out of the basin, so, for this hike, return to the four-way trail junction.

At the junction, bear south onto the trail that leads into the clearing, marked for Broken Top. This path will return you to the Green Lakes trailhead in 7 miles of level and downhill hiking, with ample dog water along the way. After 0.1 mile from the junction, turn left (east) again onto the Broken Top Trail. This trail rises gently through meadows then contours through alpine firs for about 1 mile, crossing four small streams before reaching the base of Cayuse Crater on Broken Top's south flank. This cinder cone is thought to be similar in age to the Devils Chain; it is

The Green Lakes Trail follows aptly named Fall Creek for much of its distance.

a very young volcanic feature. As the trail swings around Cayuse Crater, it offers a view of Broken Top to the north.

Here, 2.8 miles from the four-way trail junction, the trail splits. The path to the left leads eventually to Broken Top. Take the right, downhill path that leads to Soda Spring and Soda Creek. This path follows the headwaters of Soda Creek, leading to another junction—this time with the Todd Lake Trail—in 0.7 mile. Turn right (west) again onto the Soda Creek Trail. This trail leads gently downslope toward alpine fir and Douglas fir woodland for about a half-mile, then turns south and begins a more rapid and switchbacking descent along the steepening canyon of Soda Creek. It reaches the creek again in another half-mile, hanging above Soda Creek Falls, and then turning west abruptly to follow the creek's canyon, crossing the stream twice in the next 0.8 mile. After the second creek crossing, the Soda Creek Trail follows a gentle slope through lodgepole forest and open spaces to reach the trailhead in another 1.4 miles.

38. Three Sisters Wilderness: Sisters Mirror Lake

Round trip: 12 miles
Elevation range: 5400–6200 feet
Difficulty: Moderate
Hiking time: 6 hours
Best canine hiking seasons: Summer, early fall
Regulations: Northwest Forest Pass required
Map: USGS South Sister 7.5' quadrangle
Information: Bend/Fort Rock Ranger District, Deschutes National Forest, (541) 383-4000

Getting there: From Bend, drive 30 miles west on Cascade Lakes Highway (Forest Road 46). Turn right (north) into a small parking area marked as the Mirror Lake trailhead.

The name of this trail and its destination, Sisters Mirror Lake, conjures visions of high alpine splendor. Instead, what you get is a rather level hike through lodgepole pines, a fleeting glimpse of higher peaks, and a satisfactory romp in a huge heather-filled meadow along the shore of a placid little pond. There are other lakes in the vicinity, and most of the day can be spent sampling each one for size.

From the trailhead, the path plunges into lodgepole pines, dropping in 0.5 mile into a small valley of fir and spruce with springs and bogs along Sink Creek. Here, the trail crosses a broader trail—part of a road to Rock Mesa crafted when a mining company threatened to turn Rock Mesa into

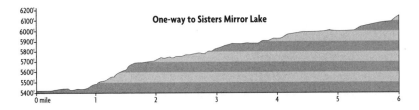

One-way to Sisters Mirror Lake

kitty litter in the 1960s. Continue straight across this broad, tempting path. The trail to Sisters Mirror Lake climbs out of the small valley, sideswipes a small forest pond at the top of the grade, and then circumnavigates several large rock outcroppings. These make inviting play areas for dogs, and a climb to the top offers a view of Kokostick Butte and a rare glimpse of South Sister peeking over the pine-fringed landscape.

From the rock outcroppings, the trail ambles 3 miles through a lodgepole stand. There is no dog water here, and it can be a long stretch on hot days, so carry dog water for this portion of the hike.

At 3.8 miles from the trailhead, the path intersects the Pacific Crest Trail. If you continue straight ahead, the path circles around the lake basin and leads about 4 miles through still more lodgepoles, meandering downslope through firs to Sphinx Creek and Nash Lake (4920 feet). To reach Sisters Mirror Lake (6200 feet) and a welter of other small alpine lakes and ponds, turn left (southwest) here onto the Pacific Crest Trail. The path leads across a heather-floored meadow—a former lake-bottom— to reach the shore of Sisters Mirror Lake in 0.6 mile.

The view of South Sister is disappointing here, but it improves slightly as you travel farther south and west along the trail. Once at Sisters Mirror

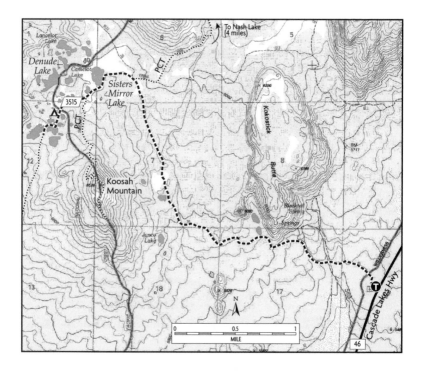

Meesha contemplates a plunge into the water along the trail to Sisters Mirror Lake, Three Sisters Wilderness.

Lake, the trail (which can be a challenge to find among the heather and sedges) splits. One branch leads northwest away from the lake, the other heads southwest along the lakeshore. There are other lakes in this basin to explore, including Denude Lake 0.6 mile along a trail to the northwest and a cluster of slightly smaller, unnamed lakes along the trail about 1 mile to the southwest. Return to the trailhead as you came.

39. Todd Lake

Round trip: 5.6 miles
Elevation range: 6120–6840 feet
Difficulty: Moderate
Hiking time: 4 hours
Best canine hiking seasons: Summer, early fall
Regulations: Northwest Forest Pass required
Map: USGS Broken Top 7.5' quadrangle
Information: Bend/Fort Rock Ranger District, Deschutes National Forest, (541) 383-4000

Getting there: From Bend, drive 27 miles west on Cascade Lakes Highway (Forest Road 46). Just past Sparks Lake, turn right (north) onto FR 370,

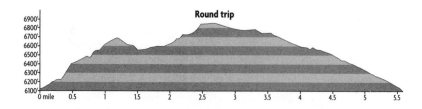

marked for Todd Lake. Drive 0.6 mile to the trailhead and campground parking area.

This hike tours a varied landscape, rising from a large lake lined with fir and hemlock into a subalpine environment with less than 1000 feet of climb. Most of the hike is forested; open meadowlands offer streams or marshes.

The first half of this almost 6-mile hike follows well-maintained Forest Service trails; the second portion tracks along roads, most of which are abandoned or gated off. They are really nothing more than luxuriously wide hiking paths, though there is occasional use by vehicles on the last half-mile, so as you return be vigilant for the sound of approaching engines and keep dogs close.

From the trailhead, the broad path to Todd Lake and its walk-in campground is well marked and offers an easy stroll to the popular lake's well-trampled beach. For dogs, this is a good spot for a wetting before heading out. The likely proximity of campers and picnickers here during the peak summer season recommends that dogs remain on leashes here.

The Todd Lake Trail leaves to the left along the east side of the lake, climbing quickly and steadily away from the water and into dense Douglas fir forest, leaving the lake only a blue glimmer through the trees. After gaining about 300 feet in the first half-mile, the path moderates its climb.

At 1.2 miles, a trail leads to the right. If you wish to make this a shorter hike than the 4-hour route outlined here, you can turn right (east) here, reaching a two-track gravel road in 0.5 mile, followed by boggy subalpine meadows and a small stream in about 1 mile, and continuing on the road 2.6 miles back to the trailhead for a 4-mile loop. This option forgoes the best views of Broken Top, however.

To continue on the main hike, go straight at the intersection heading northwest. At 1.7 miles, the trail intersects the Soda Creek Trail. For a good view of Broken Top, a mountain that owes its craggy countenance to glaciers rather than explosive eruptions, turn left onto the Soda

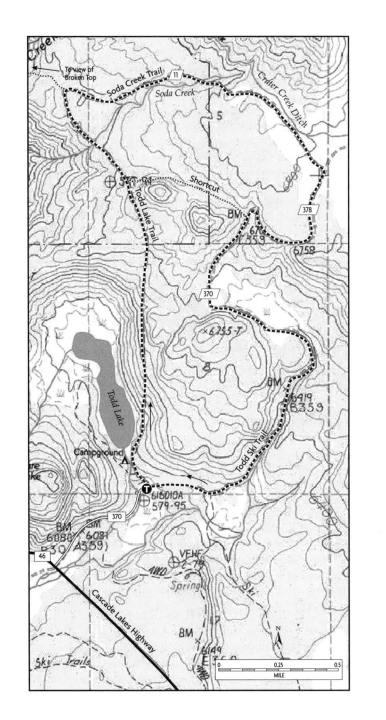

Broken Top, an extinct, glaciated Cascade volcano, rises above the trails from Todd Lake and Green Lakes.

Creek Trail and continue for 0.5 mile to alpine meadows and the head-waters of Soda Creek before turning around and retracing your steps to the intersection.

To return to the Todd Lake trailhead, head east (right) on the Soda Creek Trail. This path intercepts the Crater Creek Ditch in 0.9 mile, then merges with abandoned Spur Road 378 about 1 mile from its beginning at the intersection with the path that leads up from Todd Lake. In 0.5 mile, the two-track path leads past boggy meadows, then merges into a more traveled road—Spur Road 370. Like Spur Road 378, this road is not maintained for vehicular traffic and is gated most of the year. However, use caution when hiking with dogs, as it is open at times during the fall and mountain bikers occasionally use the roads.

In 1 mile, Spur Road 370 joins the upper reaches of Todd Creek, a small stream that leads you, your dog, and the road 1.5 miles back to the Todd Lake trailhead.

40. Newberry National Volcanic Monument: Peter Skene Ogden Trail

One-way trip: 9.5 miles
Elevation range: 4300–6350 feet
Difficulty: Moderate
Hiking time: 6 hours
Best canine hiking seasons: Early summer, early fall
Regulations: Northwest Forest Pass required
Maps: USGS Paulina Peak and Finley Butte 7.5' quadrangles
Information: Bend/Fort Rock Ranger District, Deschutes National
    Forest, (541) 383-4000

Getting there: Reach the beginning of this hike by following U.S. Highway 97 south 23.5 miles from Bend. Turn left (east) onto Forest Road 211, which is the main entrance road to Newberry National Volcanic Monument. Drive 2.8 miles to Forest Road 2120, then turn left (north) into Ogden Group Camp.

To leave a second vehicle at the far end of this one-way hike, continue east on Forest Road 21 for 12 miles past the entrance to Ogden Group Camp. Turn left into a service road marked Paulina Lake Lodge.

This hike on the Peter Skene Ogden National Scenic Trail follows Paulina Creek for 9.5 miles to Paulina Lake. En route to the lake, the trail passes several waterfalls and provides a tour of how a forest changes with increasing altitude. Mountain bikers ride this trail uphill, but their downhill run is supposed to be on the road or a separate path. Horses, however, share the trail both uphill and down, though there is a separate parallel trail just for them.

From the trailhead in a large parking lot just before Ogden Group Camp,

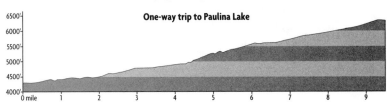

One-way trip to Paulina Lake

the trail points upstream along Paulina Creek. In 0.25 mile it crosses the creek on a sturdy bridge, then moves across grassy meadows and into lodgepole pine stands with an understory of bitter-brush and manzanita. These trees are well adapted to Newberry's ash-rich soils and to the eruptions and distur-bance cycles of volcanoes.

The trail jogs right at 0.7 mile then left at 0.9 mile, crosses another wooden foot-bridge, and then emerges onto a narrow-gauge railroad grade well above the creek. At 2.5 miles, Paulina Creek be-gins a retreat into its gorge, making creek access next to impossible for the next 0.5 mile until the campground at McKay Crossing. Here, a pretty 15-foot waterfall marks Paulina Creek's renewed ac-cessibility.

The path uphill for the next 5.7 miles is uninterrupted by campgrounds or other dis-tractions. This forest includes occasional old-growth ponde-rosa pines and an understory of kinnikinnick—a low man-zanita. This segment of the trail is rocky in places, and Paulina Creek is not always ac-cessible, especially in the

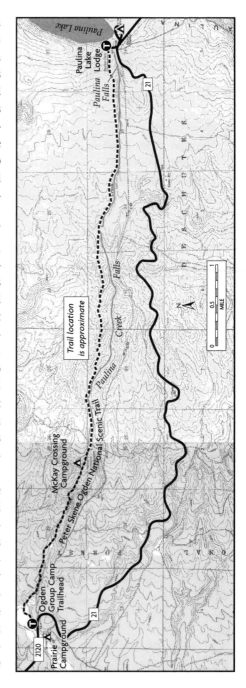

Hot dogs. Dundee and Meesha on the Peter Skene Ogden Trail, Newberry National Volcanic Monument.

stretch between mile 4.6 and mile 5.2 where the creek cuts through another gorge just downstream from an unnamed 10-foot falls. From this falls to Paulina Falls is another 3 miles of trekking through a fragrant lodgepole forest, interspersed with more ponderosa pine and eventually Douglas fir as the trail moves higher. The path moves away from the stream at 7.9 miles into the hike, remaining safely atop the rims of a deepening gorge—the entree to Paulina Falls. Where the path encounters the falls at 8.5 miles, it offers only a rudimentary glimpse of the rushing water from the north side of the stream. For a better view, visit the developed interpretive trails on the south bank at the conclusion of your hike.

The trail continues 0.3 mile past Paulina Falls to the entrance road to Paulina Lake Lodge. To reach the main Paulina picnic area, cross the bridge and follow a path along the highway guardrail 0.3 mile to the west.

NORTH UMPQUA TRAIL

Built over an eighteen-year period from 1978 to 1996, the North Umpqua Trail (NUT) is one of the newest pathways along Oregon's scenic rivers. It extends for 79 miles from just east of Glide on State Route 138 upstream to Maidu Lake, the North Umpqua River headwaters. The trail is divided into nine easily accessible segments that follow the river, offering a variety of hiking environments with old-growth cedar and spruce forest and high-altitude hikes amid lodgepole pine and subalpine fir. Trailheads are easily accessible, but the trail itself is remote from traffic, even on the segments that follow the Umpqua along the main highway—the trail is across the river from the road and well screened by forest. The entire North Umpqua Trail is excellent for hiking with dogs, though this book covers just four segments of it.

Because of the frequent access points, three of the hikes along the North Umpqua Trail are described as one-way trips. Hikers can use a two-vehicle shuttle system to hike the trail in only one direction. An alternate way to enjoy these hikes is to walk the whole distance to the next trailhead and return, or walk part of the distance from one trailhead, return, and then hike from the next trailhead.

41. North Umpqua Trail: Tioga Segment, Miles 1–16

One-way trip: 15.7 miles
Elevation range: 770–1800 feet
Difficulty: Moderate
Hiking time: 6 hours
Best canine hiking season: Fall
Regulations: Northwest Forest Pass required
Maps: USGS Old Fairview and Mace Mountain 7.5′ quadrangles (this trail is too new to appear on maps)
Information: North Umpqua Ranger District, Umpqua National Forest, (541) 496-3532; Coos Bay-Umpqua Office, Bureau of Land Management, (541) 756-0100

Getting there: To reach the west trailhead where this hike begins, start at the North Umpqua Ranger Station at Glide and head east for 2 miles

One-way trip to Forest Service Road 4711

on Oregon Route 138. At the Swiftwater Bridge, turn right (south) across the bridge, marked for the North Umpqua Trail, Tioga segment. Turn left into the trailhead parking area.

To reach the east trailhead, where you can leave a shuttle car to make this a one-way hike, return to ORE 138. Drive 18 miles east on ORE 138 to Forest Road 4711 (Wright Creek Road). Turn right onto FR 4711 and drive across the bridge. The trailhead is almost immediately across the bridge.

The Tioga segment of the North Umpqua Trail (NUT) is the lowest elevation portion of the trail and lies closest to Roseburg and other towns. Ironically, this popular and most accessible segment, mostly on land operated by the Bureau of Land Management (BLM) and Douglas County Parks, is also one of the NUT's longest and most rigorous. It climbs over Bob Butte, one of the few strenuous uphill stretches in the 79-mile trail.

Watch for poison oak in sunny or open places. The North Umpqua is a big and powerful river along this segment, so exercise caution when you take Fido for a dip. You also might encounter inexperienced hikers whose destination is the river overlook along a handicapped-accessible interpretive trail to Deadline Falls, so be sure to keep dogs on a leash.

From the west trailhead (Tioga, also the start of the 79-mile trek to Maidu Lake on the north flank of Mount Theilsen), the path follows the river and in 0.1 mile offers a short, interpretive side trail to an overlook of a riparian wetland and Deadline Falls—a 6-foot cataract jumped by migrating salmon and steelhead in the fall. From this side trail, the main route turns back into the forest, following the river at a respectful and generally inaccessible distance. Periodic encounters with small side creeks provide adequate doggie dunkings in spring and early summer. Douglas fir, Alaska yellow cedar, and bigleaf maple form most of the forest canopy along the Tioga trail segment. Maidenhair and sword ferns and manzanita form most of the low understory. Watch for kingfishers, with their clicking, ratchety call along the river.

At 1.8 miles, the path provides an overlook of Fern Falls, a misty curtain of water that plummets off a rock outcrop and scampers into a deep blue hole in the adjacent North Umpqua. Beyond this falls, the trail

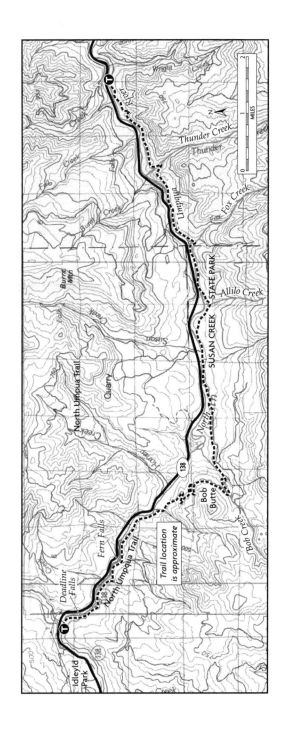

The North Umpqua River plunges over numerous small falls and rapids near the North Umpqua Trail's Tioga Segment.

maintains some distance between itself and the river, though with a little perseverance you can scamper down the slopes (sometimes steep) to find the shore. After maintaining its distance from the river, the path begins a climb up the west shoulder of Bob Butte at about 3.5 miles into the hike. It climbs about 900 feet in a switchbacking ascent through mostly Douglas fir forest. Look for pileated woodpeckers here. In summer, the call of hermit thrush sounds like a distant flute.

The ascent of the northern shoulder of Bob Butte is the only real climb on this segment of the trail, but there is no water along it, so carry extra for your dog and be prepared to take a break on hot days. Westbound mountain bikers relish the downhill challenge, so keep your dog under close control here and be ready for hurtling two-wheelers.

The trail reaches its summit at 1800 feet (Bob Butte's northern shoulder) and begins a much straighter descent to Bob Creek. The creek provides an adequate doggie dip to compensate for a long, hot climb. There's still another 10 miles ahead before reaching the next trailhead.

Once across the creek, the trail ducks beneath a powerline and then joins an old two-track road. It follows this road for about 2 miles, including a stint though the south side of Smith Springs County Park. At the end of this road near the riverbank, the NUT resumes its more familiar form as a single-track trail. At 10 miles into the hike, a side trail invites you up a canyon with a small creek. This trail leads to a very pretty, 45-foot waterfall. It's best explored in spring and early summer, though the stream, Allilo Creek, is perennial. For the next 5.7 miles, the trail continues through a diverse fir and cedar forest, generally keeping away from the riverbank, and at times perching on steep slopes above the water. It crosses ten more creeks, so even if you cannot access the North Umpqua River, there are enough doggie dips to keep even Labrador retrievers happy.

At its end, the Tioga segment of the North Umpqua River Trail emerges from a dark, sheltered forest at the small trailhead area on Forest Service Road 4711 near the small community of Steamboat.

42. North Umpqua Trail: Hot Springs Segment, Miles 47–54

One-way trip: 6.2 miles
Elevation range: 2512–3135 feet
Difficulty: Moderate
Hiking time: 4 hours
Best canine hiking seasons: Summer, fall
Regulations: Northwest Forest Pass required
Maps: USGS Potter Mountain and Toketee Falls 7.5′ quadrangles
Information: Diamond Lake Ranger Station, Umpqua National
    Forest, (541) 498-2531

Getting there: To reach the start of the hike, from Interstate 5 at Roseburg drive 59 miles east on Oregon Route 138. Turn left (north) onto

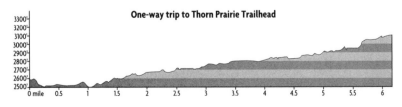

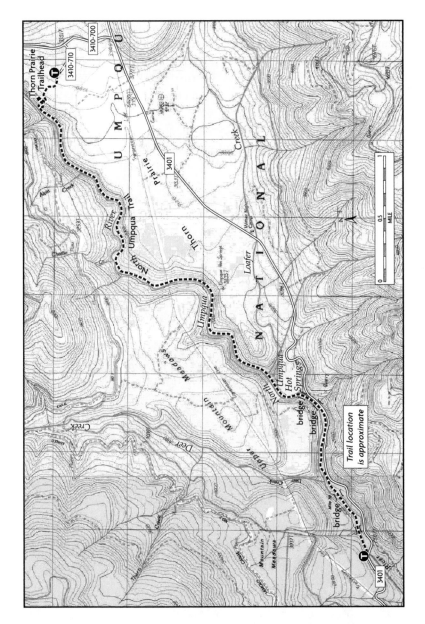

Forest Road 34, the Toketee Lake turn-off. Continue 2 miles on FR 34, past a noisy generator plant and Toketee Campground, and bear right onto FR 3401, marked Hot Springs. Park at a small trailhead parking turn-out on the right on FR 3401, about 0.6 mile beyond the turn-off from FR 34, just after a bridge across the river.

To reach the Thorn Prairie trailhead, where you can leave a shuttle car to make this a one-way hike, return to FR 3401. Drive an additional 4 miles on FR 3401 and turn left (west) onto Spur Road 700, marked NORTH UMPQUA TRAIL. Drive 0.5 mile on Spur Road 700, then bear left onto Spur Road 710 and drive another 0.5 mile to the Thorn Prairie trailhead parking area.

The Hot Springs segment of the North Umpqua Trail (NUT) sets off briskly through a Douglas fir and Alaska yellow cedar forest, then encounters a thinned forest segment where there is more daylight. An understory of thorny ceanothus is struggling here. This plant has such robust thorns that Forest Service planters who had to work here dubbed the ceanothus-covered ridge to the east "Dread and Terror Ridge." The remaining trees provide too little shade for this plant to flourish, but the thorns here will likely keep Fido pretty close to the trail. Sunlight has its upside, though. Look for huckleberry bushes among the thorns.

The path winds past one of many springs on this segment, then crosses Deer Creek, a broad tributary stream, on a narrow log bridge at 0.7 mile. In spring, this creek roars. In summer and fall, it's an ideal place for a

Shouldn't we be wading through the stream instead of going up here on the bridge? Meesha crosses a log bridge on the North Umpqua Trail, Hot Springs Segment.

dog to play. In about a mile, the trail meets the path to Umpqua Hot Springs. Venturesome soakers will turn left, uphill, to relax in the warm waters. The hot spring water is far too warm for dogs, however, so it's best to save your luxurious soak for a time when your dog doesn't have to wait. Follow the main trail right, or southeast, across a sturdy bridge to resume the hike at the north end of a parking lot.

Just past this crossing, the trail crosses a copious spring, then in 0.2 mile dips into a small riverside meadow and passes a moist and mossy outcrop of columnar basalt along the river's edge. This rock is a harbinger of the higher country, an outlying flow of the young lavas of the High Cascades.

Beyond this outcrop, the spring-saturated trail follows the river closely. In 0.3 mile it passes a fern-fringed waterfall and crosses a footbridge across Loafer Creek, offering another nice view of the river. For the remaining 3 miles, the path splashes across more springs and wetlands, traversing a Douglas fir, cedar, and hemlock forest. At 5.6 miles from the trailhead a spur trail from the right leads steeply to the Thorn Prairie trailhead. This path climbs about 350 feet in 0.6 mile of rough, switchbacked trail. The trailhead area, marked with sharp, spiky white ceanothus, is aptly named.

43. North Umpqua Trail: Dread and Terror Segment, Miles 54–63

One-way trip: 8.1 miles
Elevation range: 3020–4025 feet
Difficulty: Moderate
Hiking time: 4 hours
Best canine hiking seasons: Spring, summer, fall
Regulations: Northwest Forest Pass required
Maps: USGS Potter Mountain and Lemolo Lake 7.5′ quadrangles
Information: Diamond Lake Ranger Station, Umpqua National Forest, (541) 498-2531

Getting there: To find the west trailhead at Thorn Prairie where this hike begins, from Interstate 5 at Roseburg drive 59 miles east on Oregon Route 138. Turn left (north) onto Forest Road 34, the Toketee Lake turn-off. Continue 2 miles on FR 34, past a noisy generator plant and

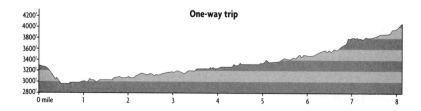

Toketee Campground, and bear right onto Forest Road 3401, marked Hot Springs. Drive an additional 4.6 miles on FR 3401 and turn left (west) onto Spur Road 700, marked for the North Umpqua Trail. Drive 0.5 mile on Spur Road 710 to the trailhead.

To reach the trailhead where you can leave a shuttle car to make this a one-way hike, return to Oregon Route 138. Turn left (north) onto Forest Road 2610, marked for Lemolo Lake. Drive 6 miles, crossing Lemolo Lake dam, and turn left (west) 0.2 mile past the dam and continue 0.6 mile on gravel road to the trailhead.

From the Thorn Prairie trailhead, an access path plunges 0.3 mile downward into Douglas fir, yellow pine, and Alaska cedar forest along the river. Once at the main North Umpqua Trail (NUT), the path follows the North Umpqua River religiously, hugging the banks, then rising and falling gently to cross several small drainages. The path offers a variety of springs and seeps—more than enough to keep dogs happy. A road to a power plant occupies the opposite (north) shore, and occasionally you can hear a pickup rumbling along it.

At 4.7 miles into the hike, the hum of the plant can be discerned, and it makes a fleeting appearance, along with a set of transmission lines, at 5 miles into the walk. The annoying contact with civilization subsides quickly as you enter a deeper and steeper canyon and head for scenic Lemolo Falls.

About 1 mile from the power plant the trail rounds a sharp river bend and heads purposefully for Lemolo Falls, crossing the stream on a solid wooden bridge at 1.5 miles from the plant, and then angling steadily uphill. The trail levels a half-mile before the falls, following the precipitous cliffs above the North Umpqua, now raging far below. Dogs should be on leashes along this segment.

Lemolo Falls can better be heard than seen from this trail. The roar of the 108-foot waterfall (*lemolo* is an Umpqua word thought to mean "untamed") lures hikers closer and closer to the edges of cliffs and outcrops for a view that never quite materializes. The best views can be had

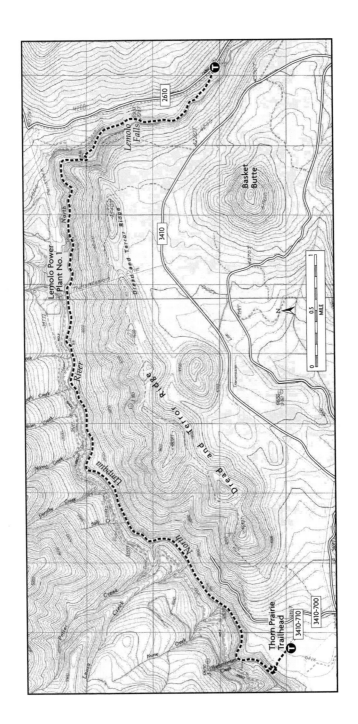

Lemolo Falls, where the North Umpqua River plunges more than 200 feet, appears near the north end of the Dread and Terror trail segment.

from the path just before it passes the falls, about 2.5 miles from the power station, or about a mile before the Lemolo Falls (NUT) trailhead.

The trail rejoins the river just beyond the falls. The waters within a few hundred yards of the falls' dangerous brim are deceptively smooth and placid. They look like a perfect place to cool overheated dogs. However, the water is exceptionally swift here. Continue at least another 0.1 mile up the trail before allowing dogs to cool off in the water.

Above the falls, the North Umpqua flows over a superb sequence of lesser falls, like a gymnast practicing routines before attempting a death-defying leap. The sound of the big falls fades rapidly, leaving you with the songs of many other beautiful and more accessible waterfalls. Watch for dippers (water ouzels) along this upper segment where the trail is close to the stream. These gentle upper falls are beautiful and pleasantly soothing after the disconcerting plunge and cliffs at Lemolo Falls.

The trail rises gradually through old-growth Douglas fir and ponderosa pine for another mile, seeming to linger along the stream before emerging at the Lemolo trailhead 8.1 miles from the segment's beginning.

From this point, the NUT follows forests above the north shore of Lemolo Lake. The Lemolo segment, miles 62–69, offers no water along its length and no access to the lake, either. Its only redeeming virtue is that it connects the Dread and Terror segment with the final segment, Maidu.

44. North Umpqua Trail: Maidu Lake Segment, Miles 69–79

Round trip: 18 miles
Elevation range: 4245–5990 feet
Difficulty: Moderate
Hiking time: 9 hours
Best canine hiking seasons: Summer, early fall
Regulations: Northwest Forest Pass required
Map: USGS Tolo Mountain 7.5' quadrangle
Information: Diamond Lake Ranger Station, Umpqua National
    Forest, (541) 498-2531

Getting there: From Interstate 5 at Roseburg, drive 73.5 miles east on Oregon Route 138. Turn left (north) onto Windigo Pass Road (Forest Road 60). Drive 4.5 miles on FR 60 to its crossing of the North Umpqua River. Just before a bridge across the North Umpqua, park in the small parking area on the left (west) side of the road. The trailhead is on the right.

At this uppermost trailhead on the North Umpqua Trail (NUT), the North Umpqua River is just another pretty alpine stream, serene and placid as it winds through alpine meadows and marshes. The landscape here owes its gentle flatness to Mount Mazama. Much of the valley at

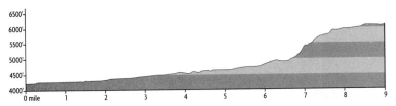

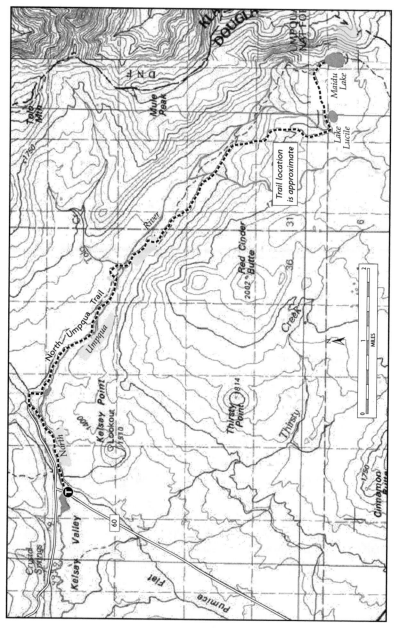

the trailhead is filled with pumice and ash from the cataclysmic eruption 6500 years ago. The river is only now beginning to cut its way
downward again. The lower portions of the trail explore peaceful mead-

ows and stands of lodgepole pine and subalpine fir. But as the trail rises, the North Umpqua retreats into a steep-sided canyon. The path climbs out of the canyon to find two lakes—petite Lake Lucile, and then Maidu Lake a mile farther—the end of this hike and the headwaters of the North Umpqua River.

The trail saunters into the lodgepole pines, heading northeast along the crystal-clear stream. It seems the perfect river for a dog—just enough depth to allow a swim, but not too much speed and few rocks. The banks here are low and lined with huckleberries in August. Dogs who have learned to pick and eat them might need a reminder to keep up.

The river meanders through ashy sand. Lodgepoles provide sporadic shade through the first third of the hike before denser forest appears. Watch for kingfishers along the open meadows. At 1.8 miles, the trail crosses an off-road vehicle trail. Watch for mountain bikers here as well. In the open lodgepole woodland, pine squirrels scold both dogs and hikers.

North Umpqua River is just a pretty alpine stream along the Maidu segment of the North Umpqua Trail.

From this point, the NUT swings away from the river, occasionally crossing wetlands and fragile meadows via sturdy boardwalks. The path maintains an easy grade as it enters denser forests with grand fir and sub-alpine fir and fewer lodgepole pines about 4 miles into the hike. Though the path has abandoned the river, now several hundred yards to the north, there is ample water for canine cooling at 5.3 miles into the hike where the trail encounters wetlands and crosses an unnamed creek.

At 6.5 miles, the trail's gradient steepens noticeably and the vegetation shifts to dense fir. This marks the approach to Lake Lucile, 1.5 miles farther and 1000 feet higher. This relatively small lake squats in a fir-lined basin. The trail circumvents the lake and heads back into the trees to find the true headwater lake—Maidu Lake, an easy and short 1-mile hike farther.

Maidu Lake, a bit larger than Lucile, is entrenched in forest at the north base of Mount Thielsen—there are spectacular views of the needle-shaped peak from the wooded shore. The NUT intersects the Pacific Crest Trail on the far (south) side of the small lake, offering an opportunity to climb the peak in another day's hike. The 5-mile approach to Mount Thielsen is definitely hikeable with a dog, but the final, mile-long trail to the summit is extremely narrow with abrupt cliffs, so it is not recommended for dogs.

Maidu Lake offers a number of camping sites along its shore and outlet—the beginning of the North Umpqua. Return as you came.

THE UPPER ROGUE RIVER TRAIL

The Upper Rogue River Trail is 48 miles long, popular, and exquisitely maintained. Divided into seven segments, it provides easy to moderately easy hiking over its entire length. The river is close at hand in most segments. Leashes are required or recommended on all trail segments. The most northern segment is the least dog-friendly, but even it has adequate cooling water and enough shade to make it a comfortable stroll for most dogs. The trail is best hiked in spring, early summer, or fall to avoid the warmest weather. Southern portions of the Upper Rogue Trail can be accessed in winter. Mountain bikers share the trail, though they are few in number as of this writing.

Because of the frequent access points, two of the hikes along the Upper Rogue River Trail are described as one-way trips. Hikers can use a two-vehicle shuttle system to limit the hike to one direction. An alternate way to enjoy these hikes is to walk half the distance desired, then turn around and return to your vehicle the way you came.

45. Upper Rogue River Trail: Takelma Gorge Segment, Miles 6–10

One-way trip: 4 miles
Elevation range: 2815–2960 feet
Difficulty: Moderate
Hiking time: 2 hours
Best canine hiking seasons: Spring, fall
Regulations: Northwest Forest Pass required; dogs must be on leash
Maps: USGS Whetstone Point and North Prospect 7.5' quadrangles
Information: Prospect Ranger District, Rogue River National Forest, (541) 560-3400

Getting there: To reach the start of this hike, from Medford drive north and east on Oregon State Route 62 until you reach milepost 49. Turn right (west) onto Forest Road 6210, marked for River Bridge Campground. Drive 0.5 mile to the trailhead.

To reach the Woodruff Bridge trailhead where this hike ends, return to Oregon Route 62 and head south to milepost 68 (0.75 mile north of the Mammoth Pines Picnic Area). Turn left (west) onto Forest Road 68, marked for Woodruff Bridge Picnic Area. Drive 1.75 miles on this paved road—it can seem as though you will never reach the river, but eventually the picnic area appears on the right, the bridge and river are straight ahead, and trailhead parking is on the left.

The Takelma Gorge segment of the Upper Rogue River Trail is scenic and dog-worthy. The river is an affable companion almost the entire way—

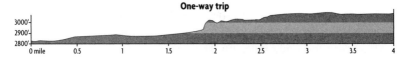

One-way trip

although for a mile or so the stream runs through narrow and steep-walled Takelma Gorge while the trail follows along the top, making water inaccessible for this section only. You will also encounter buildings and likely some people at the Rogue Baptist Camp, so keep dogs on leash or under close control here.

From the River Bridge trailhead, the path follows a broad, calm, almost quiescent river. The river is only resting, however, from its labors upstream where it has notched a 100-foot canyon through young lava and mud flows that blocked its way about a million years ago. Many of the boulders along the stream here were quarried from the gorge walls. Their angular shapes indicate that they have not been carried far by the bouncing, rolling, and rounding power of high-energy river water.

Along the pumice-strewn flats near the trailhead, huge ponderosa pine and sugar pine vie for sky space, dwarfing fir and an understory of vine maple and alder. This portion of the trail glows with fluorescent reds, oranges, and yellows when frost kindles fall colors in October.

For the first mile, the trail hugs the riverbank, allowing easy dog access. This trail segment is also a favorite place to fish, so while your dog explores the riverbank, be wary of possible fishhooks and even possible dead or discarded fish. Most of the time, the worst-case scenario is a doggie roll in dead and pungent fish—an odor that your dog will relish, but you might be less enthusiastic about—but see the section on first aid in this book's introduction for information on salmon poisoning and other riverside risks.

At the end of the first mile of nearly level hiking, you'll catch a glimpse of low-slung buildings ahead through the thinned forest. The trail hugs the river but still cruises close to the Rogue Baptist Camp—an unoccupied facility for much of the year. Keep dogs leashed and under control as you approach and continue past the facility.

Beyond the camp, the trail enters a section of trail that appears wild and pristine, although it is never far from the gravel entry roads that lead to the camp. The river's pace quickens a bit; the forest closes its canopy, and the trail picks up its pace, steepening ever so slightly though it remains essentially flat by most hiking standards.

About 0.7 mile beyond the Rogue Baptist Camp, the trail moves away from the river as the stream recedes into Takelma Gorge.

This gorge is a channel cut by the Rogue River through a relatively young lava flow—one that is less than one million years in age. The gorge is about 100 feet deep and 1 mile in length. The path along its rim offers occasional

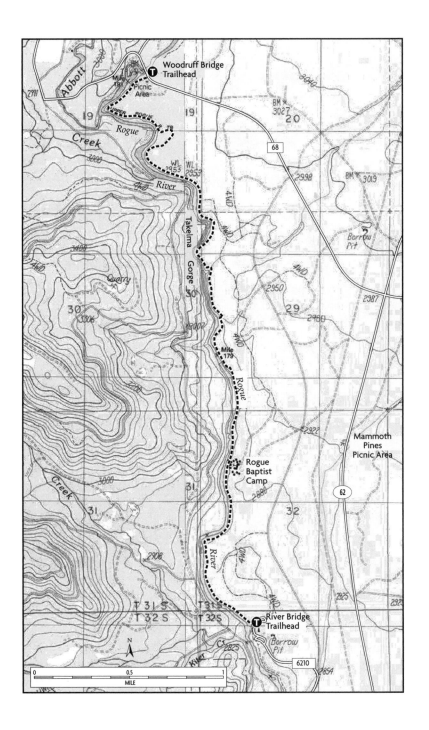

The Rogue River carves steep-sided Talkema Gorge through soft volcanic debris flows.

glimpses into the chasm. You will have to leave the trail for the best views—keeping an eye and a grip on Rover. The gorge walls reveal a sequence of rubbly basalt flows, as well as more fragile mudflows. Because the relatively thin lava flows were underlain by soft and unconsolidated mudflow deposits, the river was able to erode its channel easily once it had worn its way through the harder basalts.

Near the north end of the hike along the gorge, the trail steps over ropy, pahoehoe basalt—now relatively subtle after a million years of rain and organic acids—and twenty years of human feet—have weathered it.

After exploring the rim of Takelma Gorge, the trail remains remote from the river for another half-mile, then plays tag with the stream, dropping to a wetland area in 3 miles from the River Bridge trailhead, and reaching the Woodruff Bridge trailhead in 4 miles from the start of the hike.

46. Upper Rogue River Trail: Knob Falls Segment, Miles 10–14

One-way trip: 3.5 miles
Elevation range: 2960–3200 feet
Difficulty: Easy
Hiking time: 2 hours
Best canine hiking season: Fall
Regulations: Northwest Forest Pass required; dogs must be leashed on interpretive trail
Maps: USGS Whetstone Point, Prospect North, Abbott Butte, and Union Creek 7.5' quadrangles
Information: Prospect Ranger District, Rogue River National Forest, (541) 560-3400

Getting there: To find the beginning of the hike, take Oregon Route 62 from Medford to milepost 68 (0.75 mile north of the Mammoth Pines Picnic Area). Turn right (west) onto Forest Road 68, marked for Woodruff Bridge Picnic Area. Drive 1.75 miles on this paved road—it seems as though you will never get to the river, but eventually the picnic area

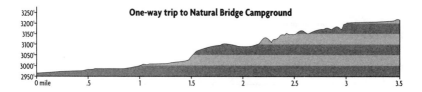

One-way trip to Natural Bridge Campground

appears on the right, the bridge and river are straight ahead, and the trailhead parking is on the left.

To reach the end of this hike where you can leave one car, return to Oregon Route 62 and drive to milepost 52. Turn left (west) at the sign for the Natural Bridge Campground. Drive west 0.4 mile and bear left (south) into a parking area for the Natural Bridge Interpretive Trail. The paved interpretive trail leads toward a bridge across the Rogue. The southbound Upper Rogue River Trail is an unpaved trail that ducks into the forest about 200 feet before the snazzy, arching footbridge across the river.

This relatively short segment of the Upper Rogue River Trail is one of the easiest and prettiest touring some of the Upper Rogue River's most spectacular gymnastics. Most of the river is accessible for doggie dips, with the sole exception being the slightly daunting stretch at Knob Falls and another point where the river makes a sharp curve about 0.5 mile south

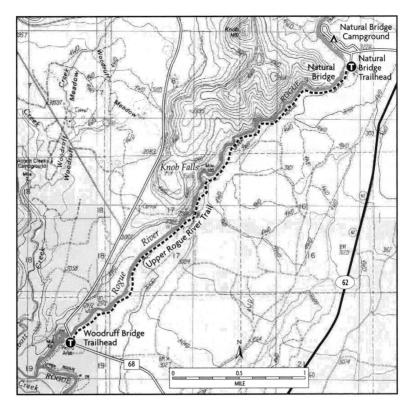

A blacktailed squirrel bears watching along the Knob Falls segment of the Upper Rogue River Trail.

of the Natural Bridge trailhead. Leashes are required along the paved interpretive trail at the northern end of this hike. Expect to find many people on the paved trail, but very few venture onto the wilder, unpaved Upper Rogue River Trail—or even know it is there.

This forest is adapted to slightly colder and wetter conditions than the forest at the lowest trailhead near the town of Prospect. Manzanitas disappear at about 3000 feet and above. But the amazing multiplicity of tree species still provides surprises galore. Look for mixed forests that include three different pines—sugar pine, western white pine, and ponderosa pine—that often grow adjacent to one another, as well as incense cedar, western hemlock, and Douglas fir. Huckleberries appear along portions of this trail.

The path that heads upstream from Woodruff Bridge Picnic Area follows a calm and pretty stretch of the Upper Rogue River. The path is nearly flat for the first mile, weaving through an open forest and swinging to meet the stream at 0.4 mile into the hike. For the next mile, the trail follows the Rogue's bidding, never departing from the stream. Look for many wet-dog opportunities along this mile. For aquaphilic dogs, the easy-going stream is irresistible here.

At 1.4 miles into the hike, the Rogue begins to prove it is not just a placid stream. The gradient picks up, rocks become numerous, the banks are steeper, and water roils over stony cataracts. This is all in preparation for Knob Falls, where the river performs a brief disappearing act. At 1.5 miles, the trail pulls away from the river, climbing upward about 100 feet. Here, a torrent of water funnels through a remnant lava tube and then emerges with a roar. A short, steep side trail provides an overview of the river's brief vanishing act—a practiced and common magic for this portion of the Rogue. If you indulge your dog's penchant for wading before you reach Knob Falls, she will be less likely to think this might be a good place for a swim. It's not. A trail leads out onto the promontory above Knob Falls, but the view is disappointing. Take the side trail just a bit before the trail climbs to the oxbow's "summit" for a better view.

Once past Knob Falls, the trail rejoins the river. The forest is rich in Douglas fir and ponderosa pine. Tree trunks are charcoaled, hinting at past fires that cleared the understory but left large trees standing. The path climbs one more overlook of a river bend before connecting with the paved trail and parking area at Natural Bridge, a huge lava tube that briefly swallows the Rogue River. Be sure to keep dogs leashed while on the paved interpretive trail.

47. Upper Rogue River Trail: Natural Bridge to Big Bend Segment, Miles 14–21

One-way trip: 6.8 miles
Elevation range: 3200–3740 feet
Difficulty: Moderate
Hiking time: 5 hours
Best canine hiking seasons: Summer, early fall
Regulations: Northwest Forest Pass required; dogs must be leashed on interpretive trails
Map: USGS Union Creek 7.5' quadrangle
Information: Prospect Ranger District, Rogue River National Forest, (541) 560-3400

Getting there: To reach the Natural Bridge trailhead where this hike begins, from Medford take Oregon Route 62 east to milepost 52. Turn left (west) at the sign for Natural Bridge Campground. Bear left into the

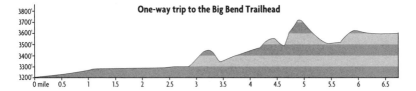

parking area. To reach the northbound Rogue River trailhead from the interpretive trail, follow the paved trails northward along the east bank of the Rogue, bypassing the Natural Bridge Campground and keeping to the riverbank behind the campsites. Dogs should be leashed for this 0.4-mile stretch, and it's best to keep them leashed until you cross the footbridge to the west bank of the Rogue about 1 mile from the start of the interpretive trail.

To reach the end of this hike where you can leave a shuttle, return to Oregon Route 62 and drive northeast to the junction with Oregon Route 230 in 2.6 miles. Follow ORE 230 north 0.9 mile, then turn left (west) onto Forest Road 6510, marked for Big Bend. Cross the Rogue on this road and drive 0.6 mile to a well-marked Big Bend, Upper Rogue River Trail trailhead.

One of the best things about the superbly designed Upper Rogue River Trail is that even amid the crowds at tourist attractions, such as Natural Bridge and the popular campground at Union Creek, you and your dog can find solitude along the trail. At Natural Bridge and the Rogue Gorge interpretive site to the north, the Rogue River Trail accomplishes this miracle by taking refuge on the west side of the river—a position it occupies for most of this hike.

Both these interpretive sites are well worth touring, however, with your dog on a leash. If you charge through them en route to the next trailhead, don't forget to return for a more leisurely examination. The name Natural Bridge evokes a mental image of red sandstone arches such as those found in Utah's Arches National Park. But there is no sandstone within a hundred miles or so of this spot. Instead, this "natural bridge" is a lava tube that swallows the Rogue River whole, and then disgorges it a hundred yards or so downstream. The Rogue Gorge is a former lava tube that probably contained the river underground until the top of the lava tube gradually collapsed, leaving the river visible and confined to a narrow but rather deep channel where the water is incredibly swift.

Here, the Upper Rogue River Trail achieves its solitude at a cost—

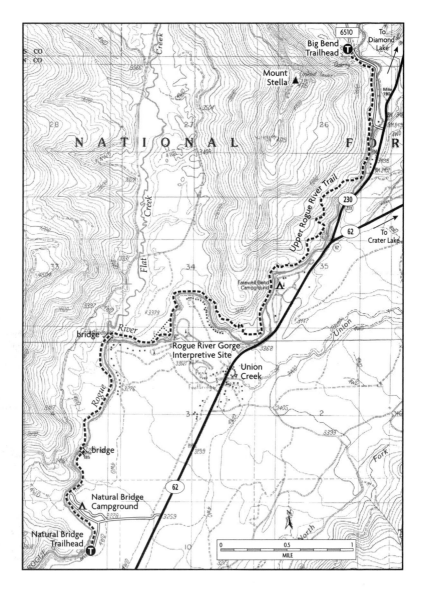

especially for canine hikers. This stretch of the trail abandons the riverbank for a substantial portion of its length. The trail climbs about 300 feet above the riverbed at its highest deviation on this trail segment. But to hikers who have gotten used to an almost flat, watery route, the sudden imposition of this climb comes as a rude reminder that this is Oregon and there are hills here.

Furthermore, the hilly segment of the hike has no reliable water along the way, so be sure to carry ample dog water, especially in hot weather. The trail does have shade by early afternoon, however, mitigating canine temperature concerns somewhat.

Once you and your pup are on the west side of the river and away from the chatter of campers, the trail follows the river quite faithfully for 1.5 miles. There are plenty of opportunities for doggie dunks along this stretch of the trail. The west trail bypasses a set of cabins and yurts along the river's east bank—part of Union Creek and the Union Creek Campground. The hike here moves through stately yellow and sugar pines, crosses a footbridge over Flat Creek, and follows a river bend to the east. You will have to endure another mile of hiking along the west bank with views of cabins and campers as the river bends north and then east.

At 2.8 miles from the trailhead, the trail begins to climb up the bank to avoid steep shores along the river and the Rogue Gorge. This first digression from the river rises about 100 feet in a gradual switchback. The trail then winds back to the river in another 0.3 mile. This segment of the river is swift and uninviting as the Rogue begins to settle into its fast trip through the short gorge. You might want to leash your dog here should the river pose a temptation.

After a fleeting glimpse of the water, the trail moves away again, and then upslope, this time climbing well above the river into a forest dominated by Douglas fir along fairly steep slopes. This part of the trip is cool, even on hot summer days. There are springs along this uphill stretch in spring and early summer, but it is a good idea to carry dog water as there is no reliable stream or spring for the last 3.7 miles of this 6.8-mile hike. The upper trailhead appears at the end of a downhill stretch, when the trail finds Forest Road 6510.

The Rogue River enters a system of topless lava tubes as it nears its narrow gorge and Natural Bridge.

48. Union Creek Trail

Round trip: 7.5 miles (or 3.7 miles one-way)
Elevation range: 3330–3767 feet
Difficulty: Easy
Hiking time: 4 hours
Best canine hiking season: Fall
Regulations: Northwest Forest Pass required
Map: USGS Union Creek 7.5′ quadrangle
Information: Prospect Ranger District, Rogue River National Forest, (541) 560-3400

Getting there: From Medford, take Oregon Route 62 to Prospect then continue 10 miles to Union Creek Campground at the community of Union Creek. Turn left (west) at the campground entrance and find the parking area just before you enter the campground. The trail begins at the opposite (east) side of the highway just south of the small bridge. Alternatively, to avoid crossing the highway, there is a small parking area on the east (right) side of ORE 62 near the trailhead. Parking is very limited here. The Union Creek Store is on the north side of Union Creek here, and permission is needed to park in its parking lot.

To reach the trailhead at Union Creek Falls, continue 3 miles past the community of Union Creek on ORE 62, turn right (south) onto Forest Road 600, marked for Union Creek Falls. Follow FR 600 for 0.25 mile then bear left onto FR 610 for another 0.1 mile to the trailhead parking area.

This hike follows closely along Union Creek, a stream that starts 15 miles away and 3000 feet higher on the western flanks of Union Peak in Crater Lake National Park. The portion of the waterway covered by this hike traverses a bit of the Rogue River's famously diverse forest. The path is broad and flat and offers dogs the opportunity to take frequent dips in an inviting

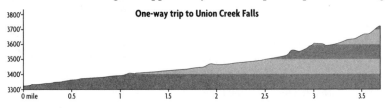

One-way trip to Union Creek Falls

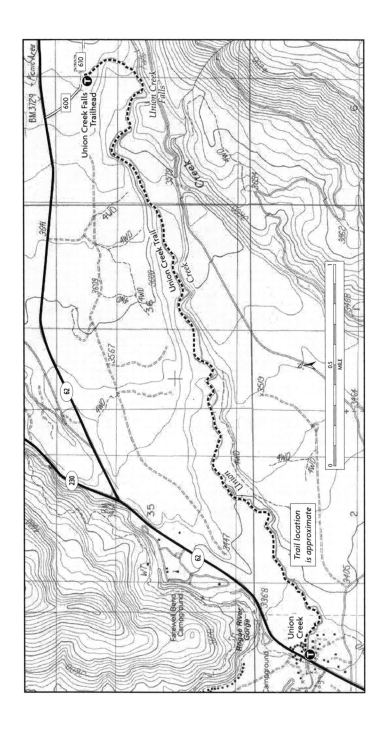

Taking a break on the bridge across Union Creek.

and accessible stream. For those (dogs) who like to wade in mud up to their elbows, there are several opportunities here.

From the trailhead, the Union Creek Trail moves into the open forest, crossing a solid bridge a hundred yards or so from the highway, then moving past a wetland area before turning upstream. Look for kingfishers, redtailed hawks, and water ouzels. Beaver have left chiseled stumps along the creek. Incense cedar, Douglas fir, hemlock, bigleaf maple, and alder comprise a diverse forest along the creek's banks. Sugar pine and ponderosa pine appear on higher slopes or on drier sites. Look for the huge, curving sugar pine cones along the trail. The old-growth trees are huge, and many show scars from fires here early in the twentieth century.

At about 1.5 miles, the creek burrows a bit deeper into the landscape, and the forest closes in. Mountain hemlock and western white pine will be your hiking companions now. Blacktailed pine squirrels scold, warning their families that there are dogs on the trail. In the fall, dogs might encounter squirrels so intent on sequestering their supply of pine nuts and other succulent snacks underground that they forget to watch for predators. A cornered squirrel can give a nasty bite, so hikers and dogs should be wary and also take steps to ensure the safety of squirrels and all wildlife.

The trail rises at almost a flat grade but becomes a little narrower and less used with every step beyond about 1.5 miles. The hike follows Union Creek closely, even where the canyon becomes notably narrower at about mile 2. From here to the falls, wet areas make the path a bit mushy in spring and early summer. The moisture is welcome on dogs' feet, but chances are that they'll already be blissfully wet and cool.

At about 2.5 miles, both the creek and trail quicken their pace. The creek tumbles more urgently over rocks; the path rises at a steeper grade—though still an easy pace by almost any measure. Alder, cedar, Douglas fir, and a few stalwart pine occupy the canyon bottom and south-facing slopes. Look for a few huckleberry bushes upslope from the trail here.

At 3.5 miles from the trailhead, the trail leads to a small, 20-foot waterfall. The cataract is impressive in early summer, but by fall it is reduced to a lacy curtain of water. The pool beneath the falls is refreshingly deep for doggie dips and a swim.

At Union Creek Falls, the trail turns upslope abruptly, rising at an earnest pace and reaching the Union Creek Falls trailhead parking area in 0.3 mile and a climb of about 100 feet. End your hike here if you parked a shuttle car, or return the way you came.

49. Muir Creek Trail to Meadows Hummingbird

Round trip: 8.5 miles
Elevation range: 3905–4600 feet
Difficulty: Moderate
Hiking time: 4 hours
Best canine hiking season: Summer
Regulations: Northwest Forest Pass required
Maps: USGS Hamaker Butte and Fish Mountain, 7.5' quadrangles
Information: Prospect Ranger District, Rogue River National Forest, (541) 560-3400

Getting there: From the intersection of Oregon Routes 62 and 230 near the community of Union Creek in southcentral Oregon, head north (left) on ORE 230 and drive 10.4 miles to trailhead parking on the left (west) side of the highway just before the Muir Creek bridge.

This trail is a true delight for dogs. It tracks through meadows and splashes across a major creek on a very hikeable gradient for more than 4 miles before it climbs steeper slopes out of Muir Creek's valley into the Rogue–Umpqua Divide Wilderness.

You might encounter livestock along this route, especially in the lower meadows or even in the larger Hummingbird Meadows. Keep dogs under control and leashed if necessary to avoid confrontations and conflicts. Horse riders also use this trail as a major horse route into the higher country of the Rogue–Umpqua Divide Wilderness. Mountain bikers are prohibited from wilderness entry, but they occasionally use the lower, nonwilderness portion of the path.

From the trailhead, the Muir Creek Trail climbs quickly into a forest of western white pine and Douglas fir, with a few western hemlocks. It avoids the meadows partly to protect soils and fragile plants, partly to save hikers from wet feet, and partly to shield wildlife and livestock from human and canine intrusion. However, in 0.5 mile it drops to the flatter bottoms and meadows, following the southern side of the broad and scenic wetland meadows. Look for columbine, lupine, scarlet gilia, false hellebore, and lilies in meadows.

At 0.8 mile into the hike, as the trail rises out of the meadow slightly and flirts with the forest again, it meets a trail on the left. Continue straight here.

At 1 mile from the trailhead, the Muir Creek Trail rejoins the stream for the next half-mile—an excellent place for dogs to get a good wetting. However, as this area is grazed, it's also a good idea to provide drinking water for your dog before she decides to slake her thirst in the giardia-infected stream.

At 2.4 miles, the canyon narrows and the trail hops onto the south slope, detouring past Muir Creek Falls and entering a forest. In the next 2 miles, the trail crosses Muir Creek four times, requiring that you ford the creek or use stepping stones for most crossings. Your dog won't mind

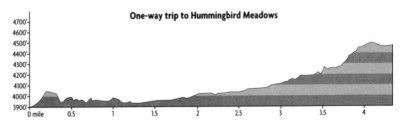

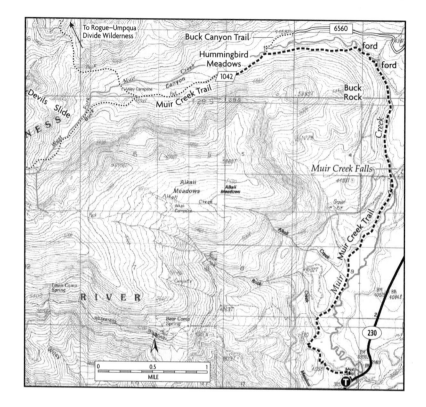

this at all. However, Muir Creek is a swift and deep stream, especially in the canyon where its gradient and velocity are authoritative, and these creek crossings can be hazardous in spring or early in the summer.

About 4 miles into the hike, the trail climbs away from the canyon bottom and Muir Creek. The grade of the creek flattens and the canyon bottom widens, though you won't notice much for the trees. At 4.5 miles, the Buck Canyon Trail joins from the north. This marks the beginning of the Hummingbird Meadows section of the hike. Look for wild berries as the canyon opens. For dogs who have learned to pick and eat these fruits along the trail, this might be the best part of the hike. After an appropriate break to enjoy the views of Buck Rock to the south and the rugged face of Devils Slide to the west, return as you came.

Five More Great Dog Hikes in the Cascade Mountains

1) Elk Lake Creek, 9 miles. Forested, with abundant water. Estacada Ranger Station, Mount Hood National Forest, (503) 630-6861.

2) East Fork McKenzie River Trail, Three Sisters Wilderness, 10 miles. Follows upper river from Cougar Reservoir almost to headwaters. McKenzie River Ranger District, Willamette National Forest, (541) 822-3381.

3) McKenzie River Trail, Three Sisters Wilderness, 26 miles. Follows McKenzie from above McKenzie Bridge to Clear Lake. McKenzie River Ranger District, Willamette National Forest, (541) 822-3381.

4) Lower South Fork Trail, 20 miles. Follows the South Fork of the Rogue River through pine-rich forest. Butte Falls Ranger District, Rogue River National Forest, (541) 865-2700.

5) Six Lakes Trail, Doris Lake to Mink Lake, 18 miles. Take the Cascade Lakes Highway .75 mile south of Elk Lake to the trailhead for Trail 3526. Many lakes for swimming. Bend/Fort Rock District, Deschutes National Forest, (541) 383-4000.

KLAMATH MOUNTAINS

50. Summit Lake

Round trip: 4 miles
Elevation range: 3080–4730 feet
Difficulty: Difficult
Hiking time: 3–4 hours
Regulations: Northwest Forest Pass required
Map: USGS Squaw Lakes 7.5' quadrangle
Information: Applegate Ranger District, Rogue River National Forest, (541) 899-3800

Getting there: From Interstate 5 at Medford, take exit 30, Jacksonville and Oregon Route 238. Follow ORE 238 for 14 miles through Jacksonville to Ruch. At Ruch, turn left (south) onto Upper Applegate Road and drive 14.5 miles to Applegate Dam. Turn left onto Forest Road 1075 to cross the dam and continue on this road for 8.5 miles to Squaw Lakes. The trailhead is on the right in the upper parking lot. Keep to your right as you navigate the many cars at the entry to popular Squaw Lakes. The last 5 miles of FR 1075 is a narrow single-track gravel road. Watch for traffic, including occasional logging trucks.

Summit Lake is a grassy, wetland depression rimmed by beautiful old-growth pine. It is somewhat boggy in the spring when the snow melts,

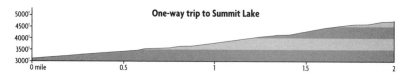

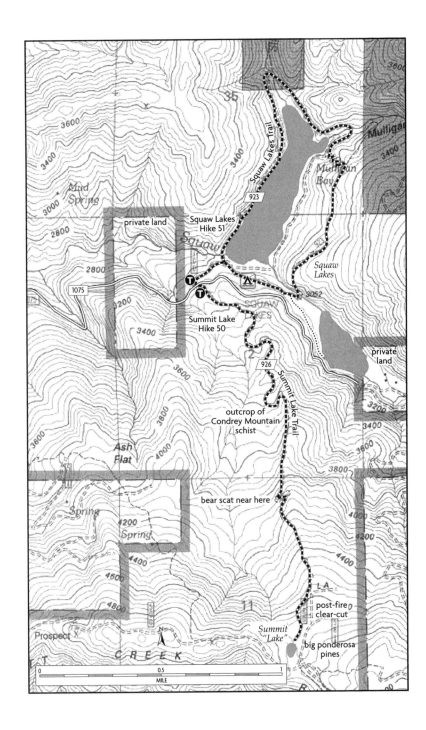

A tree-fringed grassy meadow takes the place of boggy Summit Lake in late summer.

but it's a nice soft place to rest after a hard 2-mile climb in the summer. In early July the "lake" surface shimmers with delicate violet blooms.

From the Squaw Lakes trailhead, the Summit Lake Trail climbs evenly at an easy grade for the first half-mile, crossing a wooden bridge and switchbacking gently uphill. There is no water here—at least not in late summer—so carry plenty for Fido. Look for an osprey nest in a tall pine snag just a few hundred yards up the trail. After the second bend, the trail begins to climb in earnest.

At about 1 mile, the trail ducks behind a slope, tempers its rise, and lets you explore a natural outcropping. Here, you enter bear country—look for signs including droppings, dead trees that have been ripped open in search of ants and grubs, and large rocks rolled over in similar hunts for food. The diverse forest along the way includes madrone, Douglas fir, ponderosa pine, sugar pine, and cedar.

At 1.7 miles, the trail skirts a huge clearing—the result of a 1980 forest fire that was subsequently logged so as not to "waste" wood. (Today we know that the number of birds increases in a burned area as new species including flickers, nuthatches, and pileated woodpeckers harvest the insects that come to feed on damaged or dead trees.) Only one or two lonely snags remain standing. At the upper end of the clearing, the trail zigzags and then joins Spur Road 700. Just before the junction with the Forest Service road, an unmarked trail leads gently downslope 100 yards to a clearing—Summit Lake. There are nice views of the Siskiyous from the logged-over fire area and an opportunity to explore the old-growth pine grove that encloses Summit Lake. Return as you came.

51. Squaw Lakes Trail

Round trip: 3.4 miles
Elevation range: 3020–3340 feet
Difficulty: Easy
Hiking time: 1 hour
Best canine hiking seasons: Summer, fall
Regulations: Northwest Forest Pass required
Map: USGS Squaw Lakes 7.5' quadrangle
Information: Applegate Ranger District, Rogue River National Forest, (541) 899-3800

Getting there: From Interstate 5 at Medford, take exit 30, Jacksonville and Oregon Route 238. Follow ORE 238 for 14 miles through Jacksonville to Ruch. At Ruch, turn left (south) onto Upper Applegate Road and drive 14.5 miles to Applegate Dam. Turn left onto Forest Road 1075 to

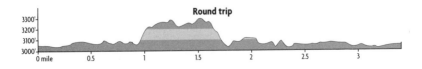

The larger of Squaw Lakes provides plenty of scenery and a nice place to swim.

cross the dam and continue on this road for 8.5 miles to the parking lot at the end of the road. The last 5 miles of FR 1075 is a narrow single-track gravel road. Watch for traffic, including occasional logging trucks.

This short hike leads to two pretty lakes. You'll find a lot of people and dogs here, along with a lot of water. Campsites are dispersed along the trails—one reason why this is such a popular spot.

The hike begins at the Squaw Lakes trailhead parking area—which is likely to be jammed on summer weekends. Follow a broad path about 0.1 mile down to the lake—it used to be a road but was blocked to protect the lakes from cars, trucks, and trampling. Bear right at the lake. You'll come to a small beach with an overview of the larger Squaw Lake and a good swimming hole for dogs. A lot of people swim here, too.

The trail marches around the east side of the lake, taking a bit more than 2 miles to make the circuit. At 0.5 mile from the parking area, a level path leads 0.5 mile to a smaller lake. Visit this lake, and then return to the main lake and trail to continue the lake circuit. Expect to find campers interspersed with the forest along the way. The forest is composed of Jeffery pines, Douglas fir, cedar, and an occasional sugar pine. The path occasionally journeys to the lake but mostly remains sequestered in the forest. The path returns you to where you started for a farewell swim and the stroll back uphill to the car.

52. Applegate Lake: French Gulch—Payette Trail

Round trip: 4.5 miles
Elevation range: 1950–2460 feet
Difficulty: Moderate
Hiking time: 3 hours
Best canine hiking seasons: Spring, early summer, fall
Regulations: Northwest Forest Pass required
Map: USGS Squaw Lakes 7.5' quadrangle
Information: Applegate Ranger District, Rogue River National Forest, (541) 899-3800

Getting there: From Interstate 5 at Medford, take exit 30, Jacksonville and Oregon Route 238. Follow ORE 238 for 14 miles through Jacksonville to Ruch. At Ruch, turn left (south) onto Upper Applegate Road and drive 14.5 miles to Applegate Dam. Turn left onto Forest Road 1075 to cross the dam and drive 1.1 miles to French Gulch Campground. The trailhead is at the east end of the parking area.

This hike leads along the shores of Applegate Lake, ensuring ample access to water. In spring, it also ensures ample mosquitoes, so bring bug repellent for yourself and your dog. After touring the lakeshore, the trail climbs away from the lake to a hilltop, then returns to the French Gulch trailhead.

To find the trail, park at the French Gulch trailhead area, and follow the Payette Trail, which leaves from the far end of the campground.

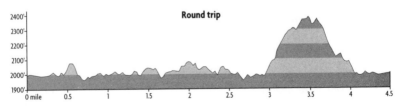

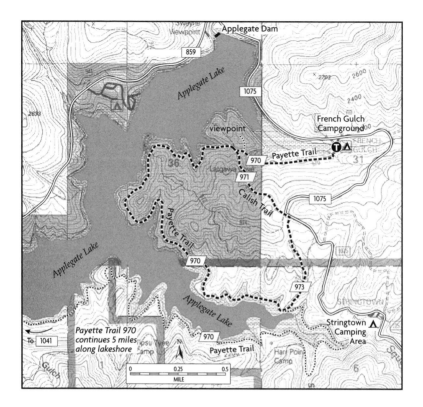

Keep dogs under control for the first few hundred yards as the trail bisects the campground. The Payette Trail is popular with mountain bikers, so keep an eye out for them throughout the hike. Wild blackberries line the trail here and appear in other locations along the way. They are ready to eat in mid- to late July. Poison oak also festoons the trail edge periodically, but it is easily avoided, at least by humans. Beyond the campground, the forest above the trail has been commercially thinned using helicopter logging. These more open woods, with abundant snags and second-growth and some old-growth trees, are habitat for pileated woodpeckers.

About 0.3 mile into the hike, watch for an accessible beach at the Latgawa Cove boat-in campground. From here, the trail heads uphill 0.2 mile to a junction with two other trails. For an interesting side jaunt, take the short side trail to the right marked VIEWPOINT. It rises through a moss- and lichen-festooned woodland of oak, manzanita, madrone, pine, and Douglas fir. The lichens, light green and diaphanous, are nitrogen

Meesha, on an overlook of Applegate reservoir along the trail.

fixers—they pull moisture and nitrogen from the air, and when they die and fall from the trees, they enrich the soils with nitrogen. This short side trail ends at what I like to call "Corps of Engineers Hubris Viewpoint." It offers a view of the dam, water-intake structure, and the campground and boat-launch across the lake.

The other trail at the junction (Calish Trail 971) will be your return path as you complete this loop hike.

Continue right on the Payette Trail. It offers a number of opportunities to visit the lakeshore—usually on points that jut out into the water. At 1.7 miles, the Payette Trail drops to the right toward the lake, while a broader path marked Old Squaw Arm Trail (an old mining road) goes straight. Follow the Payette Trail down to the lakeshore here. The trail finds coves and beaches for the next mile. Then at 3 miles from the trailhead, it meets a trail on the left.

Turn left here onto Trail 973. Watch for poison oak along the path as it rises through oak-strewn forest. There is no dog water for the next 1.5 miles of hiking, so be sure you have adequate water with you.

This trail winds through a mixed forest. It is not well maintained, and poison oak can be thick in places, but it makes a nice climb of 500 feet in a half-mile to meet a paved Forest Service road. There is a short, 100-yard walk along the road to the Calish Trail and its oversized parking lot. At the trailhead, turn left and go down the Calish Trail to intersect with the Payette Trail in 0.7 mile. Follow the Payette Trail another 0.3 mile back to the French Gulch trailhead.

53. Echo Lake

Round trip: 8 miles
Elevation range: 2200–5860 feet
Difficulty: Difficult
Hiking time: 5 hours
Regulations: Northwest Forest Pass required
Map: USGS Kangaroo Mountain 7.5′ quadrangle
Information: Applegate Ranger District, Rogue River National Forest, (541) 899-3800

Getting there: From Interstate 5 at Medford, take exit 30, Jacksonville and Oregon Route 238. Follow ORE 238 for 14 miles through Jacksonville to Ruch. At Ruch, turn left (south) onto Upper Applegate Road. Continue 19 miles to a T intersection at the upper end of Applegate Reservoir. Turn left and follow Forest Road 1040 1.3 miles to a large open area where FR 1040 turns sharply right downhill. Follow FR 1040—a good but narrow single-lane gravel road—for 5.8 miles along the Middle Fork of the Applegate River to a parking loop at the trailhead.

Technically this hike is located in California, but it is only accessible by roads from Oregon. The Echo Lake Trail (Trail 958) leads to an alpine lake in the Red Butte Wilderness. The ridge above the lake offers outstanding views and access to short hikes over the tawny outcrops of Red Butte. The hike has two major creek crossings as well as Echo Lake itself—a smallish tree-cloistered pond. Dogs will enjoy the wild character of the hike. The second half of the trail is not maintained, so expect a real workout.

From the trailhead, the path follows a small stream for first 0.25 mile, shouldering by several dark, heat-radiating outcrops. The trail begins to switchback upslope and splits at 0.5 mile, with Butte Fork Trail 957 sauntering right and your path, Trail 958, sprinting ominously uphill straight ahead.

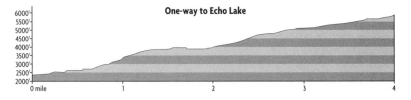

The trail's steep pitch soon moderates. It passes through a forest of ponderosa pine, sugar pine, madrone, and Douglas fir where hermit thrush provide fluty music. After a 0.5-mile stretch straight uphill, the path switchbacks across black-and-white-striped outcrops to several nice views of the Butte Fork landslide. Red Butte—at the head of the trail's destination—peers over the top of the slide.

You might have to clamber over fallen trees along the next segment of the trail—a more level path that rises to 4000 feet in elevation amid giant sugar pine and ponderosa pine in an area known as Horse Camp

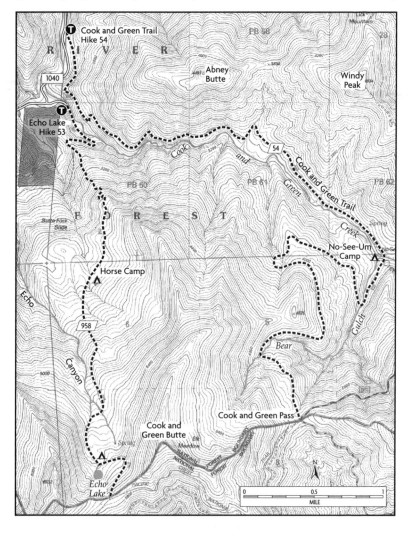

Sugar pines en route to Echo Lake and Red Butte, Red Butte Wilderness.

before dropping about 100 feet to meet Butte Fork Creek at mile 1.8. This is a welcome wet place. The cool, shallow water is an ideal place for dogs to cool off.

Beyond the creek, the trail is less traveled and less well maintained. It also rises more steeply. More fallen trees require detours. After another uncivilized mile the trail enters the meadows below Echo Lake. These meadows were once lakes, but in the ten thousand years since the retreat of the glaciers, the lakes have filled in to become marshes. Small streams flow through them. These wetlands are important reservoirs of upland water retaining cool water in their soils through the long, dry summer when a surface lake might have evaporated. They also make mighty fine splashing places for dogs.

The trail is challenging to follow through these meadows. Rock cairns mark the route here and there.

To find Echo Lake, a tiny wet refuge below hulking Red Butte, continue on the trail as it leads east, seemingly away from the valley. After winding about 0.25 mile thorough a thinly forested slope, a spur trail leads to the left. Marked Echo Lake, this trail leads slightly downward to the shore of the shallow lake. Half-submerged logs line the shore, and accessing the water can be difficult. Marshes and a small exit stream also provide places for dogs to cool off. The main trail continues left to the ridge top (5860 feet). From here, the landscape of northern California and southwest Oregon is at your feet, including Mount Shasta, the Trinity Alps, and Grayback

Mountain. Red Butte rises just to the west. The trail connects with the Pacific Crest Trail here. Return as you came.

54. Cook and Green Trail

Round trip: 16 miles
Elevation range: 2280–4765 feet
Difficulty: Moderate
Hiking time: 7 hours
Best canine hiking season: Spring
Regulations: Northwest Forest Pass required
Map: USGS Kangaroo Mountain 7.5' quadrangle
Information: Applegate Ranger District, Rogue River National Forest, (541) 899-3800

Getting there: From Interstate 5 at Medford, take exit 30, Jacksonville and Oregon Route 238. Follow ORE 238 for 14 miles through Jacksonville to Ruch. At Ruch, turn left (south) onto Upper Applegate Road. Continue 19 miles to a T intersection at the upper end of Applegate Reservoir. Turn left and follow Forest Road 1040 1.3 miles to a large open area where FR 1040 turns sharply right downhill. Follow FR 1040—a good but narrow single-lane gravel road—along the Middle Fork of the Applegate River for 4 miles.

The Cook and Green Trail is named for three miners, Robert Cook and the Green brothers, who used it between 1860 and 1870. It climbs through old-growth sugar pine and Douglas fir. It offers minimal dog water along the way, so on hot days offer your dog the opportunity for a drink at the car and a cooling dunk before starting. An informal trail leads from the trailhead parking area to the stream. Technically, this hike is in California, but its only access is from the Oregon side.

The trail begins through a shaded forest of oak, bigleaf maple, and

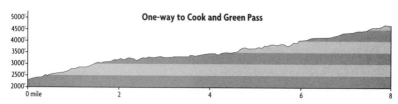

One-way to Cook and Green Pass

Beagles Tasha (7 years old) and Taz (2 years old) are still ready to go after a hike along the Cook and Green Trail.

madrone but soon becomes more conifer-dominant. About 0.25 mile into the hike, the trail encounters a huge old-growth Douglas fir and crosses an old placer ditch. Here, the path begins a series of switchbacks that weave across a seasonal stream and carry you up about 500 feet in elevation. As the trail straightens, the forest changes to a typically dry, south-facing slope assemblage of madrone, fir, and sugar pine. The trail is more open and sunnier here, and on warm days, occasional stops for water from your pack will help your dog endure the long hike to the end. A good place for a break is at No-See-Um Camp about 3.5 miles into the hike. Above this point, the trail encounters a more diverse conifer forest that includes old-growth Douglas fir, sugar pine, and ponderosa pine. A few Brewer's spruce and noble fir also can be spotted from the trail. There is another small but usually reliable spring just before reaching Cook and

Green Pass and a junction with the Pacific Crest Trail (PCT). From here, you can further explore the Red Butte Wilderness along the PCT or return to the trailhead as you came.

55. Middle Fork Applegate River

Round trip: 6 miles
Elevation range: 2660–3670 feet
Difficulty: Moderate
Hiking time: 3 hours
Best canine hiking seasons: Spring, early summer
Regulations: Northwest Forest Pass required
Map: USGS Kangaroo Mountain 7.5′ quadrangle
Information: Applegate Ranger District, Rogue River National Forest, (541) 899-3800

Getting there: From Interstate 5 at Medford, take exit 30, Jacksonville and Oregon Route 238. Follow ORE 238 for 14 miles through Jacksonville to Ruch. At Ruch, turn left (south) onto Upper Applegate Road. Continue 19 miles to a T intersection at the upper end of Applegate Reservoir. Turn left and follow Forest Road 1040 1.3 miles to a large open area where it turns sharply right downhill. Follow FR 1040—a good but narrow, single-lane gravel road—along the Upper Applegate 5.8 miles to a junction with FR 1035. FR 1035 goes straight while FR 1040 turns left and crosses a bridge. Continue straight on FR 1035 for 0.2 mile to a curve. The trailhead is a subtly marked path at this curve.

This Middle Applegate Trail, located in California but only accessible from Oregon, is an ideal summer hike with dogs. It begins as a broad mining road, then narrows to a well-maintained single track that periodically veers away from Middle Fork of the Applegate River to bypass narrow chasms but always returns to the river. Spend a few hours on this trail

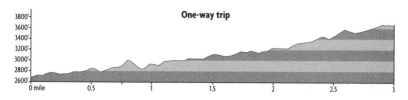

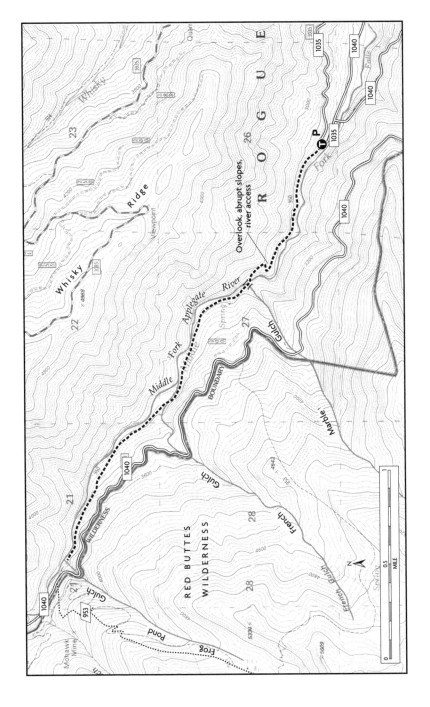

Oh, PLEEEEEEEEEEEZE throw the stick!! Meesha and friends along the Middle Fork of the Applegate River.

and you'll begin to think that 5-foot-diameter trees are normal.

From the trailhead, the broad path heads purposefully along a bank above the river. In about 0.5 mile a tempting trail bears left downhill and toward the river. This unnamed, unmarked spur dead-ends at the riverbank though, so if you take it, you'll have to backtrack. The real trail goes straight, suddenly narrowing to a single-track path. It curves into a shady dell, where a side stream offers a second opportunity for a cooling dog bath, and continues well above the river for another 0.2 mile. Here, a steep side trail plunges to a deep swimming hole; however, a better option is to continue along the trail, which begins a gradual descent to stream level and offers multiple opportunities for safer dog swims.

This forest is a mix of old-growth and younger Douglas fir. Madrones arch upward where light permits and are more abundant on upper, south-facing slopes. Vine maple and manzanita populate the understory. A few white oaks and bigleaf maple struggle to grow on upper slopes. At 1.1 miles, the trail crosses the river on a bridge hewn from a single huge log. The bridge has a rickety handrail for humans and is broad enough for dogs to cross with ease—though they likely will splash across the stream instead.

The best part of the trail lies ahead. It is more rugged, but the trees are spectacular. Jeffery pines 3 to 4 feet in diameter begin to appear. Douglas firs exceed 4 feet with such regularity that big trees begin to seem normal. The trail swings away from the stream periodically. In this segment, the forest canopy permits occasional glimpses of the rugged slopes and rock cliffs in the Applegate canyon. The Applegate River remains accessible periodically. At 1.8 miles the path scoots through wetland areas and crosses a stream at French Gulch. A mile farther, just before it reaches FR 1040, the path crosses another side stream at Frog Gulch. The intersection with the road marks the end of this hike, although the trail jogs up the road and continues steeply upward for another 2 miles without any trailside water to Frog Camp. Return as you came.

56. Big Pine Loop

Round trip: 3 miles
Elevation range: 2180–2580 feet
Difficulty: Easy
Hiking time: 1.5 hours
Best canine hiking season: Year-round
Regulations: Northwest Forest Pass required; $5 camping fee; leashes required on the lowland interpretive trail
Map: USGS Chrome Ridge 7.5' quadrangle
Information: Galice Ranger District, Siskiyou National Forest, (541) 471-6500

Getting there: From Grants Pass, drive north on Interstate 5 to exit 61, Merlin. Head west on the Merlin-Galice Road. Continue 12 miles through Merlin and past Indian Mary Park to Forest Road 25 (also called Taylor Creek Road and Briggs Valley Road). Turn left here and follow this narrow, curving, paved road 13.4 miles to Big Pine Campground. The trail to Big Pine leaves from the day-use parking lot.

Ecologically intact old-growth stands are a rarity. This hike takes you through an outstanding grove of mixed forest at an elevation of 2300 feet—high enough that poison oak is absent here and southern Oregon's hot summer days are tolerable. The area was severely burned in a stand-replacement forest fire about 300 years ago. A few young ponderosa pines

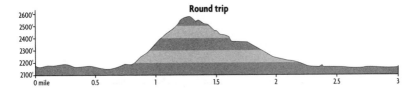

survived, including Big Pine, the tallest living ponderosa pine in the world. This 300-year-old tree towers 250 feet tall and measures almost 6 feet in diameter.

Leashes are required on the lowland interpretive trail that begins the hike. The Big Pine Loop Trail leads away from the gravel parking area, and turns right, following Briggs Creek through a riparian area that sports native thimbleberry and wild native blackberry, tanoak, and chinquapin. This trail gives you an option of crossing the creek on a bridge and hiking the opposite side of the creek, or continuing on the west side of the creek where a short side trail finds a nice wading pool on Briggs Creek. The west-side trail leads to a second bridge and then turns left across the creek.

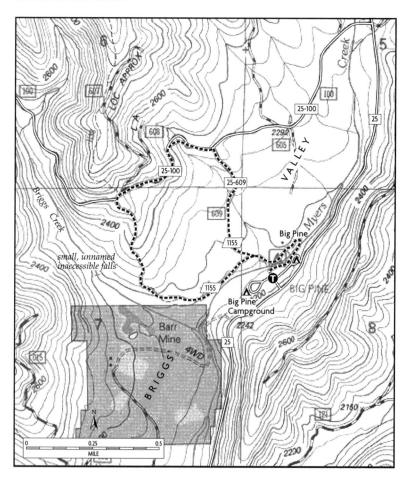

On a day when the temperature hit 100°F, Dundee and Meesha keep cool on the Big Tree Loops, Myers Creek.

Trails on both sides of Briggs Creek ultimately lead to Big Pine, a tree now ringed by a handrail and converted to a sort of shrine amid the cathedral grove. From Big Pine you can follow a longer 0.5-mile loop back to the first bridge across Briggs Creek, or venture farther into the forest. The trail that continues away (west) from Big Pine winds past trees almost as big and past burned snags—reminders of just how persistent fire-hardened snags can be. In 0.25 mile this spur trail intersects the longer loop system. There is no water along these loop trails, so you should carry water for both you and your dog.

The left trail contours gradually through the forest, rising about 300 feet in elevation in a slow meandering curve past more big trees before encountering a more typical modern "working forest" of second-growth fir and pines. This south slope forest is drier than the riparian area. Its understory includes wild hazelnut, and tanoak. At the upper reach of the trail, a few madrone trees add diversity to the conifer forest.

This trail connects with a ridge trail. Here the path climbs uphill into second and third growth, reaching Forest Service road 25–100 in 0.7 mile. Turn left along the little-used road, and walk 0.5 mile along a downhill stretch to Spur Road 609 to the right. Turn right and continue downslope, paralleling a small tributary of Myers Creek. You reach the much more civilized loop trail in 0.5 mile along 609.

Turn right to exit the old-growth stand in about 0.25 mile, turning back toward the creek where dogs will find an opportunity for a dunk. From here, the trail connects with the original Big Pine Loop Trail about 100 yards from the first bridge crossing and the trail back to the to the parking lot.

57. Taylor Creek Trail

One-way trip: 5.6 miles
Elevation range: 1515–2645 feet
Difficulty: Moderate
Hiking time: 2.5 hours
Best canine hiking seasons: Winter, spring
Regulations: Northwest Forest Pass required
Maps: USGS Mount Peavine and Chrome Ridge 7.5′ quadrangles
Information: Galice Ranger District, Siskiyou National Forest,
  (541) 471-6500

Getting there: To reach the trailhead where this hike begins, drive north on Interstate 5 from Grants Pass to exit 61, Merlin. Head west on the Merlin-Galice Road. Continue 12 miles through Merlin and past Indian Mary Park to Forest Road 25 (also called Taylor Creek Road and Briggs Valley Road). Turn left (south) on FR 25 and drive 13.4 miles to Big Pine Campground. The trailhead is on FR 25, across the road from the campground entrance.

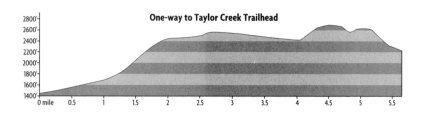

One-way to Taylor Creek Trailhead

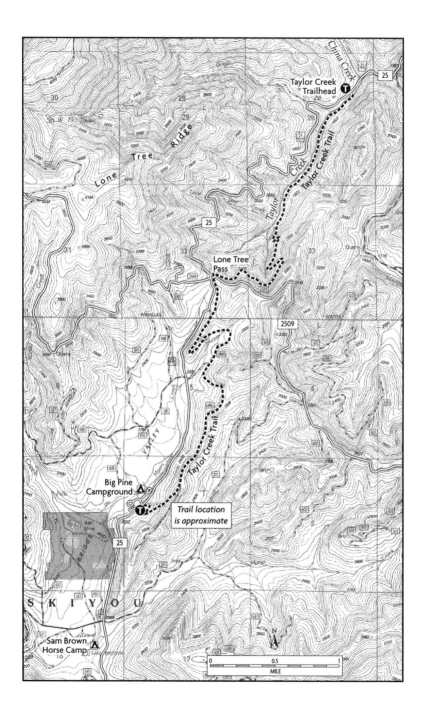

To reach the lower trailhead where this hike ends, in order to arrange a pick-up or leave a shuttle vehicle, from Big Pine Campground return to FR 25. Drive north on FR 25 for 6.3 miles to a turnout on the right labeled Taylor Creek.

Taylor Creek Trail was reconstructed in the early 1990s to accommodate horseback riders based at Sam Brown Horse Campground. However, horse use is rare. There's no water on the first 4 miles of the trail, so carry plenty of dog water and hike when it's cool. The lower portion of the trail, at and below Taylor Creek's headwaters, offers frequent access to drinks and dunks.

The hike begins at a trailhead across the road (FR 25) from Big Pine Campground. This trail is narrow and tracks easily uphill 0.7 mile through old-growth Douglas fir to meet Taylor Creek Trail. Turn left onto this somewhat broader path. The Taylor Creek Trail travels evenly along slopes paralleling FR 25, but far enough away that the road is never evident and dogs aren't at risk. At the Lone Tree Pass 3 miles into the hike, the trail veers closer to the main single-track road and also crosses FR 2509. (This is another convenient pick-up or drop-off point.) From the summit, Taylor Creek Trail drops into the basin of Taylor Creek, looping away from the roads and into second-growth forest that includes smaller firs, madrones, and ponderosa pines.

As you approach a small headwaters wetland at mile 3.2, alders become the dominant tree and moisture-loving willows and wild hazelnut are abundant. Wet places are inviting spots to cool off. Beyond the wetland, the trail resumes a more serious trek through the forest. Most of this area was logged in the 1960s and 1970s, and open areas where poison oak appears become more abundant beyond the headwaters wetland. But there are also patches of old growth or vigorous second growth where yew trees share the understory with hazelnut and occasional stunted madrone.

The trail periodically morphs into an old wagon road, a remnant of the placer and hydraulic mining that was rampant here in the 1890s. Bridges lead across the creek as the trail meanders just before emerging into the Taylor Creek trailhead parking lot 2.6 miles beyond Lone Tree Pass. The trail continues another 2 miles along the creek to Tin Cup Campground. However, this segment is loaded with poison oak and is perched on steep slopes well above the creek for most of its distance—a fine trip for hikers wearing long pants, but dubious for dogs, especially in the summer.

58. Rogue River Trail: Illahee to Paradise Bar

Round trip: 21 miles
Elevation range: 240–350 feet
Difficulty: Moderate
Hiking time: 2–3 days
Best canine hiking seasons: Winter, spring
Regulations: Northwest Forest Pass required; register for wilderness
   entry
Maps: USGS Illahee and Marial 7.5' quadrangles
Information: Gold Beach Ranger District, Siskiyou National Forest,
   (541) 247-6651; Paradise Lodge, (800) 525-2161; Clay Hill Lodge,
   (503) 859-3772

Getting there: From Gold Beach on the southern Oregon coast, turn
east onto Jerrys Flat Road (Forest Road 33) at the south end of the Rogue
River Bridge. Drive 30 miles to County Road 375, marked for the Illahee
and Rogue River Trails. Follow this road 3 miles to a large, grassy parking area and the trailhead.

The Rogue River Trail is a 40-mile adventure that follows the river from
Illahee to Grave Creek. This hike tours the lower part of this trail, as an
out-and-back trip of 21 miles, beginning on a gentle path through shady
forests. As it travels upstream, shade becomes more rare. Most of the hike
travels along rocky, bare, and poison oak–infested riverbank, with the Rogue
River not easily accessible. The lower part of this trail, described here, is
the best for dogs, as the openness of much of the trail beyond Paradise
Lodge is downright uninviting for pooches, especially on hot summer days.

That said, the lower portion of the trail, especially the first 8 miles, is
doggie heaven with shade, soft trails, and a lot of small streams to dabble
in even when the main channel of the Rogue is far below the path or a
long distance through the forest.

The trail leads from the east side of the expansive parking area at Foster

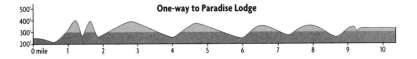

Bar, where the Rogue, a broad and relatively tame river here, makes a gracious meander. For the first mile, the trail swings away from the river through a forest of largely deciduous trees—bigleaf maple, oak, and alder.

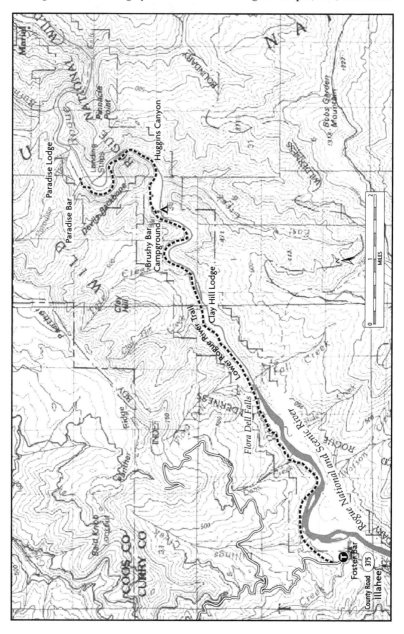

You'll want to carry water here, as there are limited side creeks for several miles.

In about a mile, the river comes into view, but well below the trail. The trail closes on the river at 1.5 miles, and then strays away. Look for doggie cooling water at Flora Dell Falls, a 30-foot cascade 3.5 miles into the hike. The trail continues through a mixed plant community that includes manzanita, sugar pine, and yellow pine. The river is fairly accessible for the next 2 miles beyond the falls. Then at 5.5 miles into the hike, the path ducks into deeper forest and encounters a small settlement and overnight lodge, known as Clay Hill Lodge. Expect people, cabins, and loose dogs here. You can arrange accommodations and obtain food here. (The next lodge offering overnight accommodations to hikers and rafters is 7 miles ahead.)

Once past this stray outpost of civilization, the trail again hugs the river, seeking the boundary be-

A refreshing waterfall greets hikers at Flora Dell Creek along the Lower Rogue River Trail.

tween forest and rocky shoreline, so that shade is never really absent—but seldom fully present either. At 7.5 miles from the trailhead, after touring river bends with rugged banks and rocky shores, the trail ducks back under forest cover at Brushy Bar Campground. There are good campsites here along almost 0.5 mile of flat, sandy ground with two creeks for water.

Beyond Brushy Bar the trail enters the steep-walled gorge of Huggins Canyon and the trail becomes markedly more rugged and less shaded. In 1.5 miles, it emerges and reaches Paradise Bar 10.5 miles from the trailhead. Paradise bar is aptly named. This is a pretty site with a historic lodge. Paradise Lodge was established in 1903. It can provide food and lodging if you reserve space ahead of time.

The Rogue River Trail continues to Graves Creek some 30 miles beyond Paradise Bar. For dogs, however, the rest of the trail is unpleasant in many places—rough, with minimal shade and abundant poison oak. It's fine in cool weather, but on hot sunny days it's a difficult trek for Fido. For most hikers, Paradise Lodge makes a great destination and turnaround spot.

59. Vulcan Lake

Round trip: 3.5 miles
Elevation range: 3740–4180 feet
Difficulty: Moderate
Hiking time: 4 hours
Best canine hiking seasons: Spring, summer
Regulations: Northwest Forest Pass required
Map: USGS Chetco Peak 7.5' quadrangle
Information: Chetco Ranger District, Siskiyou National Forest, (541) 469-2196

Getting there: From Brookings, drive east on the North Bank Road up the Chetco River. In 10 miles at Little Redwood Campground, the paved country road morphs into gravel Forest Road 1376. At 16 miles, the road crosses the Chetco River on a high bridge. Turn right at a T intersection just across the bridge and follow FR 1909 21 miles to an intersection marked for Chetco Lake Trail to the right and Vulcan Lake Trail to the left. Turn left to follow a narrow, single-lane road that is quite drivable by passenger cars, but use caution. The trailhead is at the end of the road 1.8 miles from the intersection.

From the trailhead, the path travels along a road that once led to chrome mines near here, then, in 0.25 mile, begins a 0.5-mile climb up a slope of tawny talus and outcrops, the dunnage of a collision between the North American continent with the Klamath microcontinent and sea floor about

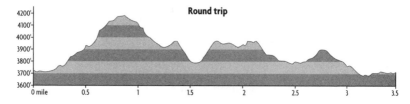

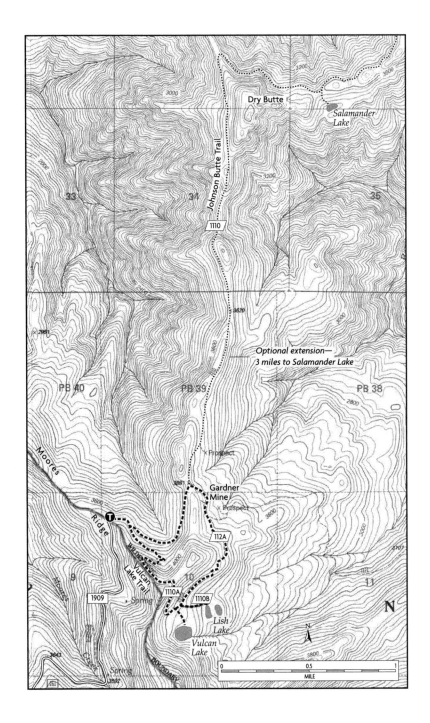

The trail to Vulcan Lake provides an overview of the Chetco River's basin and the Pacific Ocean.

130 million years ago. The peculiar orange-colored rock found here is called peridotite. It once was part of the earth's mantle. Geology is of little interest to your dog, however, who is probably more focused on the golden-mantled ground squirrels that make their homes in rock crevices. Look for Jeffrey pines along the ridge tops—these variants of three-needle yellow pines are well adapted to eeking a living from the magnesium-rich soils that stifle most other plants here.

At the ridge crest, you gain a view of the Chetco River watershed and the Pacific coast to the west, the rugged interior of the Kalmiopsis Wilderness and Big Craggies Botanical Area to the north, and Vulcan Lake, a teal-colored pool 300 feet below. Then the Vulcan Lake Trail drops, reaching Vulcan Lake in about 0.75 mile via several informal spurs. You can work your way around the small lake, which was carved out by glacial action during the Pleistocene Ice Age.

From Vulcan Lake, retrace your steps to the main trail. The path continues downslope toward Lish Lake. This lake is also reached by side paths. Lish Lake, also known as Little Vulcan Lake, sustains a substantial population of pitcher plants. Take care that dogs do not disturb these rare, wetland-loving carnivorous plants.

Retrace your path to the rather diaphanous main trail, Trail 112A, and follow it upslope through a forest of huge-coned sugar pine and Jeffrey pine. Cairns help you find your way where the path is elusive. After about 0.5 mile, the trail merges with an abandoned road and leads to the Gardner Mine. This was once a chrome mine, and you can still find shiny, black-spotted chrome ore here in places.

From the mine, the road leads to the ridge top. You can return to the trailhead by following the road to the left (south) back to your vehicle. Or you can turn right and follow the road and Johnson Butte Trail 1110 north toward Dry Butte. This trail continues for 10 miles. If you choose to venture toward Dry Butte, be sure you have extra water for you dog, as there's none along the trail for the next 5 miles until you reach Salamander Lake—which may be dry. Shade is not abundant along this ridge top either, so on hot days it's best to forego this extension of your hike.

60. Chetco Lake

Round trip: 10 miles
Elevation range: 3800–3980 feet
Difficulty: Moderate
Hiking time: 8 hours
Best canine hiking seasons: Spring, early summer
Regulations: Northwest Forest Pass required; register for wilderness entry
Maps: USGS Quail Mountain and Chetco Peak 7.5' quadrangles
Information: Chetco Ranger District, Siskiyou National Forest, (541) 412-6000

Getting there: From Brookings in the far southwest corner of the state, drive east on the North Bank Road up the Chetco River. In 10 miles at Little Redwood Campground, the paved country road morphs into gravel Forest Road 1376. At 16 miles, the road crosses the Chetco River on a high bridge. Turn right at a T intersection just across the bridge and follow FR 1909 21 miles to an intersection marked for Chetco Lake Trail to the right and Vulcan Lake Trail to the left. Bear right. The trailhead is 0.8 mile from the intersection.

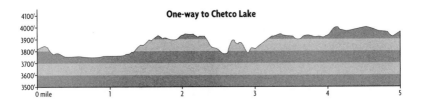

This hike in the Kalmiopsis Wilderness Area tours the south side of Vulcan Peak, following a long-abandoned mining road into the ridges east of the peak, then drops into the small Chetco Lake basin. The hike provides views of the Kalmiopsis Wilderness to the north and of Red Buttes Wilderness and Mount Shasta to the south and east. There is shade periodically and two springs along the way for canine cooling. However, it's best to hike this trail in cooler weather.

From the roadside trailhead, the broad, rocky path climbs the south side of Vulcan Peak. The trail is very rocky, and while the orange-red bedrock looks smooth, in truth it has tiny, sharp protrusions of minerals that can be tough on unseasoned paws. This is a good place for dog booties.

The odd-looking rocks are peridotite—a rock that is characteristic of the earth's mantle. Like the rocks at Vulcan Lake, these were uplifted many miles by folding and faulting when North America collided with the Klamath microcontinent about 130 million years ago.

The trail tours upward through largely open slopes—the magnesium-rich

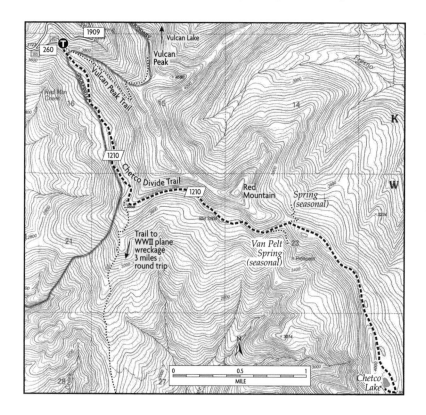

Barren outcrops above Chetco Lake provide a great perch for a dog on cool days.

soils here discourage most plant growth. Jeffrey pines and brushy junipers provide sporadic shade. Oregon grape and stunted manzanitas form an understory, and a few azaleas show off spring flowers. At 1.3 miles, an informal trail leads downslope about 1.5 miles to the site of a 1944 plane crash and a monument to its Navy crew. The main trail plods into the wilderness and toward the ridge. Once at the ridge crest 2 miles into the hike, you're treated to amazing vistas.

At 2.7 miles, a side trail leads about 0.25 mile downhill to Van Pelt Spring. You can fill water bottles here to douse the dog. Bountiful iris and other wildflowers make the side trip doubly worthwhile. At 3.5 miles, the trail reaches the ridge top and levels out. The surrounding landscape is rugged, with Chetco Lake in view, beckoning but still a mile ahead. At 4.5 miles into the hike, there is a junction. The path to the right drops gently into the lake's small basin lined with pine and juniper. Campsites and shady spots are available for a well-deserved rest among the trees. Return as you came.

Five More Great Dog Hikes in the Klamath Mountains

1) Briggs Creek Trail, 8 miles. Begins at Sam Brown Campground and follows then fords Upper Briggs Creek. Galice Ranger District, Siskiyou National Forest, (541) 471-6500.

2) Mount Ashland Trail/Pacific Crest Trail, 12 miles. This trail above Forest Road 1050 offers great views; carry plenty of water. Ashland Ranger District, Rogue River National Forest, (541) 482-3333.

3) Pilot Rock, 2 miles. No water, but an interesting geological formation. Ashland Ranger District, Rogue River National Forest, (541) 482-3333.

4) Mount Elijah and Bigelow Lakes, 4 miles. Begins at Oregon Caves National Monument. Applegate Ranger District, Rogue River National Forest, (541) 899-1812.

5) Frog Pond, Red Buttes Wilderness, 8 miles. Alpine meadows and small ponds. Applegate Ranger District, Rogue River National Forest, (541) 899-1812.

BLUE MOUNTAINS, WALLOWA MOUNTAINS, AND EASTERN OREGON

61. Twin Pillars Trail

Round trip: 10 miles
Elevation range: 3750–5360 feet
Difficulty: Moderate
Hiking time: 5–6 hours
Best canine hiking seasons: Spring, summer, fall
Regulations: Northwest Forest Pass required; camping fee at Wildcat Campground; register for wilderness entry
Map: USGS Steins Pillar 7.5' quadrangle
Information: Lookout Mountain Ranger District, Ochoco National Forest, (541) 416-6500

Getting there: From Prineville, drive 8 miles east on U.S. Highway 26. Turn left (north) onto Mill Creek Road. Follow Mill Creek Road (which

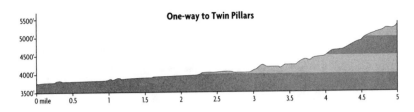

becomes Forest Road 33) 10.7 miles to Wildcat Campground. The trail-head parking is just before the campground entry.

This hike follows Mill Creek for much of its distance, then strikes off cross country to visit an ancient volcanic vent about 23 million years old, now a rock outcrop known as Twin Pillars. It also tours the recovery of the vast area burned in August 1996 in the 18,000-acre Hash Rock Fire.

The Twin Pillars Trail begins at the official parking lot on the right just before you enter Wildcat Campground. Walk down the road. Just across the bridge, the trail follows the creek to the left. There is another trailhead in the campground. Both spurs join 0.4 mile from the bridge.

For its first 2.5 miles, the nearly flat Twin Pillars Trail meanders back and forth across Mill Creek, allowing plenty of opportunities for dogs to splash and play in shallow summer water. Hikers must ford the stream at several crossings, and a pair of Gore-Tex–lined boots is a boon here. Mill Creek can be a raging torrent in the spring, so be prepared to contend with a vigorous stream from late March through mid-June.

The first portion of the hike leads through the outer fringes of the Hash Rock Fire burn area, where many trees survived and the landscape is little changed. You might not notice the fire scars at first, but by 2.5 miles into the hike, as you approach the junction with Belknap Trail, it's obvious that a fire has marred the landscape.

At 2.5 miles, the trail splits—the Belknap Trail heads up the hill to the right. The Twin Pillars Trail continues straight along the creek. Evidence of the fire increases as you continue along the Twin Pillars Trail.

At 3 miles, the trail climbs away from the creek and enters an area where the fire burned hotter, a stand-replacement blaze that killed at least 80 percent of the older pines and tamaracks. This gaunt but recovering landscape is fascinating. Grass, some seeded after the fire, some native, flourishes on the nitrogen-enriched soils. Native bull thistle, aster, and snowberry have sprouted. Ceanothus, a nitrogen-fixing shrub whose seeds sprout only after being heated by fire, is beginning to grow.

And mosses and lichens are restoring the forest's microbiotic crust in places where the ground might seem completely bare and sterile. Woodpeckers, including black-backed and flickers, are busy drilling the trees (woodpecker, nuthatch, and chickadee populations typically increase dramatically after fires) while rufous hummingbirds patrol the creekbanks for mint, columbine, shootingstar, and fireweed.

The 2-mile trek from the creek to Twin Pillars—a very obvious landmark now, given the absence of trees—has only a few spots of shade and little water, save in one small creek crossing, so plan accordingly for your dog and carry water for this stretch.

You reach Twin Pillars 5 miles from the trailhead. To explore these dual

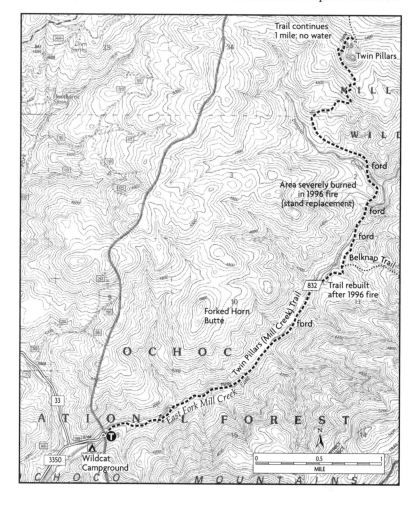

An informal bridge crosses Mill Creek on the trail to Twin Pillars.

rocks, you will have to leave the trail and scramble upslope a bit. The rock here is crumbly. Note the layers in the smaller pillar and on the flanks of the larger spire. Here, light-colored volcanic rocks erupted in layers of hot, pasty lava accompanied by blasts of steam from the vent. It's hard to imagine this as a volcanic vent, but 23 million years ago this spot might have resembled the slopes of modern Mount Kenya, complete with grassland savannah and antelope.

The Twin Pillars Trail continues past Twin Pillars, but there is no water farther along the path and very little shade in the burned-over forest. For dog hikers, this is a good place to turn around and return as you came.

62. Lookout Mountain Trail

Round trip: 15 miles
Elevation range: 4030–6926 feet
Difficulty: Moderate
Hiking time: 6 hours
Best canine hiking seasons: Spring, summer, fall
Regulations: Northwest Forest Pass required
Maps: USGS Gerow Butte and Lookout Mountain 7.5' quadrangles
Information: Lookout Mountain Ranger District, Ochoco National Forest, (541) 416-6500

Getting there: From Prineville in the middle of Oregon, drive 14.7 miles east on U.S. Highway 26, and bear right (east) onto County Road 23 (Lookout Mountain Road). Continue 8 miles to Ochoco Ranger Station. The trailhead is on the right (south) side of the road just past the Ochoco Ranger Station.

The hike to Lookout Mountain's flat, wind-blown summit travels through a diverse landscape with spectacular groves of ancient ponderosa pine and south-facing, sun-blasted stands of mountain mahogany. Along the way you might encounter wild horses (they are more wary than truly wild). Take water and a camera. And, of course, your dog. This hike joins Hike 63, Independent Mine, at the summit.

From the roadside trailhead, the Lookout Mountain Trail winds upslope through a Douglas fir forest. This is not a straight-up climb, but more of a shambling up-and-down affair, rising and falling over the small hills along Lookout Mountain's generous northern slope. As the trail rounds the first summit about 1 mile into the hike, it offers a view of

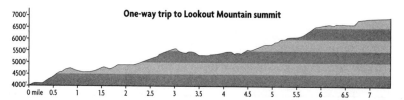

One-way trip to Lookout Mountain summit

nearby Round Mountain to the east. Then it curves back down a moist forest slope—look for wild iris here and along the rest of the trail in midsummer. At 1.7 miles, the trail finds a beautiful stand of ponderosa pine, along with a grassy, iris-lined meadow. Wild horses like to hang out here

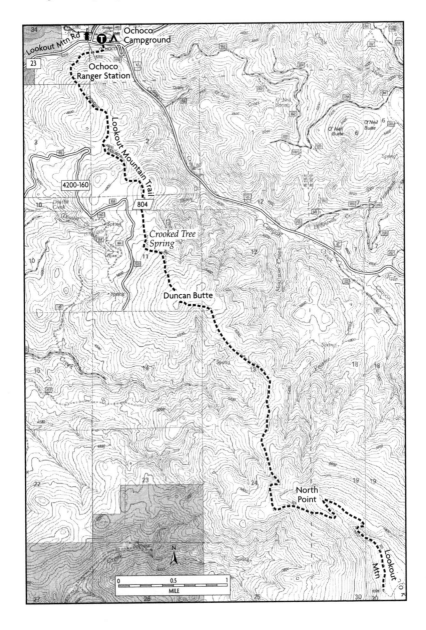

in the spring. They might have foals, so keep dogs close at hand here.

The trail turns and climbs again, leaving the ponderosa behind. It reaches Crooked Tree Spring—the only reliable water along the entire hike—at 2.3 miles from the trailhead. The spring is located just downhill from the trail. An informal trail leads to the spring and a set of water troughs.

The path tops Duncan Butte at 3 miles. You can scramble west through the forest here for a few hundred yards for a preview of the Cascades. From the butte, the trail plunges down through thicker forest to a saddle. Mountain mahogany grows on this warm and rocky site.

Beyond the saddle, the trail climbs toward the top of Lookout Mountain, bypassing the rocky basalt outcrops at North Point. To reach the summit, the trail switchbacks along a narrow ridge, finally topping out on the mountain's broad plateau (6926 feet) at about 7 miles from the trailhead. Take time to explore this top area—redtailed hawks and other raptors ride the thermals to hunt ground squirrels that live in this summit grassland. Return as you came.

63. Independent Mine to Lookout Mountain Summit

Round trip: 5 miles
Elevation range: 5810–6920 feet
Difficulty: Moderate
Hiking time: 5 hours
Best canine hiking seasons: Spring, early summer
Regulations: Northwest Forest Pass required
Map: USGS Lookout Mountain 7.5' quadrangle
Information: Lookout Mountain Ranger District, Ochoco National Forest, (541) 416-6500

Getting there: From Prineville, drive 14.7 miles east on U.S. Highway 26, and bear right (east) onto County Road 23 (Lookout Mountain Road).

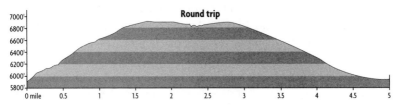

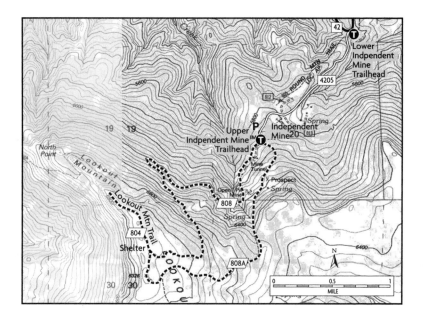

Continue 8 miles to Ochoco Ranger Station, and bear right onto Forest Road 42 and drive 6.3 miles to a junction with Spur Road 4205 and the parking lot for the Independent Mine Trail. This 1-mile trail segment is shown as Round Mountain Trail on the map. To shorten your hike by almost 2 miles, continue on the gravel road 0.9 mile to a second and easily accessible trailhead for the Independent Mine Trail.

This hike takes you past an old mine along a trail to the top of Lookout Mountain where you'll find outstanding views of the Cascade and Ochoco Mountains. Three routes—808, 808A, 808B—lead to the summit of Lookout Mountain from the trailhead. Trail 808 heads out toward the north and provides a slow, but easy and shaded, 4-mile ascent to the top. It's the return trail for this loop hike, but dogs who need a lot of water and shade might prefer Trail 808 as an out-and-back hike. Trail 808A follows an old mining and logging road. It's direct, partly shaded, and a bit rocky with no water along the way. Watch for mountain bikers on this route.

Begin the loop hike on Trail 808A, which heads west (straight) from the parking area. This path tackles Lookout Mountain directly, after circling past a danger zone underlain by abandoned mine shafts that are prone to collapse. Heed the Forest Service warning signs here. In 0.2 mile, the trail joins an abandoned road that leads almost straight to flat meadows on Lookout Mountain's southern end. Here you can catch a first glimpse of the view to come in about 0.9 mile.

As it nears the summit, the trail rises gradually through a basalt-capped landscape that is wet and marshy in the spring. In late summer it supports false hellebore (skunk cabbage), silver sage, stunted rabbitbrush, lupine, and tarweed. There is virtually no grass, except for cheatgrass, ripgut brome, and bottlebrush squirreltail—plants designed with strong defenses against being eaten by sheep. They also have seeds that embed themselves in dog paws. The absence of grass and domination of unpalatable plants is the result of severe overgrazing of Lookout Mountain (and most eastern Oregon alpine areas) by sheep in the late 19th and early 20th centuries. Restoration takes a very long time in such a harsh alpine environment. Most of the thin topsoil on Lookout Mountain's summit was eroded as a result of overgrazing.

The trail from Independent Mine to the summit of Lookout Mountain encounters outcrops of ancient mudflows near the trailhead.

In 1.5 miles, Trail 808A reaches a junction with Trail 808. For a short loop, you can return downhill here—but once you have made it this far, you should explore the true summit areas of Lookout Mountain that still lie ahead. At 1.8 miles, there is a snow shelter that was built in 1989 by the Forest Service. Continue north along the trail and in 0.6 mile, you will reach the true summit area of Lookout Mountain, with views of the Cascades to the west, and the Ochocos to the north and east.

Return as you came to the trail junction of 808 and 808A. Here, turn downslope onto Trail 808—a shaded path that is much easier on the knees and on hot, tired dogs. This trail heads gently downhill, then turns in a seemingly wrongheaded direction to the north when your instincts scream for you to hike to the south. The route crosses a bog and leads along a stream. And after a half-mile of hiking, the trail switchbacks and turns toward home.

In another 1.4 miles, after crossing two more streams, it brings you into sight of the stamp mill and refinery of the Independent Mine—a long-abandoned operation. In 0.5 mile from your first view of it, you pass just below the mine, and also pass an abandoned and unsafe mine shaft. Walk uphill and find the short trail connecting to the trailhead.

64. Round Mountain Trail

Round trip: 8.4 miles
Elevation range: 5350–6785 feet
Difficulty: Moderate
Hiking time: 4 hours
Best canine hiking seasons: Spring, fall
Regulations: Northwest Forest Pass required
Map: USGS Ochoco Butte 7.5' quadrangle
Information: Lookout Mountain Ranger District, Ochoco National
   Forest, (541) 416-6500

Getting there: From Prineville in the middle of Oregon, drive 14.7 miles east on U.S. Highway 26 and bear right (east) onto County Road 23 (Lookout Mountain Road). Continue 8 miles to Ochoco Ranger Station, and bear left onto Forest Road 22, marked for Walton Lake. Continue 6.5 miles to the Walton Lake Campground entrance. The road to the trailhead is a right turn just past the campground entrance. Follow this road 0.2 mile to the trailhead.

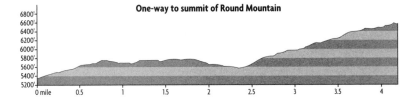

This hike explores a part-wooded, part-open landscape and climbs to the summit of Round Mountain for panoramic views of Big Summit Prairie and distant Cascade peaks. There's not much water for dogs on the hike, but there's plenty of opportunity for pre- and post-hike swims in Walton Lake just across the road from the trailhead.

Meesha checks out the route to Round Mountain.

From the trailhead, the path toward Round Mountain heads through a grassy meadow and then enters a forest dominated by Douglas fir. The woods here are an example of "forest health problems"—the forest is replete with snags, many of which bear the telltale huge holes left by pileated woodpeckers. For most of its length, the trail plays tag with a Forest Service road—the trail is the straighter route to the summit.

After switchbacking up a ridge, the trail crosses an open, rocky meadow with views of Round Mountain's antennae-cluttered summit, distant Cascade peaks, and Big Summit Prairie to the south. From here, the path heads toward a forested saddle and reaches Scissors Spring—the only water on the trail—at 2.4 miles from the trailhead. Beyond the spring, the trail again enters open grassland then begins a switchbacking ascent of Round Mountain's north slope. A few juniper trees, undernourished yellow pine, and scruffy Douglas fir provide

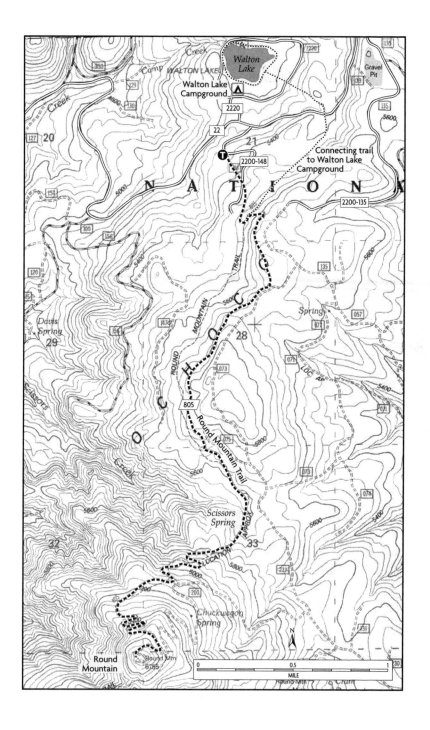

little shade on the upper half of this mile-long, 1000-foot climb, so let dogs take their time here. The path joins a gravel road just below the summit and reaches Round Mountain summit (6785 feet) at 4.2 miles from the trailhead. The summit bristles with communication towers and offers a great view. Return as you came.

65. Elkhorn Crest Trail to Anthony Lake

Round trip: 8 miles
Elevation range: 7130–8180 feet
Difficulty: Moderate
Hiking time: 5 hours
Best canine hiking season: Summer
Regulations: Northwest Forest Pass required
Map: USGS Anthony Lakes 7.5' quadrangle
Information: Baker Ranger District, Wallowa-Whitman National Forest, (541) 523-4476

Getting there: From Interstate 84, 25 miles south of La Grande, take exit 285 at North Powder. Drive west on County Road 101 marked for Anthony Lakes. In 3.5 miles, turn left (south) at a four-way intersection, drive 0.6 mile, and turn right (west) onto the Elkhorn Scenic Byway. This road becomes Forest Road 73 when it crosses into the Wallowa-Whitman National Forest. At about 19.2 miles from I-84, turn left (south) into a Forest Service parking area marked for Elkhorn Crest Trail. If you reach the Anthony Lake Campground, you've gone about 0.8 mile too far.

This loop hike takes you into truly alpine landscapes—the realm of Rocky Mountain goats, whitebark pine, and Clark's nutcrackers. A few springs provide minor stops for cooling in midsummer, and you are likely to find

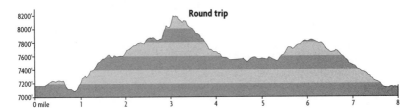

a bit of lingering snow if you hike this trail before the Fourth of July. Overall, however, there's not much shade or water on the trail, so carry extra water for your pooch.

The trail begins at a parking area about 0.8 mile east of the Anthony Lake Campground. This trailhead is the main point of departure for horseback riders touring the Elkhorn Crest Trail, so in midsummer you might meet horses on the path.

The Elkhorn Crest Trail leads unabashedly upslope, climbing through a lodgepole and subalpine fir forest into whitebark pine. It reaches an unnamed pass (8180 feet) just east of Angell Peak in 3 miles of steady going. En route, it passes a small spring at about 2 miles. This is a highly scenic route, with clear views of the Wallowa Mountains to the east and Baker Valley below.

Beyond the pass, the trail ducks behind a small peak then emerges to provide a view of the valley of Dutch Flat Creek—a forested, U-shaped valley that sprawls to the east. At 3.7 miles into the hike, you reach a four-way intersection at Dutch Flat Pass. Dutch Flat Lake lies temptingly

Erika and Wolf, a 9-year-old Alaskan malamute, stroll along the trail around Anthony Lake.

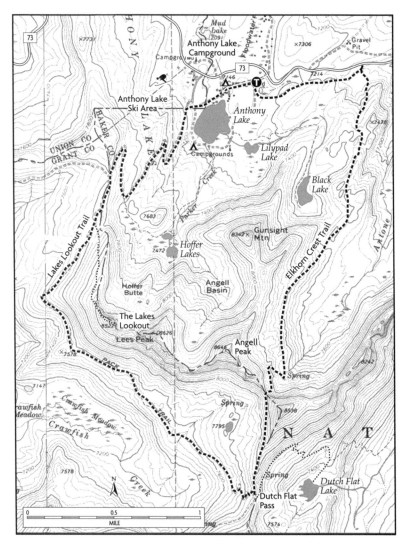

below. The trail to the east leads to the lake, 600 feet below you, in about 1 mile.

The loop route turns west onto the Lakes Lookout Trail here, following signs to The Lakes Lookout. The trail contours along a slope of granitic boulders and craggy outcrops where subalpine fir and whitebark pine provide the major vegetation. At 4.3 miles, the trail crosses a boggy area, part of the headwaters of Crawfish Lake far below.

The trail continues along this south-facing slope—a place that, despite its 7500-foot altitude, can become quite warm on hot days. Paint-brush and buckwheat vegetate the barren alpine landscape. At 6.2 miles into the hike, the path reaches another saddle—this provides an over-look of Hoffer and Anthony Lakes. Here, a two-track gravel road switchbacks down to Anthony Lake, allowing an easy descent. At the bottom of the grade, follow the lakeshore path into the campground. The connecting trail to the Elkhorn Crest trailhead is located at the east end of the campground. From here, the trail leads back to the trailhead in 0.8 mile.

66. Hoffer Lakes

Round trip: 2 miles
Elevation range: 7150–7430 feet
Difficulty: Easy
Hiking time: 1 hour
Best canine hiking season: Summer
Regulations: Northwest Forest Pass required
Map: USGS Anthony Lakes 7.5′ quadrangle
Information: Baker Ranger District, Wallowa-Whitman National
Forest, (541) 523-4476

Getting there: From Interstate 84, take exit 285 at North Powder. Drive west on County Road 101 marked for Anthony Lakes. In 3.5 miles, turn left (south) at a four-way intersection. Drive 0.6 mile from the intersec-tion and turn right (west) onto the Elkhorn Scenic Byway. This road becomes Forest Road 73 when it crosses into the Wallowa-Whitman National Forest. Follow FR 73 to the Anthony Lake Campground 20 miles from the exit off I-84. At the main campground intersection, turn right past a gazebo into the day-use area. Continue 0.3 mile to the road's end. Follow the path past campsites 0.1 mile to a trailhead on the right.

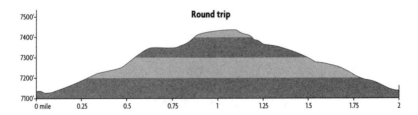

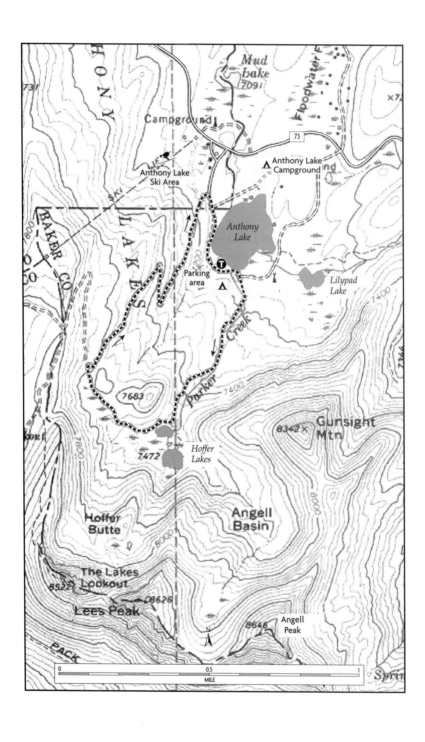

This short, popular hike leads from Anthony Lake to scenic Hoffer Lakes, which seem quite wild and very alpine. Expect dogs and children here. It's a great hike for both. The soft alpine meadows blaze with wildflowers in early summer, including dogtooth violet, shootingstar, and paintbrush; trout dart through the alpine streams, tempting dogs to make futile leaps to catch them.

From the trailhead parking lot, follow the broad path that leads east around Anthony Lake. In about 100 yards a side trail marked for Hoffer Lakes heads to the left (south). The path marches quite purposefully upslope, passing huge boulders as it parallels Parker Creek, which it crosses on several bridges. In 0.5 mile the path emerges from the lodgepole pine forest at the bank of Hoffer Lake. Informal trails travel left around the lake and right to marshy meadows with views of this small but serene lake basin.

To continue the loop hike, when you reach the lake bear right along a well-worn path that follows the shoreline. In 0.3 mile the trail emerges from the lodgepole pines and subalpine fir into alpine meadows; at 0.6 mile it joins a gravel roadway that turns right and leads back to the Anthony Lake picnic areas in another 0.4 mile. At the picnic area and gazebo, turn right again and follow the road to the parking area and trailhead.

Small streams and creeks make the basin around Hoffer Lakes a perfect early summer hike.

67. Crawfish Lake

Round trip: 2.5 miles
Elevation range: 6840–7160 feet
Difficulty: Moderate
Hiking time: 2 hours
Best canine hiking season: Summer
Regulations: Northwest Forest Pass required
Map: USGS Crawfish Lake 7.5' quadrangle
Information: Baker Ranger District, Wallowa-Whitman National Forest, (541) 523-4476

Getting there: From Interstate 84, take exit 285 at North Powder. Drive west on County Road 101 marked for Anthony Lakes. In 3.5 miles, turn left (south) at a four-way intersection. Drive 0.6 mile from the intersection and turn right (west) onto the Elkhorn Scenic Byway. This road becomes Forest Road 73 when it crosses into the Wallowa-Whitman National Forest. Follow FR 73 20 miles from the I-84 exit past Anthony Lakes Ski Resort (7500 feet) to a Forest Service spur road on the left marked for Crawfish Lake. Drive 0.2 mile to the parking area.

This hike is simply a short walk to a picturesque lake tucked in glacial basin. The Sloan Ridge Fire burned the pine and fir forest upslope from here in 1996, while a 1962 fire, the Anthony Lakes Burn, affected ridges along the north fringe of the hike.

The Crawfish Lake Trail (Trail 1606) departs enthusiastically downhill, but it quickly tempers its plunge, moderating to a more gradual descent across open slopes with gaunt, charcoal-girdled snags. There has been little regrowth and forest recovery at this higher elevation, even after decades of time. Pearly everlasting, horsemint, wild delphinium, lupine,

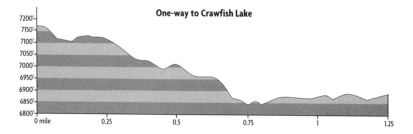

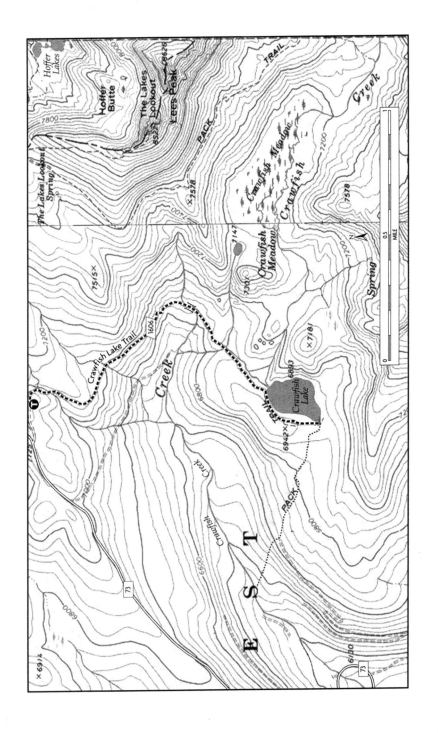

and paintbrush are the masters of these open meadows now, and the flowers are at their best in mid-July.

After a half-mile tour of the fire zone, the trail retreats to forest and levels off for the remainder of its trip to Crawfish Lake. This small, glacier-carved lake is sequestered in lodgepole pine and fir forest, with granitic outcrops above its scenic eastern shore. There is plenty of room for a 0.5-mile hike around the lake on informal trails, and the easy clamber up the granite rocks is fun for both dogs and people. Watch for fishing debris that might snare a dog.

A second trail to Crawfish Lake, also Trail 1606, leaves from the opposite shore, descending steeply at first toward the drainage of Crawfish Creek, then leveling off to an easier grade in a half-mile. This portion of Trail 1606 briefly flirts with the 1966 Sloan Ridge fire area before it

Belgian Malois pups cool off in Crawfish Lake.

plunges back into denser cover to arrive at a second Crawfish Lake trailhead 1.3 miles from the lake. This second trailhead on FR 73 is 3.5 miles from the first, with the road the only option for connecting the two, so trying to make this a loop hike is not a good idea unless you and Fido like long walks uphill along busy, paved, and shadeless roadways. Instead, from Crawfish Lake return to the start of the hike the way you came.

68. Baldy Creek Trail

Round trip: 12 miles
Elevation range: 5600–7100 feet
Difficulty: Moderate
Hiking time: 8 hours
Best canine hiking season: Summer
Regulations: Northwest Forest Pass required
Maps: USGS Crawfish Lake and Mount Ireland 7.5' quadrangles
Information: Baker Ranger District, Wallowa-Whitman National Forest, (541) 523-4476

Getting there: From Interstate 84, take exit 285 at North Powder. Drive west on County Road 101 marked for Anthony Lakes. In 3.5 miles, turn left (south) at a four-way intersection. Drive 0.6 mile from the intersection and turn right (west) onto the Elkhorn Scenic Byway. This road becomes Forest Road 73 when it crosses into the Wallowa-Whitman National Forest. Follow FR 73 20 miles from the I-84 exit to Anthony Lakes, then continue 11.5 miles to a Forest Service spur road marked for Baldy Creek trailhead. The trailhead is at the end of this 0.2-mile road.

This hike is a gentle excursion along a clear stream through quite wild country. It leads to a tree-rimmed alpine lake below a clean granite peak. It's one of the best dog hikes Meesha and I have ever done.

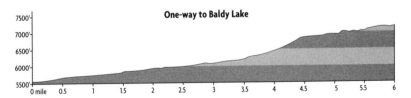

One-way to Baldy Lake

From the trailhead, the Baldy Creek Trail crosses a shaky two-log bridge across the North Fork John Day River then heads through forest. The trail is lined with huckleberry bushes, which are food for grouse, bear, dogs, and humans. With a little encouragement, many dogs learn to eat huckleberries right off the bush. The advantage is that they will alert you to the presence of huckleberries, even off-trail. The disadvantage is that they can find and eat them faster than you can.

In 1 mile the trail crosses Baldy Creek, providing humans with another informal two-log bridge—this is the last true "bridge" across the creek. From here on, rely on downed logs and/or waterproof boots.

For the next mile the creek remains discreetly east of the trail but is accessible. At mile 2.1, the trail veers away from a burned area—the outer limit of the 1996 Sloan Ridge Fire. Here the trail wallows across the confluence of two streams. It next veers west, taking the high ground through a primitive forest of spruce and Douglas fir for the next 1.2 miles.

You might encounter elk and deer here, and in the early

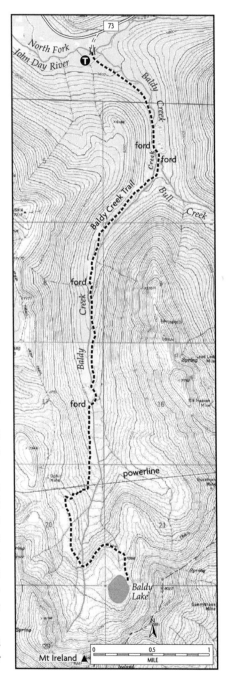

Pooped pup: Dundee rests on rocks above Baldy Lake.

summer be aware that vulnerable calves and fawns are present. A family of goshawks is resident in an old-growth Douglas fir on the edge of the stand-replacement burn. Gray jays, hermit thrush, and flickers make the forest come alive. You also will hear the serious percussion of pileated woodpeckers and watch energetic dippers negotiating the rushing stream.

At 2.5 miles from the trailhead, the path rejoins the creek and plays tag with the stream for the next mile. The path steepens and the trail is rougher as it begins a serious climb from flat forest floor to the top of moraines and Baldy Lake. The approach of the switchbacking portion of the climb is signaled rather rudely when the trail ducks beneath a huge powerline. Switchbacks maintain an even grade and easy pace.

Once at the top of the climb, the trail flattens and contours to the southern end of the basin in another mile. Here, a spur trail leads to the right for another 0.25 mile south and 100 feet up to find Baldy Lake—surrounded by forest, but a nice view of the imposing granite cliffs above that lead to the summit of Mount Ireland. This is a calm, wild, secluded place to camp. Wildlife abounds. Return as you came.

69. North Fork John Day Wilderness: Elkhorn Crest Loop

Round trip: 9 miles
Elevation range: 5870–7960 feet
Difficulty: Difficult
Hiking time: 8 hours
Best canine hiking season: Summer
Regulations: Northwest Forest Pass required
Maps: USGS Crawfish Lake and Anthony Lakes 7.5' quadrangles
Information: Baker Ranger District, Wallowa-Whitman National Forest, (541) 523-4476

Getting there: From Interstate 84, take exit 285 at North Powder. Drive west on County Road 101 marked for Anthony Lakes. In 3.5 miles, turn left (south) at a four-way intersection. Drive 0.6 mile from the intersection and turn right (west) onto the Elkhorn Scenic Byway. This road becomes Forest Road 73 when it crosses into the Wallowa-Whitman National Forest. Follow FR 73 24 miles from the I-84 exit past Anthony Lakes Ski Resort (7500 feet) to Forest Road 73/380 marked for Peavy Cabin, an historic ranger cabin. Turn left onto FR 73/380 and drive 3.4 miles to a trailhead at road's end. The trailhead is at the end of the road 0.1 mile past Peavy Cabin. If you park closer to the cabin, you'll be a bit closer to the return trailhead.

This hike ranges from subalpine meadows to stark granitic ridge crests. Mountain goats live in this high country. Keep dogs under control. The hike provides a good lesson that a burned forest is not a dead forest. Deer, coyotes, kingfishers, owls, hawks, and woodpeckers are abundant, even

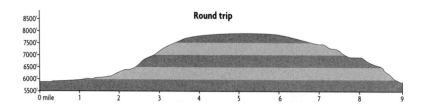

though for the first 2 miles you hike through the bleached and skeletal remnants of a mixed forest that burned in the 1996 Sloan Ridge Fire.

From the trailhead, the trail enters the North Fork John Day Wilderness almost immediately to follow the North Fork John Day River.

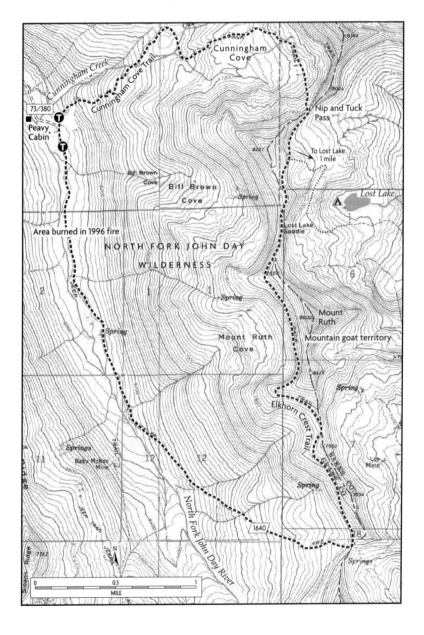

There are ample opportunities to visit the stream. Water is also abundant in small tributary streams early in the season. At 1 mile into the hike, the trail enters a wet meadow that is one of the main headwaters springs for the North Fork. The trail remains a respectful, but accessible, distance—between 20 yards and 0.25 mile—from the nascent river for the first 2 miles. Watch for woodpeckers cavorting in the snags and an abundance of flowers—including lupine, mules ears, paintbrush, and fireweed—that attract a proliferation of butterflies.

At 2 miles, the trail forks. Bear left here on Trail 1640. You'll be leaving your free-flowing canine cooling water supply behind for a time. This trail scrambles away from the North Fork, gaining altitude rapidly. It navigates talus, then thin alpine soils where yellow buckwheat blooms in midsummer, arriving at the ridge crest (7500 feet) 1.7 miles from the junction. At the ridge top, turn left (north) onto the Elkhorn Crest Trail (Trail 1611). This well-worn path follows the top of the ridge, providing cool breezes and exquisite views of Baker Valley and the Wallowa Mountains to the east, and the Greenhorn and Strawberry Ranges to the west.

Rocky Mountain goats like these can be found along the Elkhorn Crest trail. Keep dogs close at hand to avoid harassing these rare goats and other wildlife.

The trail continues for 3 miles along the ridge. Watch for white—and relatively tame—mountain goats. Control dogs in the event that you encounter them.

After an excursion west around the granitic pinnacle of Mount Ruth, the trail drops to Nip and Tuck Pass. Here, it meets the Cunningham Cove Trail that heads to the left—and down. Within a half-mile of the junction, the Cunningham Cove Trail lowers you into a granite-lined emerald basin replete with springs. Below you and spread out across much of the landscape to the east are the gray snags of fire-killed trees. The Cunningham Cove Trail drops at a fairly steady and rapid pace, returning you to the Peavy Cabin and trailhead area in 2.5 miles, playing tag with Cunningham Creek on the way down.

70. North Fork John Day Wilderness: North Fork Campground to Granite Creek

Round trip: 26 miles
Elevation range: 3980–5200 feet
Difficulty: Moderate
Hiking time: 2–3 days
Best canine hiking season: Summer
Regulations: Northwest Forest Pass required
Maps: USGS Trout Meadows and Olive Lake 7.5' quadrangles
Information: North Fork John Day Ranger District, Umatilla National Forest, (541) 427-3231

Getting there: From Interstate 84, take exit 285 at North Powder. Drive west on County Road 101 marked for Anthony Lakes. In 3.5 miles, turn left (south) at a four-way intersection. Drive 0.6 mile from the intersection and turn right (west) onto the Elkhorn Scenic Byway. This road becomes

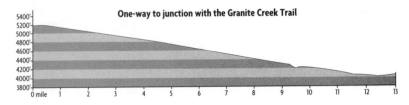
One-way to junction with the Granite Creek Trail

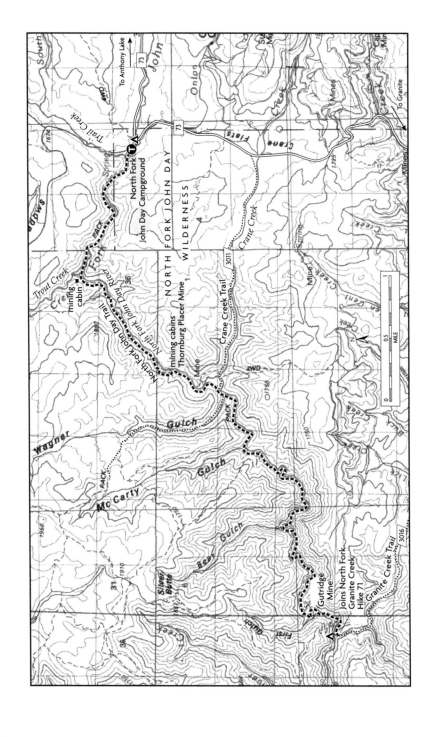

Forest Road 73 when it crosses into the Wallowa-Whitman National Forest. Follow FR 73 28.5 miles from the I-84 exit past Anthony Lakes Ski Resort (7500 feet) to the North Fork Campground. The trailhead is at the campground entrance.

This trail has a civilized beginning that lures you into one of Oregon's wildest places. Expect bears and maybe even wolves here. The path follows the North Fork John Day River religiously. Water for canine cooling is almost always within easy reach.

From the campground entry, the trail heads across a grassy, pine-studded meadow. The landscape is fairly open for the first mile, and lodgepole pines dominate the trees. Look for lupines and spring camas here. An old mining cabin looms in a mile, and the trail becomes increasingly cloistered in the John Day's deepening canyon. The hike leads pleasantly through groves of ponderosa pine and Douglas fir.

At 2.5 miles, the trail finds another old mining cabin and crosses Trout Creek—a vigorous stream in early summer. Beyond the creek, the path slips around a bend and then crosses a broad floodplain where fragrant pines provide a great place to watch for deer. This is an area favored by does with fawns, so keep dogs close at hand in June and early July.

At 4.5 miles, the trail climbs along the outside of a steeply banked river meander. On the opposite bank you can glimpse piles of gravel. This is the abandoned Thornburg Placer Mine—worked in the late 1800s

Meesha and the author crossing a bridge near the confluence of the North Fork John Day River and Granite Creek.

and early 1900s and yet another reminder that even when left alone wilderness recovers slowly from human abuse. The trail clings to the hillside, then makes a switchbacking descent to the river at 5.5 miles into the hike.

Once back at river level, the valley opens, leading to meadows and open ponderosa stands. There are many suitable camping spots here. This is also a doe-fawn area, so be watchful, especially if you choose to camp.

At 6 miles, the trail meets the Crane Creek Trail and continues into the deepening canyon. Douglas firs and occasional spruce are more abundant now. The river is bigger and more serious. At 8 miles, the canyon bottom broadens briefly, opening into a grassy meadow that again invites thoughts of camping. Dogs accustomed to trotting along a forested trail might want a brief romp in this open grassy paradise. But the trail quickly plunges into a starker canyon, where the forest that fringes the canyon top occasionally provides a skeletal reminder of past fires. At 9.5 miles, the trail crosses the North Fork on a narrow bridge. From this bridge to the junction with Granite Creek about 2.5 miles ahead, the path spends about half its time perched on slopes well above the river. At 13 miles, the path joins the Granite Creek Trail (Hike 71) at a small open meadow where there are inviting campsites. Turn around here to return as you came.

71. North Fork John Day Wilderness: Granite Creek to Big Creek

Round trip: 24 miles
Elevation range: 3370–4270 feet
Difficulty: Difficult
Hiking time: 4–5 days
Best canine hiking season: Summer
Regulations: Northwest Forest Pass required
Maps: USGS Olive Lake, Silver Butte, and Kelsay Butte 7.5' quadrangles
Information: North Fork John Day Ranger District, Umatilla National Forest, (541) 427-3231

Getting there: From Interstate 84, take exit 285 at North Powder. Drive west on County Road 101 marked for Anthony Lakes. In 3.5 miles, turn

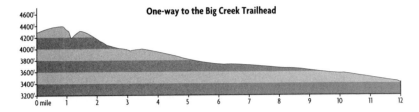

left (south) at a four-way intersection. Drive 0.6 mile from the intersection and turn right (west) onto the Elkhorn Scenic Byway. This road becomes Forest Road 73 when it crosses into the Wallowa-Whitman National Forest. Follow FR 73 28.5 miles from the I-84 exit past Anthony Lakes Ski Resort (7500 feet) to an intersection with Forest Road 51 at North Fork Campground. Continue left (south) on FR 73 another 8 miles to Granite. There is a store and gasoline at Granite. From Granite, take Grant County Road 24 (Forest Road 10) west 1.5 miles to Forest Road 1035. Bear right onto FR 1035, drive 4.5 miles to Spur Road 1035/70. Drive 0.2 mile to the trailhead.

This hike tours the rugged and remote canyon of the North Fork John Day River. This is true wilderness, with craggy scenery and solitude. There are also old mines and plenty of wildlife. Expect bears. You might hear a wolf. One of Oregon's first documented wild wolves—in recent times—was captured here and returned to Idaho in 1998. Since then, the policy has changed and wolves are allowed to stay. Good campsites are rare in the narrow canyon, but they can be found at Granite Creek (3.5 miles), Silver Creek (5.4 miles), Dixon Bar (7 miles), and Fitzwater Gulch (10 miles), as well as Big Creek at the downstream trailhead. This trail joins the end of the Hike 70 route at the confluence of the North Fork John Day River and Granite Creek.

From the trailhead, the narrow path leads along south-facing slopes high above Granite Creek. At 0.7 mile, the trail crosses a small tributary stream, a good opportunity for dog water. At 0.8 mile, the trail joins with a path from the creekside road, which permits another access to Granite Creek. For the next mile the trail continues far above the creek on south-facing slopes, then finds a bridge and crosses to the cooler north slope. It is quite rough here as the trail pushes through bogs and a small willow grove, then rises onto drier ground. It finds a junction with Trail 3018 at mile 2 and a small spring at Snowshoe Spring—a good place to replenish both human and canine water supplies. In 2.3 miles from the trailhead, the trail crosses a major bridge and finds the confluence of Granite Creek and the North Fork John Day River. Here, the Granite Creek Trail (Trail 3016) joins the North Fork Trail (Trail 3022).

To continue downstream to Dixon Bar, cross the bridge over the North Fork and turn left. This portion of the trail explores the most remote and rugged parts of the North Fork Canyon—it also contains several narrow rocky segments. There are more rock outcroppings, including Wind Rock, a looming dark crag about 2 miles downstream from the North Fork–Granite Creek junction. The trail remains on the south side of the river for the remaining distance to Dixon Bar, as well as for the remainder of the trail in general, but provides a crossing to flat, forested areas and small meadows suitable for camping sites near Dixon Bar. Side trails lead to the canyon rim (Paradise Trail to the east and Glade Creek Trail to the

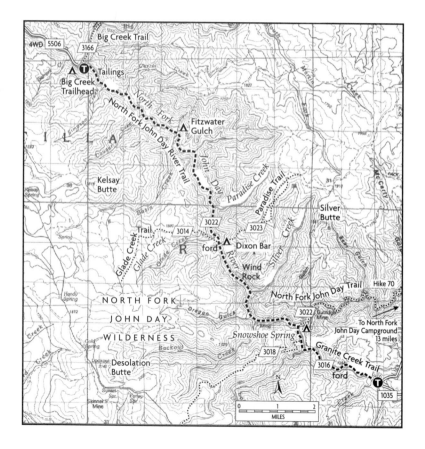

Meesha in backpacking gear along Granite Creek.

west. Both climb about 2000 feet to reach campgrounds at Forest Service roads). Tributary streams provide additional water. At Dixon Bar, the river trail changes its number to Trail 3022. From here, it becomes slightly broader and somewhat more traveled.

Downstream from the broad pine and fir glades at Dixon Bar, the canyon narrows again, traversing outcrops on the trail while the river rushes past. The trail also narrows here, becoming quite rocky in places. The trail keeps close to the river, however, and also crosses eight more side streams between Dixon Bar and the trail's end at Big Creek trailhead, so there is adequate opportunity to keep dogs cool. Watch for snakes along the rockier lower stretches of the trail.

A mining cabin appears along the river about 4 miles downstream from Dixon Bar, a reminder that this wilderness has not been free of human disturbance for very long. More evidence—piles of mining tailings—appear along the open riverbanks just a few hundred yards above the end of the trail and FR 5506. Return as you came.

72. Eagle Cap Wilderness: Bear Creek

Round trip: 35 miles
Elevation range: 3720–7900 feet
Difficulty: Moderate first 5 miles, difficult thereafter
Hiking time: 2–3 days
Best canine hiking season: Summer
Regulations: Northwest Forest Pass required
Maps: USGS Wallowa, Jim White Ridge, and North Minam Meadows
7.5′ quadrangles
Information: Eagle Cap Ranger District, Wallowa-Whitman National
Forest, (541) 426-4978

Getting there: From the town of Wallowa on Oregon Route 82, 40 miles
from La Grande, turn west onto Bear Creek Road (Forest Road 8250).
Continue west (right), then south on this road 8 miles to Spur Road 040.
Drive south on Spur Road 040 for 1 mile to Boundary Campground and
the Bear Creek trailhead.

This long backpack trip explores some of the wildest country in the Eagle
Cap Wilderness. You could encounter bears or cougars on this trail, as
well as elk calves and mule deer fawns in the spring and early summer.
A few horseback riders use the trail in the summer, but the heaviest horse
traffic is for fall hunting. If you hike this path in late August or fall,
consider putting an orange hunting vest on your dog so she won't be
mistaken for a game animal.

From the trailhead, the Bear Creek Trail enters a forest of mixed Douglas fir and ponderosa pine. For the first 2.3 miles from the trailhead to
Bear Creek Guard Station (now abandoned), the trail follows the creek
closely, crossing the stream twice and finally settling in on the east bank.

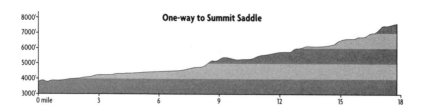

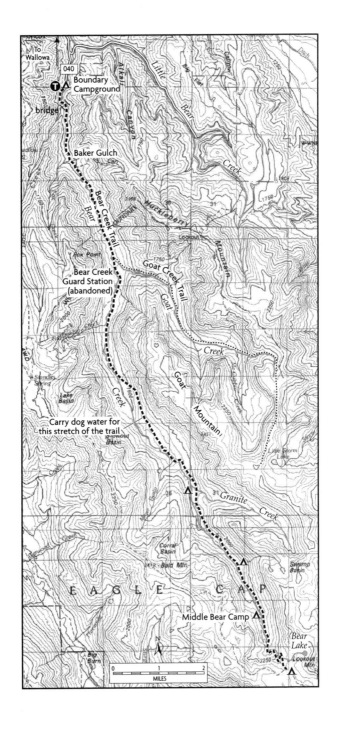

To
Wallowa

040

Boundary
Campground

bridge

Baker Gulch

Bear Creek Trail

Bear

Alkali Canyon

Little Bear

Creek

Huckleberry Mountain

Goat Creek Trail

Goat

Creek

Bear Creek
Guard Station
(abandoned)

Fox Point

Creek

Lake
Basin

Carry dog water for
this stretch of the trail

Goat

Mountain

Creek

Little Storm
Lake

Granite Creek

Swamp
Basin

Corral
Basin

Bald Mtn

E A G L E   C A P

Middle Bear Camp

Bear
Lake

Big
Barn

Lookout
Mtn

0   1   2
MILES

The forest here is dense old-growth Douglas fir, grand fir, and Engelmann spruce; the trailside understory includes sword ferns, syringia, and snowberry. Then the path moves a little farther from the creek, but it still keeps the stream in sight and sound, seldom rising more than 40 feet above it. The trail reaches the Eagle Cap Wilderness boundary in 3.3 miles from the trailhead. The canyon is relatively narrow here, with steep walls rising about 2500 feet above the trail.

Approximately 1 mile past the wilderness boundary and 4.2 miles from the trailhead, the main trail meets a little-used spur trail that heads southeast up Goat Creek. Bear Creek Trail then crosses the creek and encounters another path that leads about 0.2 mile to the abandoned Bear Creek Guard Station. The old guard station is a popular destination for a day hike.

From this point, the canyon bottom is relatively broad and the forest cool, but the Bear Creek Trail becomes rougher and a higher percentage of its users are horse packers bound for a longer stay in the high Wallowa Mountains.

The trail stays within easy reach of Bear Creek for the next 2 miles, following the flat canyon bottom and climbing at an easy pace. At 6 miles into the hike, the trail edges away from the stream and a mile farther begins a much steeper and steady climb up the canyon's sides. This portion of the trail continues for the next 5 miles. Four intermittent streams and several seeps might provide a chance for cooling along this stretch, but in warm weather you should carry dog water for this portion of the trail. The trail makes one sudden trip to the creek at 12.2 miles (5400 feet), a good spot for a break. Grand fir and spruce dominate here. Then the path abruptly climbs 200 feet before moderating its rise. But it remains aloof from the stream to about mile 14. Numerous unnamed side streams provide water along this portion of the trail during summer, but some can be dry by September.

Dundee, ready to go after a dip in Bear Creek.

At 15.5 miles from the trailhead, the trail reaches Middle Bear Camp, a small meadow at elevation 6800 feet. Bear Creek meanders through the landscape here, and the meadow, ringed by grand and subalpine fir, is a fine camping site.

From Middle Bear Camp, the trail scrambles to the summit above Bear Creek, rising 1000 feet in 2 miles. The major climb is along a lung-numbing, switchbacking segment that begins a mile south of Middle Bear Camp and heaves itself upward from 6900 feet to 7900 feet in a mile. The summit saddle offers views of the high Wallowas and North Minam Valley. From here, you turn east for a cross-country scramble along the last portion of Bear Creek that leads to the creek's headwaters at Bear Lake. Return as you came.

73. Eagle Cap Wilderness: Hurricane Creek

Round trip: 6.4–24 miles
Elevation range: 5020–7700 feet
Difficulty: Moderate
Hiking time: 4 hours–2 days
Best canine hiking season: Summer
Regulations: Northwest Forest Pass required
Maps: USGS Chief Joseph Mountain and Eagle Cap 7.5' quadrangles
Information: Eagle Cap Ranger District, Wallowa-Whitman National Forest, (541) 426-4978

Getting there: From the town of Joseph, turn west onto West Wallowa Avenue. In 3 miles, at the white Hurricane Creek Grange building, make a hard left onto a gravel road, the westward extension of Hurricane Creek Road. Continue 2.9 miles to the parking area at the end of the road.

This trail leads into the Lake Basin of the Eagle Cap Wilderness. It is far less popular than nearby trails up the Lostine River or the path from

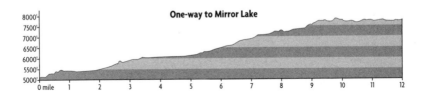

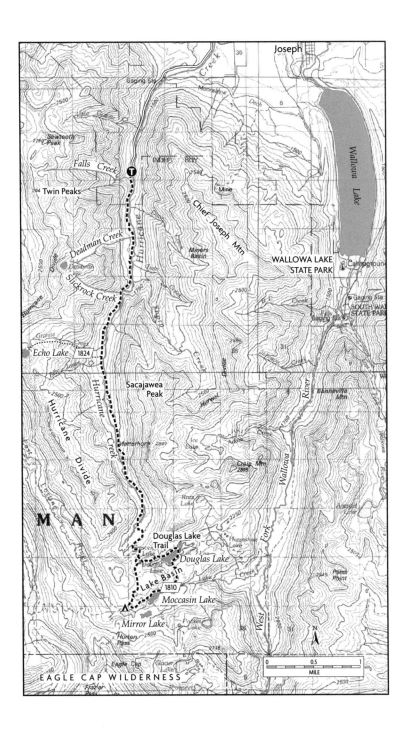

Horseback riders and packers frequently share the Hurricane Creek and other trails with hikers in the Wallowa Mountains.

Wallowa Lake. There is some use by horse packers. You might glimpse mountain goats on the slopes high above you.

From the trailhead, the Hurricane Creek Trail moves through lodgepole pine, tamarack, and grand fir forest for 0.3 mile to a water crossing of Falls Creek—getting across can be a challenge in early summer. Just upstream is a 70-foot waterfall. Informal trails lead to the base of this inviting cascade. This destination alone makes Hurricane Creek a worthy route.

Beyond this detour, the trail crosses a treeless expanse that appears to be a clear-cut. It is a natural clear-cut, however—a forest mowed down by snow avalanches in the 1960s. Beyond this natural, brushed-over area, the trail slips into lodgepole pine and larch woodland, then emerges into subalpine meadows at Deadman Creek 1.5 miles from the trailhead. The meadows offer views of Twin Peaks to the west and Sacajewea Peak to the south. If you watch the ridges to the west closely, you might see white dots—mountain goats frequent the rocky upper slopes.

Beyond Deadman Creek, the trail reenters a lodgepole-dominated forest for another 1.7 miles, switchbacking along outcrops and tiptoeing at the edge of an abrupt drop into Hurricane Creek and emerging into the open as it nears Slickrock Creek. This stream comes by its name honestly. The bedrock is coarse marble—a soft stone that has been polished and smoothed by running water. Approaching the Slickrock crossing (5780 feet), the trail teeters above cliffs and then crosses the slippery outcrops at the creek's junction with Hurricane Creek. It's a nice watering spot and, at 3.2 miles, a popular destination for day hikes.

At Slickrock Creek the trail steepens slightly, continuing through a forest increasingly composed of grand fir and Englemann spruce along with lodgepoles. Tamaracks are less abundant at this higher altitude. As you proceed up the trail, look for increasing numbers of spindle-topped subalpine fir.

At 5.1 miles from the trailhead, the path meets a junction with Trail 1824 to Echo Lake. This trail is steep and very rough, climbing about 2500 feet in 3.1 miles to the rocky alpine environment of Echo Lake (8372 feet). If you wish to put more grunt and challenge into your trip, this trail provides it. There is no water along the way, so if you choose to try this side trip, carry plenty for your dog.

Just past the junction with Trail 1824, the Hurricane Creek Trail jogs left and crosses Hurricane Creek. There is no bridge and few stepping-stones, so expect to wade through cold, knee-deep water. Use caution, as this crossing can be hazardous in early summer. There are numerous good camping sites near this junction and crossing, and many hikers make this crossing, combined with the crawl to Echo Lake, an early-summer backpacking destination.

After plunging across Hurricane Creek, the trail steepens and strays away from the stream, though it crosses two hefty tributaries in the next mile. It encounters several abandoned and decaying cabins at about 8.3 miles from the trailhead, where the path tempers its uphill pace and encounters pretty meadows of paintbrush and lupine as it climbs from 6800 to 7000 feet. Look for Clark's nutcrackers here, and a stunning view up the adjacent, rugged, glacially polished marble slopes of Sacajewea Peak. At the end of this series of meadows the path steepens again for its final climb to the Lakes Basin.

At 9.4 miles the trail crests at 7700 feet. It then drops for 0.3 mile to meet a well-worn trail (Douglas Lake Trail) to the left (east). This trail, which heads for Douglas Lake and the Wallowa River, is also the beginning of a 4.3-mile

Lakes Basin loop hike that makes a superb day hike during your stay here. To hike the loop, turn east onto this trail for 1.6 miles past Douglas Lake to a junction with Trail 1810. Turn right (west) at this sharply angled junction and follow Trail 1810 to Moccasin Lake at 2.6 miles and back (west) to Mirror Lake.

To reach campsites near Mirror Lake, continue straight here, toward Eagle Cap and the Lakes Basin 1.2 miles ahead. The Lakes Basin is an overused area with many campsites roped off for restoration. Choose campsites well away from lakeshores, and enjoy the stunningly beautiful landscape. Return as you came.

74. Eagle Cap Wilderness: Maxwell Lake

Round trip: 7 miles
Elevation range: 5450–7730 feet
Difficulty: Moderate
Hiking time: 5 hours
Best canine hiking season: Summer
Regulations: Northwest Forest Pass required; register for wilderness entry
Map: USGS North Minam Meadows 7.5′ quadrangle
Information: Eagle Cap Ranger District, Wallowa-Whitman National Forest, (541) 426-4978

Getting there: From the town of Lostine on Oregon Route 82, turn south onto Lostine River Road. Drive 17 miles to Shady Campground and the Maxwell Lake trailhead on the right (west) side of the gravel road.

This hike leads to a pretty alpine lake in the Eagle Cap Wilderness. Hikers and hikers with dogs are the only users of the trail, one of the less-hiked paths that lead up from the Lostine River.

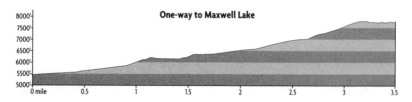

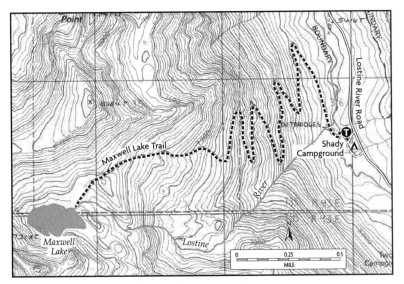

The Maxwell Lake Trail begins at the west side of a large parking area that serves both campers and hikers. It crosses the Lostine River on a sturdy footbridge and leads through a small wetland before crossing Maxwell Creek, hitting the side of the valley in 0.3 mile, and beginning a well-graded, switchbacking ascent. Maxwell Creek can be boisterous in early summer, and there is no bridge here, though stepping across the water on several large rocks can keep your feet dry. This is the last real and reliable water until the trail's end, so be sure to take advantage of it here, especially in warm weather.

The trail maintains a steady pace for the next 2 miles as it climbs long switchbacks. The trail occasionally emerges from the Englemann spruce and Douglas fir forest into sunlit meadows. Most of these meadows are fairly moist and glow with blooms of mules ears, lupine, and paintbrush in early summer. Occasionally, you can catch a fleeting view of the high Wallowa peaks to the south, including Eagle Cap.

At 2.6 miles from the trailhead, the path reaches the top of a gravelly moraine and its switchbacks, and it abruptly changes its character from Dr. Jekyll to Mr. Hyde. It turns west and begins a rough, serious crawl up the last 1000 feet to the Maxwell Lake basin. As the trail ascends, it crosses springs and wet meadows, though these can be dry by midsummer. At 3 miles from the trailhead, the route enters alpine meadows where it leads around huge, glacially sculpted outcrops and "rouche mounenee," or glacially polished sheep-shaped rocks, before descending sharply to Maxwell

Snow roll: Dundee relaxes on a June hike at Maxwell Lake in the Eagle Cap Wilderness.

Lake and its cool, gray, granite-lined basin at 3.5 miles. The views from the meadows and outcrops above the lake are mostly to the Lostine Canyon and peaks on the west side of the river, including Sawtooth Peak and Twin Peaks. After refreshing yourself and your pooch at the lake, return as you came.

75. Eagle Cap Wilderness: West Fork Lostine River to Sky Lake

Round trip: 15 miles
Elevation range: 5600–8525 feet
Difficulty: Moderate to difficult
Hiking time: 2 days
Best canine hiking season: Summer
Regulations: Northwest Forest Pass required; register for wilderness entry
Maps: USGS Eagle Cap and Steamboat Lake 7.5' quadrangles
Information: Eagle Cap Ranger District, Wallowa-Whitman National Forest, (541) 426-4978

Getting there: From downtown Lostine on Oregon Route 82, turn south onto Lostine River Road. Continue 18 miles down the initially paved, then gravel road to the Two Pan trailhead at road's end.

The trail up the West Fork Lostine River turns right or slightly west into the forest. It is generally the trail less traveled and trampled, except during hunting season when it bears more horse traffic than the East Fork.

From the trailhead, the Lostine River Trail leads into spruce and Douglas fir forest at a respectful distance from the rushing, tumbling West Fork Lostine River. In about 0.2 mile, the trail splits. The left trail (East Fork Trail) leads up the East Fork Lostine to the Lakes Basin. Instead of taking this overused, suffocatingly dusty, and badly eroded path, bear to the right, up the West Fork. This trail (West Fork Trail) carries substantially less traffic than the East Fork. Still, you can expect horses, other hikers, and even llama trekkers in the next 2.6 miles until you turn off onto the less-used Copper Creek Trail.

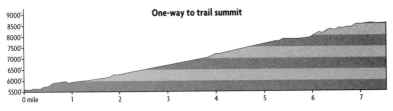

The West Fork Trail crosses the East Fork Lostine on a solid bridge, then for the next 0.7 mile switchbacks upward 500 feet as it maneuvers across open landscapes that are old avalanche scars, keeping well away from the river. At mile 1.1, it returns to Douglas fir and spruce forest, moving closer to the unruly river, and continues to climb.

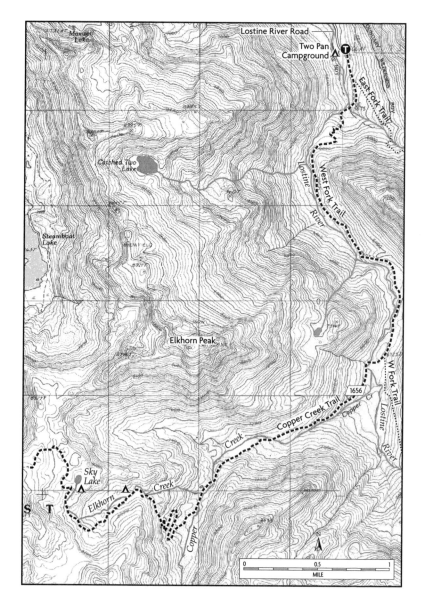

The Copper Creek Trail (Trail 1656) is well marked and bears to the right at mile 2.6. This path crosses the West Fork at a bridgeless crossing, providing a challenge to keeping dry feet. If you are not adept at balancing on rounded, slippery rocks, there is an easier, broader and shallower, sand-bottomed ford just upstream. On warm days this is a great spot to frolic in the water with your dog before continuing along the steepening trail. Expect to hear hermit thrush in these woods, as well as the busy hammering of flickers. Water ouzels (dippers) dance along the water's edges.

The Copper Creek Trail splashes through several small creeks in the next mile, though in late summer of a dry year you should not rely on these for canine cooling or as water sources. The trail follows well above Copper Creek, crossing the stream and affording another opportunity for water 1.6 miles from the junction with the West Fork Trail when it traverses a moist area and then crosses a second creek (Elkhorn Creek).

Beyond these creek junctions, the trail begins a serious climb at 4.5 miles into the hike, switchbacking upward and then rendezvousing again with Elkhorn Creek in 1.2 miles. Here the landscape opens to alpine vistas and the vegetation changes to alpine fir and whitebark pine. Clark's nutcrackers call this landscape, at about 7500 feet, their summer home. At 5.75 miles from the trailhead, the path reaches a bountiful spring at a lung-numbing 8000 feet in elevation. It's best to keep dogs out of the water here, as the spring is used as a reliable source of water for human hikers. There is plenty of access to nearby Elkhorn Creek for dogs. Sky Lake appears at 6.5 miles from the Two Pan trailhead, an excellent site for camp. The trail's summit at 8500 feet is still 0.8 mile ahead, and it offers a nice glimpse into the glacially carved basin of Swamp Lake and its surrounding emerald-green meadows. Return as you came.

Five More Great Dog Hikes in the Blue Mountains, Wallowa Mountains, and Eastern Oregon

1) Summit Point to Crater Lake, Eagle Cap Wilderness, 14 miles. Wallowa Mountains Visitor Center, (541) 426-5546.
2) Pine Creek, Cornucopia to Pine Lakes, Eagle Cap Wilderness, 10 miles. Wallowa Mountains Visitor Center, (541) 426-5546.
3) South Fork Imnaha River Trail, Indian Crossing to Hawkins Pass and Frazier Lake, Eagle Cap Wilderness, 18 miles one-way. Four-day backpacking trip into alpine grandeur. Wallowa Mountains Visitor Center, (541) 426-5546.

4) Fish Lake trailhead to Sugarloaf Reservoir and Sugarloaf Mountain, Southeast Wallowa Mountains, 8 miles. Features streams, views, lakes. Wallowa Mountains Visitor Center, (541) 426-5546.

5) Fish Lake trailhead to Clear Creek Reservoir, Southeast Wallowa Mountains, 6 miles. Features lakes, streams, forests. Wallowa Mountains Visitor Center, (541) 426-5546.

APPENDIX A: CONTACT INFORMATION

Applegate Ranger District
Rogue River National Forest
6941 Upper Applegate Road
Jacksonville, OR 97530
Phone: (541) 899-3800

Ashland Ranger District
Rogue River National Forest
645 Washington Street
Ashland, OR 97520
Phone: (541) 482-3333

Baker Ranger District
Wallowa-Whitman National Forest
3165 10th Street
Baker City, OR 97814
Phone: (541) 523-4476

Banks-Vernonia State Trail
Phone: (503) 324-0606

Bend/Fort Rock Ranger District
Deschutes National Forest
1230 NE 3rd Street, Suite A-262
Bend, OR 97701
Phone: (541) 383-4000

Cape Perpetua Visitor Center
2400 Highway 101 South
P.O. Box 274
Yachats, OR 97498
Phone: (541) 547-3289
TDD: (541) 547-3251

Chetco Ranger District
Siskiyou National Forest
555 5th Street
Brookings, OR 97415
Phone: (541) 412-6000

Columbia River Gorge National
    Scenic Area
902 Wasco Avenue, Suite 200
Hood River, OR 97031
Phone: (541) 386-2333

Deschutes National Forest Headquarters
1645 Highway 20 East
Bend, OR 97701
Phone: (541) 383-5300

Detroit Ranger District
Willamette National Forest
Highway 22
Detroit, OR 97342
Mail: HC-73, Box 320
Mill City, OR 97360
Phone: (541) 854-3366

Diamond Lake Ranger District
Umpqua National Forest
2020 Toketee Ranger Station Road
Idleyld Park, OR 97447
Phone: (541) 498-2531

Dufur Ranger Station
Mount Hood National Forest
780 NE Court Street
Dufur, OR 97021
Phone: (541) 467-2291
TTY: (541) 467-5170

Eagle Cap Ranger District
Wallowa-Whitman National Forest
88401 Highway 82
Enterprise, OR 97828
Phone: (541) 426-4978

Estacada Ranger Station
Mount Hood National Forest
595 NW Industrial Way
Estacada, OR 97023
Phone: (503) 630-6861

Galice Ranger District
Siskiyou National Forest
200 NE Greenfield Road
P.O. Box 440
Grants Pass, OR 97526
Phone: (541) 471-6500

Gold Beach Ranger District
Siskiyou National Forest
1225 South Ellensburg
P.O. Box 7
Gold Beach, OR 97444
Phone: (541) 247-3600

Hebo Ranger District
Siuslaw National Forest
31525 Highway 22
P.O. Box 324
Hebo, OR 97122
Phone: (503) 392-3161

Hood River Ranger District
Mount Hood National Forest
6780 Highway 35
Mount Hood–Parkdale, OR 97041
Phone: (541) 352-6002

Lane County Parks and Recreation
    Department
90064 Coburg Road
Eugene, OR 97408
Phone: (541) 682-2000

Lookout Mountain Ranger District
Ochoco National Forest
3160 NE 3rd Street
P.O. Box 490
Prineville, OR 97754-0490
Phone: (541) 416-6449

McKenzie River Ranger District
Willamette National Forest
57600 McKenzie Highway
McKenzie Bridge, OR 97413
Phone: (541) 822-3381

Medford District Bureau of Land
    Management
3040 Biddle Road
Medford, OR 97630
Phone: (541) 770-2200

Mount Hood Information Center
Mount Hood National Forest
65000 E Highway 26
Welches, OR 97067
Phone: (503) 622-7674

Mount Hood National Forest
    Headquarters
16400 Champion Way
Sandy, OR 97055
Phone: (503) 668-1771
TTY: (503) 668-1431

Mount Pisgah Arboretum
34901 Frank Parrish Road
Eugene, OR 97405
Phone: (541) 741-4100

North Fork John Day Ranger District
Umatilla National Forest
P.O. Box 158
Ukiah, OR 97880
Phone: (541) 427-3231

North Umpqua Ranger District
Umpqua National Forest
18782 N Umpqua Highway
Glide, OR 97443
Phone: (541) 496-3532

Ochoco National Forest Headquarters
3160 NE 3rd Street
P.O. Box 490
Prineville, OR 97754-0490
Phone: (541) 416-6500

Oregon Bureau of Land Management
Oregon State Office
333 SW First Avenue
Portland, OR 97204
Phone: (503) 808-6002

Oregon Dunes National Recreation
    Area
855 Highway Avenue
Reedsport, OR 97467
Phone: (541) 271-3611

Oregon State Parks and Recreation
    Department
1115 Commercial Street NE
Salem, OR 97301
Phone: (800) 551-6949

Pine Ranger District
Wallowa-Whitman National Forest
General Delivery
Halfway, OR 97834
Phone: (541) 742-7511

Portland Bureau of Parks and
    Recreation
1120 SW 5th Avenue
Portland, OR 97201
Phone: (503) 823-2223 or
    (503) 823-7529

Prospect Ranger District
Rogue River National Forest
47201 Highway 62
Prospect, OR 97536
Phone: (541) 560-3400

Rogue River and Siskiyou National
    Forests Headquarters Office
Federal Building
333 W 8th Street
Box 520
Medford, OR 97501-0209
Phone: (541) 858-2200
TTY: (541) 858-2203

Salem District
Bureau of Land Management
1717 Fabry Road SE
Salem, OR 97306
Phone: (503) 375-5646

Silver Falls State Park
Phone: (503) 873-8681

Sisters Ranger District
Deschutes National Forest
Highway 20 and Pine Street
P.O. Box 249
Sisters, OR 97759
Phone: (541) 549-7700

Siuslaw National Forest Headquarters
4077 Research Way
P.O. Box 1148
Corvallis, OR 97339
Phone: (541) 750-7000
TDD: (541) 750-7006

Tryon Creek State Park
Phone: (503) 636-9886

Umatilla National Forest Headquarters
2517 SW Hailey Avenue
Pendleton, OR 97801
Phone: (541) 278-3716

Umpqua National Forest Headquarters
2900 NW Stewart Parkway
Roseburg, OR 97470
Phone: (541) 672-6601

Waldport Ranger District
Siuslaw National Forest
1094 SW Pacific Highway
Waldport, OR 97394
Phone: (541) 563-3211

Wallowa Mountains Visitors Center
Wallowa-Whitman National Forest
88401 Highway 82
Enterprise, Oregon 97828
Phone: (541) 426-5546

Wallowa-Whitman National Forest
    Headquarters
1550 Dewey Avenue
P.O. Box 907
Baker City, OR 97814
Phone: (541) 523-6391

Willamette National Forest Headquarters
211 E 7th Avenue
P.O. Box 10607
Eugene, OR 97440-2607
Phone: (541) 225-6300
TDD: (541) 465-6323

Zigzag Ranger Station
Mount Hood National Forest
70220 E Highway 26
Zigzag, OR 97049
Phone: (503) 622-3191 or
    (503) 668-1704

Ginger, Dusty, and Leo, three very happy golden retrievers, head for Green Lakes in the Three Sisters Wilderness.

APPENDIX B: RECOMMENDED READING

Acker, Randy. *Field Guide: Dog First Aid Emergency Care for the Hunting, Working, and Outdoor Dog.* Wilderness Adventures Press, 1994.

Carlson, Liisa and James M. Giffin. *Dog Owners Home Veterinary Handbook*, 3rd ed. John Wiley and Sons, 1999.

Coren, Stanley. *The Intelligence of Dogs: A Guide to the Thoughts, Emotions, and Inner Lives of Our Canine Companions*, reprint edition. Bantam, 1995.

Fogle, Bruce and Amanda Williams. *First Aid for Dogs: What to Do When Emergencies Happen.* Penguin, 1997.

Knapp, Caroline. *Pack of Two: The Intricate Bond Between People and Dogs.* Bantam Dell, 1998.

Masson, Jared Moussaieff. *Dogs Never Lie About Love: Reflections on the Emotional Lives of Dogs.* Crown Publishers, 1997.

McConnell, Patricia. *The Other End of the Leash.* Ballantine Books, 2003.

Pennisi, Elizabeth. "Canine Evolution: A Shaggy Dog Story." *Science*, November 22, 2002: pp. 1540-1542.

Pryor, Karen. *Don't Shoot the Dog: The New Art of Teaching and Training.* Bantam Dell, 1999.

Rugaas, Turid. *On Talking Terms with Dogs: Calming Signals.* Legacy-by-Mail, 1997.

A treat before hitting the trail is a good way to start the day. In camp, Maidu segment, North Umpqua River Trail.

INDEX

ABOUT THE AUTHOR

Ellen Morris Bishop is the author of numerous books on geology and the outdoors, including *Hiking Oregon's Geology*, second edition (The Mountaineers Books, 2004). Dogs have accompanied her on virtually all the hikes she took while preparing *Hiking Oregon's Geology* and doing geology fieldwork. Her present dog, Meesha, is a certified Animal Assisted Therapy dog, providing canine companionship to Alzheimer's patients, nursing home patients, and children in Dorenbecher Children's Hospital in Portland. Meesha also has her Basic Obedience Certificate and Basic

Agility Certificate and is a Dove Lewis Clinic blood donor dog. Ellen Bishop's previous work with dogs includes working with stock dogs to work cattle and sheep and training a Newfoundland to be a certified Water Rescue Dog.

THE MOUNTAINEERS, founded in 1906, is a nonprofit outdoor activity and conservation club, whose mission is "to explore, study, preserve, and enjoy the natural beauty of the outdoors. . . . " Based in Seattle, Washington, the club is now the third-largest such organization in the United States, with seven branches throughout Washington State.

The Mountaineers sponsors both classes and year-round outdoor activities in the Pacific Northwest, which include hiking, mountain climbing, ski-touring, snowshoeing, bicycling, camping, kayaking and canoeing, nature study, sailing, and adventure travel. The club's conservation division supports environmental causes through educational activities, sponsoring legislation, and presenting informational programs. All club activities are led by skilled, experienced volunteers, who are dedicated to promoting safe and responsible enjoyment and preservation of the outdoors.

If you would like to participate in these organized outdoor activities or the club's programs, consider a membership in The Mountaineers. For information and an application, write or call The Mountaineers, Club Headquarters, 300 Third Avenue West, Seattle, Washington 98119; 206-284-6310.

The Mountaineers Books, an active, nonprofit publishing program of the club, produces guidebooks, instructional texts, historical works, natural history guides, and works on environmental conservation. All books produced by The Mountaineers fulfill the club's mission.

Send or call for our catalog of more than 500 outdoor titles:

The Mountaineers Books
1001 SW Klickitat Way, Suite 201
Seattle, WA 98134
800-553-4453
mbooks@mountaineersbooks.org
www.mountaineersbooks.org

The Mountaineers Books is proud to be a corporate sponsor of Leave No Trace, whose mission is to promote and inspire responsible outdoor recreation through education, research, and partnerships. The Leave No Trace program is focused specifically on human-powered (nonmotorized) recreation.

Leave No Trace strives to educate visitors about the nature of their recreational impacts, as well as offer techniques to prevent and minimize such impacts. Leave No Trace is best understood as an educational and ethical program, not as a set of rules and regulations.

For more information, visit *www.lnt.org,* or call 800-332-4100.

OTHER TITLES YOU MIGHT ENJOY FROM THE MOUNTAINEERS BOOKS:

BEST HIKES WITH DOGS: Western Washington
Dan A. Nelson
Head to the hills with a four-legged friend and the only Washington guidebook for hiking with your dog.

BEST SHORT HIKES IN NORTHWEST OREGON
Rhonda & George Ostertag
Discover the best of northwest Oregon—from the Pacific coast to the Cascade crest—with 82 short hikes perfect for families and anyone short on time.

100 CLASSIC HIKES IN OREGON
Douglas Lorain
Written by an Oregon hiking legend, this is the only full-color guide to the best hikes throughout the state.

HIKING OREGON'S GEOLOGY, 2nd edition
Ellen Morris Bishop
Ninety hikes help you unlock the mysteries of Oregon's landscape.

TENT AND CAR CAMPER'S HANDBOOK:
Advice for Families & First-Timers
Buck Tilton
The lowdown on family car and tent camping—no experience necessary!

CONDITIONING FOR OUTDOOR FITNESS:
Functional Exercise & Nutrition for Every Body, 2nd Ed.
David Musnick, M.D., Mark Pierce, A.T.C.
Pick a sport; find the exercises that will get you fit to participate.